RE-UNITED STATES

The Common Sense Guide to
Defending America in the Age of Terror

by

Dr. Marc Weisman

CAMBRIDGE HOUSE PRESS
NEW YORK

Published by
Cambridge House Press
New York, NY 10001
www.camhousepress.com

Most Cambridge House Press books are available at special quantity discounts for bulk purchase for sales promotions, premiums, fund-raising, and educational needs. Special books or book excerpts can be created to fit specific needs. For details, contact specialsales@camhousepress.com.

Library of Congress Cataloging-in-Publication Data

Weisman, Marc F.
Re-United States : the common sense guide to defending America in the age of terror / Marc Weisman.
p. cm.
Includes bibliographical references.
ISBN 978-0-9821391-0-3 (hardcover)
1. Terrorism--United States--Prevention. 2. National security--United States. 3. Jihad. I. Title.

HV6432.W384 2009
363.325'160973--dc22

2009036793

Cover design by Caroline Maher
Book design by Rachel Trusheim

Printed in the United States of America
10 9 8 7 6 5 4 3 2 1

I dedicate this book to the brave and selfless American men and women in harm's way protecting our nation and its people.

They include the armed forces, law enforcement, firefighters, and emergency medical professionals.

You are more appreciated than you know.

ACKNOWLEDGMENTS

Special thanks to my wife and children, who have somehow endured my never-ending medical practice and now have to put up with my writing. Without their encouragement, understanding, and support I could not have undertaken the monumental task of writing my first book. Thanks to America herself, for inspiring me to write *Re-United States*. Although far from perfect, this great country is the national embodiment of human hope, liberty, tolerance, and aspiration for a better world. I also wish to express gratitude to Brigitte Gabriel, Nonie Darwish, and Dr. Zuhdi Jasser for offering me their support and friendship. I hope that my contribution can, in some small way, help you enlighten Americans and the Western world to the dangers of Islamic extremism in all of its forms. As a first-time author venturing outside of my profession, I required a lot of encouragement and guidance from my editors and publisher. I want to thank Clayton Walker for his early editing and encouragement. Thanks to Drew Nederpelt, Caroline Maher, Giselle Mazur, Maryann Yin, Nadina Persaud, Aritz Bermudez Monfort, Jamie Metrick, Melissa Darcey, and everyone at Cambridge House Press. A very special thanks to my editor Rachel Trusheim for her patience and expertise. Rachel served as my "true north," keeping me on course.

TABLE OF CONTENTS

INTRODUCTION

There is a serious danger that you probably do not know exists and it's growing with each passing day. I am referring to the current deep political divisions in America and, more specifically, how this polarization places our nation at serious risk from Islamic extremism, particularly of the nonviolent variety.

Re-United States is an unapologetically candid (and maybe provocative) approach to this subject intended to educate and inform, not indict. It is replete with the necessary world and religious history, geopolitical analysis, and candid self-assessment of America and Americans to frame this subject. I have always believed that average people can change the world, and often do. Americans of all stripes, armed with new knowledge, will be encouraged to revisit this subject of radical Islam (Islamism) as it relates to America and to see it in a new light. Bottom line: knowledge breeds awareness, awareness influences expectations, and these expectations will be heard by our media and politicians. As a result, real change will occur because we the people expect and demand it.

Too many books on the subject of Islamic extremism seem, well, extreme. There exists an increasing national division in knowledge on this subject between those of us who lean conservative from those who lean liberal. I ask all readers, regardless of political affiliation, for a chance to educate and reveal a new perspective on this sensitive issue. This is not an anti-Islamic book; it is an anti-Islamic extremism book. America is and has always been the land of opportunity and peaceful coexistence for all people who respect both freedom and each other. This, of course, includes Muslims but excludes radical Islamists, who as you will soon learn, disrespect the very nature of America.

For years, possibly due to my Jewish heritage or perhaps my entrenched sense of patriotism, I have been more aware of the threat of radical Islam than most. One reason may be that I cannot help but see a strong similarity between the fascist hate-ideology of Nazism (including Nazi Germany) and Islamic extremism. Both are supremacist, skilled at using disinformation to obfuscate their masses, fiercely anti-Semitic, and violent, and both seek a new world order. We have seen the result that came from the world's appeasement of Nazi Germany—must we make the same mistake again? I am a primary care physician specializing in family and geriatric medicine, and I can tell you that early detection and "treatment" are of paramount importance.

As a medical doctor one of my many responsibilities is to help patients overcome bad habits. Nations, like people, also fall prey to destructive behaviors or habits that are often born from good intentions. An example might be the middle-aged businessman working harder than ever, which is interfering with his sleep. Sleeping medications seem to help, but before he knows it, he has become habituated to the medicine and it isn't even effective anymore. Now he has two problems. So it often is with political correctness and appeasement. Our intention as Americans is to be broad-minded and tolerant, but too often this tolerance is used by our enemies to achieve their goal of advancing the narrow-mindedness of radical Islam. There is a grave threat that America faces from radical Islam that has gone largely unrecognized. The behaviors that pose the greatest risk to our nation are political correctness, appeasement, and complacency with respect to the threat of radical Islam.

Nonviolent or "stealth" Jihad is a concept that may be new to you. That being said, it is easy to underestimate its paramount importance to the survival of American culture and our foundation of Judeo-Christian values. Overt acts of terrorism, particularly Islamic terrorism, have had a large impact on the world. Violence directed at innocents is easy to detest, vigorously denounce, and mount a response against. As I will carefully explore, our political beliefs, liberal or conservative, influence how we choose to take action against terrorism. By increasing the "average American's" awareness of these issues, our expectations and demands from leaders and pundits will grow, and in this fashion, *we the people*, can and will change our nation and the world. For instance: do we condone or condemn the assassination of Islamic terrorists? What about preemptive strikes against individuals or even nations rather than retaliate only *after* they attack us? Is it appropriate or xenophobic to demand that Islamic religious and political leaders refrain from teaching Jihad and hatred against the West, Christians, Jews, and other "infidels"? All of these are important to our nation and the world; however, they pale in comparison to the controversies surrounding the issue of nonviolent Jihad.

While radical Islamic terrorism causes great trepidation around the world, many experts and historians including Robert Spencer, Brigitte Gabriel, Daniel Pipes, and others believe that terror is not the most powerful weapon in the arsenal of Islamic extremists. And they are right. According to Islamist-Watch.org, a popular watchdog site that monitors worldwide Islamic extremism, *nonviolent* radical Islam is actually more likely than terrorism to erode the freedoms of Western civilizations over time. Discreet Islamism (radical Islam) is insidious and less likely to inspire a reaction, and therefore is more dangerous because it flies under the radar.[1] Radical Islam's prime directive isn't killing infidels; rather, its main goal lies in the worldwide implementation of *Shari'a* (Islamic law) in place of secular laws. With great patience, Islamic extremists strive to overcome the social fabric of the West and replace it with a fundamentalist and ancient brand of Islam. Nonviolent Islamism wears away at the freedoms championed by Western democracies, including women's rights, free and diverse religious worship, and all of the impediments to the ancient and repressive Islamic culture that exist in the West. The term "lawfare" has been used to describe the Islamists' rather adroit use of the extraordinary freedoms and mature legal systems that exist in America and other Western nations. Examples are many: Major U.S. universities now provide foot baths (at public expense) for Muslim students to cleanse before prayer. Public gyms have been closed to males in order to prevent offending female Muslim students. Major American publishers have pulled books that are uncomplimentary to Islam and Hollywood has changed the scripts of major motion pictures to replace Islamic terrorists with other non-Muslim villains. This appeasement only encourages and enables the ever-greater Islamization of America and the West. It is not Islamophobic to explore and understand this worldwide movement by millions of Muslims to overcome America and other Western societies. This book is not a severe indictment of Islam, but an honest exploration into the wide world of Islamic extremism. It is an indictment of our cultural obsession with politically correct behavior and other dangerous appeasements. America is increasingly susceptible to the Jihadists' cultural pressures. Jihadists hate our freedoms because they defy Shari'a, laws which they're determined to impose on us. So far, they have been less successful in repealing freedom of speech and other liberties in the U.S. when compared to Europe, but their successes have sharply increased in recent years.

Re-United States is a prescription for America in this age of Islamic extremism and terror. Most Americans are aware of but not very knowledgeable about the subject of radical Islam. The divided state of our government, our media, and our people has an enormously adverse impact on our ability to combat this threat. This book will educate and inform you about these issues and change your perception of this dangerous conflict as it comes into better focus. You are bombarded with news about wars, bombings, protests, and endless global unrest relating to this subject on a daily basis, whether you realize it or not. Too many Americans suffer from a cultural paranoia—the fear of appearing offensive or intolerant based upon anything remotely religious. This is a very dangerous national behavior and one that Islamists are successfully exploiting. American's propensity to appease through political correctness does not seem to percolate to our consciousness. Most of us just do not "get it." This, combined with the crippling state of political division in America, has resulted in an almost complete lack of response to the dangers that radical Islam poses.

Habits and other learned behaviors are difficult to break, but by applying steadfast rules, most destructive behaviors can be overcome. I have successfully treated thousands of patients with illnesses such as hypertension, diabetes, heart disease, obesity, depression, anxiety, marital and work problems, and many others. The first step in treating patients is helping them to admit to their problem and then developing an understanding of the root causes. Armed with this new understanding, chronic and often dangerous maladies can be overcome. America is currently suffering from a kind of malady or disease: a knee-jerk-like reaction to resist the ideas or perspectives of the other side, ironically, a form of intolerance. These behaviors, both personal and national, are increasing our political divisions. We are witness to very dangerous times that require our unity, not our increasing separation into inane political divisions where never the two shall meet. America's rich and proud history demands that we remember and renew our commitment to being "one nation, indivisible." The time is upon us to schedule that dreaded first doctor's appointment that will begin the process of healing—in this case the healing of America. I ask you to consider this book your first visit.

COMMON SENSE MESSAGE

Through knowledge, we the people must guide our leaders, the media, and the far right and left of the people away from useless diatribe as we reunite America with a common purpose, to stem the danger that Islamic extremism poses to America and the West.

ABOUT THE AUTHOR

I have co-authored several medical research papers, a book on geriatric medicine (one of my specialties, along with family medicine), and dozens of position papers as a primary care representative for a large Midwestern hospital, as well as articles for popular magazines in both health care and terrorism preparedness. I deeply believe that ordinary people can effect extraordinary change in the world; I've raised my three children to believe this as well. I am not an expert on Middle Eastern or Islamic history. I am not a politician. Consistent with the spirit of Thomas Paine's *Common Sense*, an inspirational 1775 pamphlet that helped spark the American Revolution, this book is written with the belief that sometimes an average person can be more credible than the pundits and leaders. I harbor a deep patriotism and a hope for this nation despite the flaws that it, like all nations, struggles with. Americans are caught in what seems to be a perpetual state of obstructive, rather than constructive, national dialogue. Through education, books such as *Re-United States* will advance our national dialogue on Islamic extremism that will bleed into the psyche of our nation. Then, finally with renewed unity, purpose, and vigor, we will effectively combat this danger.

THOMAS PAINE'S *COMMON SENSE*

A British tax collector turned author/critic of the British government, Thomas Paine visited the New World in the 1770s. During his stay in America, it became obvious to him that America was at a crossroads. Great Britain was exploiting the colonists in so blatant a fashion that he couldn't believe so many Americans were unable to realize the extent of England's injustices. Mr. Paine met Benjamin Franklin in England, and it was Ben Franklin who arranged for Mr. Paine's first job in the New World.[2] It was also Franklin who suggested to Mr. Paine that he write on the subject of England and the colonies. At the time he suggested this, Franklin had no idea how strongly Mr. Paine felt about the colonies suing for independence from Mother England. He also had no idea how successful Paine's work would be upon its release to the public, nor the role it would soon play in American independence.

Thomas Paine knew that if America was ever to be free, the country must revolt against England, no matter how objectionable this was to him, a loyal English subject. While he understood that civilized people don't generally advocate war to resolve conflict, he also understood there to be times when all other options are exhausted. Lacking fame or fortune, on January 10, 1776, he anonymously wrote the pamphlet *Common Sense*. A very well-known patriot and physician at that time, Benjamin Rush, helped Mr. Paine to publish his essay. He also suggested its title to the author. *Common Sense* described what he saw as the obvious truth: that America must unite, rise up, and expel the British. If it did not, it would be forever subservient to a tyrannical Empire. Thomas Paine arrived in America penniless, and yet he came to feel so strongly about the American cause that he transferred the copyright for *Common Sense* to the newly formed Continental Congress, and all proceeds of the more than 150,000 copies eventually sold helped to finance the Revolutionary War. So popular was this short work that on Christmas Day, 1776, before crossing the Delaware River, General George Washington read *Common Sense* aloud to his troops. At dawn the next morning, his troops would go on to win their first momentous battle in the Revolutionary War. It is in this spirit of promoting greater knowledge (of Islamic extremism in our times as opposed to tyranny in Paine's) and stimulating constructive discussion and debate that *Re-United States* is written.[3]

I

A CALL FOR UNITY

CHAPTER ONE

A Dangerous Time

THE THREAT

America finds itself at a crossroads in history. At the start of the 21st century, America is embroiled in a world war different from every previous global conflict. Compared to the wars against Nazi fascism, a hot war fought by millions of soldiers, or Soviet totalitarianism, a cold war that was essentially nonviolent and political, our current conflict with Islamic extremists is a "warm war," or somewhere in between. Islamic extremism has already resulted in the death of hundreds of thousands of people through terrorism and wars. Some say it is fundamentally a clash between ostensibly incompatible civilizations. In one corner is the modernity of America and the West, and in the other, the status quo of the Middle East, circa 900 A.D.

Islamic radicals are remnants of the despotic, misogynistic rulers and backward thinkers of Islam from a bygone era. They are generally threatened by the West for two reasons. First, they fear that the progressive concepts of democracy, equal rights for women, and *true* separation of religion from politics will infect Islam. These radicals only recognize Islamic law (Shari'a) and reject the established secular laws of nations. Second, and perhaps more threatening, they fear that Muslims living in America have already been contaminated with present-day democratic ideals, and from this perch they will successfully broadcast the message that modern Islam can evolve as the other religions have. If this were to occur, the radical Imams, despots, and chauvinists who have fomented hatred into the psyche of far too many Islamic societies would lose their toxic influence over Muslims and a peaceful and modernized Islam would prevail. In this world, Muslims, Christians, Jews, Hindus, atheists, and agnostics of all races could coexist under the liberalized and secular rule of the contemporary nations in which they live—and Islamic fundamentalism would wither. It is also in this world that devout Muslims would practice their faith in perfect harmony with peoples of all faiths in peaceful coexistence. This is the rightful destination of modern civilization, but it is an abomination to radical Islam.

Fearing this, the worldwide radical Islamic movement including Wahhabiism (Saudi extremists), wealthy extremist sheiks in the Middle East, the Muslim Brotherhood in Egypt and beyond, are indefatigably funding and promoting their propaganda to combat this modernization of Islam. Teaching hatred of Christians, Jews, America, and Israel in Islamic books, schools, mosques, radio and television broadcasts, music, movies, and sermons by Imams from the Middle East to America is a major part of their misinformation campaign. Both violent (terrorism) and nonviolent Islamism are tools used by Jihadists. Islamic terrorism is really just one method used by these zealots, and it thrives only after radical Islamic leaders and Imams first pollute the minds of young and vulnerable Muslims. Therefore, it cannot be overstated that in large part, the lasting solution to Islamic fundamentalism and terror must include enlisting the so-called moderate Muslims to root out their enemy within and stop this promulgation of hate. America and the West need to recognize that these moderates represent the best hope for successfully defeating Islamic extremism.

In America today there exists a culture of appeasement toward Islamic extremism; too many of us fall victim to the notion that it "feels wrong" or "un-American" to be critical of Islamist behavior. Mostly this is so because radical Islam blurs the line between religion and politics. Therefore their extremism, which is political, is wrapped in the cloak of the religion of Islam, and therefore protected from criticism. Much of this book is devoted to shedding light on this critical subject.

Islam has fallen from its peak that occurred in its very early years. All over the world, radical Islamists choose to hate and attack modern civilization in a pathological attempt to eliminate the gap between the West and Islam.

Author's Note: A glossary of terms is provided on page 255 to facilitate your reading and comprehension. As you read on, please recognize that it is imperative to differentiate Islam as represented by the general Muslim population from the Islamic extremists who use their twisted interpretation of Islam to achieve their odious agenda—to impose their oppressive brand of Islam onto as much of the world as possible. Although Islamic fundamentalism is much more widespread than most Americans wish to believe, we must not paint all of Islam with so broad a brush that we stereotype an entire faith. Doing so will only alienate the world's sensible Muslims, further aiding the extremists in their efforts to deceitfully portray the West's defensive war against the extremists as an example of Western aggression and intolerance against Islam itself.

COMMON SENSE MESSAGE

If we keep our eye on the ball, Americans will finally appreciate the magnitude of the danger that Jihad, in all of its forms, poses. When that time comes, we will unite and shed our culture of appeasement and demand Islam to ferret out the Islamist cancer within. Only then will the world's Muslims finally practice their faith alongside peoples of all faiths in peaceful coexistence. This "abomination" to radical Islam is the rightful fulfillment of modern civilization.

IS ISLAMIC EXTREMISM AT WAR WITH THE WORLD?

Before we go any further, let's look at two irreversibly intertwined but still distinct forms of Islamic extremism. The first, a list of Islamic terror events in America and around the world as we ask the question, is Islamic extremism at war with the Western world? The second list is one that depicts a more insidious process of nonviolent or stealth Jihad that threatens to erode American freedoms in a way that no previous threat has. Political correctness and appeasement is advancing the Islamization of America and the West. Consider these examples.

EXAMPLES OF VIOLENT JIHAD (TERRORISM) AGAINST THE WEST:

September 5, 1972: Munich, Germany. Israeli athletes are taken hostage and killed at the Olympics.

November 4, 1979: Tehran, Iran. The U.S. Embassy is taken over by Islamic extremists, resulting in the kidnapping and holding captive of 63 Americans for 444 days.

April 18, 1983: Beirut, Lebanon. A truck is bombed in the U.S. Embassy in Beirut, Lebanon, killing 63 people.

October 23, 1983: Beirut, Lebanon. U.S. Marine barracks are bombed, killing 241 people.

December 12, 1983: Kuwait City, Kuwait. The U.S. Embassy is attacked, injuring 62 people.

September 20, 1984: Beirut, Lebanon. The U.S. Embassy is attacked, killing 2 people.

April 12, 1985: Madrid, Spain. A restaurant is bombed, killing 18 and injuring 82.

June 13, 1985: Rome, Italy. TWA flight 847 is hijacked from Rome to Beirut.

October 7, 1985: Said, Egypt. The cruise ship Achille Lauro is hijacked by the Palestinian Liberation Organization (PLO). An American Jew is killed by Palestinian terrorists when thrown overboard in his wheelchair.

November 23, 1985: Malta. Egypt Air flight 628 is hijacked by 3 Arabs and forced to land at Malta International Airport.

December 27, 1985: Rome, Italy and Vienna, Austria. A massacre takes place at Rome and Vienna airports by the hands of Palestinian terrorists.

April 12, 1986: Athens, Greece. TWA flight 840 is bombed during flight, killing 4.

April 5, 1986: West Berlin, Germany. La Belle Disco bombed by Palestinian terrorists, killing 3 people.

December 21, 1988: Lockerbie, Scotland. Pan AM flight 103, carrying many U.S. military personnel, is bombed mid-air, killing all aboard.

February 26, 1993: New York, New York. The World Trade Center is bombed by Muslim terrorists, killing 6 and injuring 1,000.

June 5, 1996: Riyadh, Saudi Arabia. Khobar Towers at the U.S. compound is bombed, killing 19 and wounding 500.

August 7, 1998: Nairobi, Kenya and Dar es Salem, Tanzania. U.S. Embassies are bombed. 224 people killed, 5,000 injured.

October 12, 2000: Aden, Yemen. USS Cole is bombed, killing 17 and wounding hundreds.

September 11, 2001: New York, New York, Washington, D.C., and Shanksville, Pennsylvania. The World Trade Center and Pentagon are attacked killing 3,000 people and injuring thousands more. United flight 93 crashes in rural Pennsylvania.

October 23, 2002: Moscow, Russia. A theater is seized while some 700 people attend a performance. Russian Special Forces launch a commando raid, and the opium-derived gas they use to disable the captors kills more than 120 hostages, as well as many of the terrorists. Shamil Basayev, one of the most radical Chechen commanders, takes responsibility for organizing the raid.

October 13, 2005: Nalchik, Russia. Chechen rebels assault government buildings, telecommunications facilities, and an airport, killing 85.

November 26, 2008: Mumbai, India. A group of Islamic terrorists with ties to Pakistan terrorize Mumbai (formerly Bombay) over 3 days, killing 164 people, injuring 308. They sought out Americans and particularly Jews to torture and murder, confessed Azam Amir Kasab, one of the terrorists, to the Indian police, as reported in *Times of India*.[4] Investigations are ongoing.

In addition to these examples, the overarching concept of Muslims killing Muslims for ideology is relevant. Al-Qaeda's second in command, Ayman al-Zawahiri, as well as countless other Muslim clerics, have stated that Shari'a allows for Muslims to kill Muslims, particularly those who do not share their radical, fundamentalist views, if the end result is the annihilation of infidels.[5] Consequently, if one includes the figures from Iraq, the 50 (approximate) Muslim victims of 9/11, Israeli Arabs killed by Muslims, and the death tolls of the conflicts in Chechnya, Russia, the Philippines, India, Kashmir, and the other Islamist terror victims around the world, more than 275,000 Muslim and Arab casualties have occurred.

Even more disturbing is that we are living in an age where very little planning and few resources are necessary to perpetrate a calamity. Accomplishing the act of 9/11 took a great deal of time and planning, although not much funding. The technology has existed for decades to pack a nuclear bomb in something the size of a suitcase or backpack. It is not so difficult to imagine an Islamic fanatic gaining access to America through our porous borders or any number of ports of entry with such a weapon. Similar to 9/11, this agent of death would also "fly under our radar" but in this instance would cause unimaginable destruction that renders the 9/11 tragedy a mere harbinger.

By almost any reasonable definition, these events reveal an ongoing war of terror that is being waged by Islamic extremists upon "infidels," who are defined as nonbelievers including Christians, Jews, Hindus, as well as non-radicalized Muslims. We have answered our first question: yes, we are at war.

EXAMPLES OF NONVIOLENT (STEALTH) JIHAD AGAINST THE WEST:

Author's note: As will be described in greater detail later, unlike Christianity or Judaism, Islam is much more than just a faith or religion. It is, as S. Solomon describes in his book The Mosque Exposed, *"a universal religion with a universal mission, a message to all of mankind."[6] Islam, to millions of followers, has a responsibility to enlighten the nonbelievers and deliver them to Islam, whether they wish to be converted or not. Islamists intend to replace our secular laws, our culture, and our faiths with the one universal answer to all things: Islam in the realm of Allah. Some Islamic extremists are less patient in achieving this "utopia" and prefer terrorism as their weapon of choice. Others prefer a slow and nonviolent approach. They use our legal systems combined with the West's liberal and compassionate tolerance to insidiously Islamicize our culture and our system. These methods are referred to as "lawfare" and "slow Jihad," respectively.*

Nonviolent Jihad and the appeasement of it exists in many forms. One way to look at this concept is to label terrorism as *impatient Jihad* and nonviolent Jihad as *patient Jihad.* Impatience is a trait of the hotheaded, often young, and naïve Islamic extremist who is in a big hurry to kill the infidel by blowing himself straight to paradise where 72 virgins await him. The patient variety is a much more thoughtful and clever approach where Islamists use the West's freedoms and legal systems to slowly convert the infidels and their inferior culture to the far superior Islam. Nonviolent Jihad's goal is to insidiously replace Western societies with Islam—both as a religion and as a culture. Many Islamic extremist Imams and leaders around the world take the "long view" in an attempt to achieve the age-old goal of ridding the world of the "unclean" infidels. They believe that the radically violent Islamic terrorist approach is hotheaded and dangerous. They fear that terrorism prompts a vigorous response by the victims (America and the West) that may "awaken a sleeping giant." That phrase was used by Isoruka Yamamoto, the Japanese admiral who warned his emperor that although he could destroy Pearl Harbor in the short term, in the long term America may well rise up to defeat them. These coolheaded radical Muslim leaders prefer the "lawfare" approach where Islam wears away at America by using our own liberalism, legal freedoms, and legal systems to insidiously prevail. As horrific as terrorism is, nonviolent Islamism is more dangerous to America. I will group the following examples of nonviolent Jihad into society, military, government, and media categories.

Examples of nonviolent Jihad are plentiful. I intentionally include examples from both the greater West and America; it is imperative that we understand the global nature of this threat.

SOCIETY:

- University of Michigan, Dearborn campus: Muslim students negotiated for over four years and finally succeeded in convincing the university to construct multiple "foot baths" for their Muslim students as well as a "reflection room" for Muslim prayers—using public funds.[7]

- Harvard University, in 2008, granted Muslim female students (who typically cover hair and skin) a six-hour period per week to privately use their gym for basketball.[8]

- The Islamic Medical Association of Great Britain in 2007 argued on the behalf of certain female Muslim doctors and nurses at a Birmingham University be exempt from "baring from below the elbow in washing" and performing medical procedures, due to religious objections.[9]

- In the Netherlands, proposing that people of all faiths refer to God as Allah in order to "create more dialogue."

- The Archbishop of Canterbury's arguing that adopting elements of Shari'a law in Britain would benefit social cohesion. Shari'a courts actually do exist in several areas of England at this time, including London, Birmingham, Bradford, and Manchester.

- Sponsoring a Muslim lifeguard program for the benefit of private Muslim female sessions at the city pool in Mississauga, Canada. No other group is allowed "private" time in the "public" pool.[10]

- Dropping "Knorbert the piglet" as the mascot of Fortis Bank of Scotland due to fear of offending Muslims.

- The entertainment industry has been very culpable of cultural appeasement to Islamists. Throughout World War II, Hollywood was prolific in its efforts to legitimately reveal who our enemies were—Fascist Japan and Nazi Germany. They commissioned dozens of films and short clips that served the war effort. Today, however, films and television shows with some notable exceptions, avoid Islamic terrorism/extremism like the plague.[11]

- Muslim pressure groups have actively tried to keep movies and TV shows from portraying Islam as anything but a religion of peace. For example, the Council for American-Islamic Relations (CAIR) successfully lobbied Paramount Pictures to change the bad guys in *The Sum of All Fears* (2002) from Islamist terrorists to neo-Nazis.[12] They succeeded and the movie actually portrayed the terrorists that successfully detonated a nuclear bomb in Denver, Colorado as Eastern European mobsters. The book, on the other hand, took great pains to create a backdrop that actually made sense. In the book, Tom Clancy created a scenario where Arabs uncovered a nuclear bomb that Israel had lost, and it found its way into the hands of Islamic extremists who were obsessed with attacking the Great Satan, America.

- FOX's hugely popular series *24*, ran public service announcements during season four by the star of the show, Kiefer Sutherland, emphasizing how nonviolent Islam was. Although CAIR and other groups complained about the Islamic terrorist story line, once again self-censorship by News Corporation—the parent owner of FOX Broadcasting also played a role in these announcements. A number of conservative groups complained to FOX Network and in various blogs that this blatant apology for depicting terrorists as Muslims was an unnecessary appeasement to groups such as CAIR. These groups point out that most terrorists actually are Islamic extremists, so why apologize?

In all fairness to Hollywood, some writers, producers, and studios have braved the waters of conservative-leaning plots. I was told "off the record" by an unnamed, very successful Hollywood producer and writer that money still trumps ideology—even in Hollywood. "The entertainment business is hugely liberal, no doubt, but if a project has the potential for great profits, even the Hollywood liberals are only too happy to forego ideology." Examples include the mini-series *Sleeper Cell*, the TV series

24, and the 2008 movie *The Kingdom*. David Mamet, American playwright, television and film director agrees: "We live in oppressive times. We have, as a nation, become our own thought police; but instead of calling the process by which we limit our expression of dissent and wonder 'censorship,' we call it 'concern for commercial viability.'"

MILITARY:

- Consider this military example of political correctness gone wild. In January 2008, the Pentagon fired Stephen Coughlin, its resident expert on Islamic Jihad. He, reportedly, acknowledged that Islamic terror is motivated by religious Jihad with the West and this antagonized an influential Muslim aide. "That Coughlin's analyses would even be considered 'controversial,'" wrote Andrew Bostom, editor of *The Legacy of Jihad*, "is pathognomonic [representative] of the intellectual and moral rot plaguing our efforts to combat global terrorism." Coughlin was eventually rehired into another Department of Defense position after Bostom and others cried foul. [13]

- A few years after 9/11, President George W. Bush at last acknowledged publicly that the West was at war with Islamic fascism. A number of Muslim organizations took great umbrage with that statement and soon after their protestations, the term "Islamic fascism" was replaced with the now famous "War on Terror." Britain's Foreign Office followed suit and ordered that the phrases Islamic fascism and Islamic extremism be banned by its cabinet members. In January 2007, the Home Office decided that Islamic terrorism would henceforth be described as "anti-Islamic activity," which doesn't even make sense!

- A Minnesotan suicide bomber, a Muslim man originally from Somalia, returned to that country after living in America and blew himself up with 29 other people in October 2008. His family prevailed upon the American government to have his parts (whatever parts remained) returned at public expense.[14]

GOVERNMENT:

- Public officials led Muslim students in prayer in the spring of 2007 at Carver Elementary School in Oak Park, a San Diego, California subdivision.

- Hospitals and government officials in Scotland admonish doctors and nurses to refrain from eating within eyesight of their Muslim patients and colleagues during the month of Ramadan.

- Allowing members of polygamous Muslim marriages (illegal in Great Britain) to claim extra welfare benefits in Britain.

- The Canadian government allows Canadian cab drivers in Vancouver, B.C. to refuse certified guide dogs into their cabs for reasons of religious objection.

- The Voice of America's March 2, 2009 order to stop using these terms: "Islamic terrorist," "Islamic fundamentalism," "Islamist," and "Muslim extremist." VOA employees are to only use the term "extremist."

- The Obama administration's dictum to begin "respecting Islam" resulted in the March 13, 2009 ruling to prohibit the term "enemy combatant."

- The Homeland Security Chief, Janet Napolitano, in early March 2009 revealed to German magazine, *Der Spiegel*, America will no longer use the term "War on Terror" or the word "terrorism." Instead, these will be referred to as "man-caused" disasters.

MEDIA:

- A long-hyped and risqué historical novel based on the

Prophet Muhammad's young bride, A'isha, was slated to be released in August 2008.[15] In a poignant example of censorship, after the book had been accepted by the Book of the Month Club and had been shipped to bookstores, it was pulled by Random House, Inc. Sherry Jones, author of *The Jewel of Medina*, said she was notified by Random House, Inc. that the book's release would be "postponed indefinitely."[16] At issue is the book's depiction of the prophet's wife A'isha, whom Muhammad is said to have married when she was nine years old. In her novel, Jones describes the consummation of their marriage when A'isha was 14. "My book is a respectful portrayal of Islam, of A'isha, and of Muhammad. And anyone who reads it with [an] open mind will come away with an understanding of Islam as a peaceful religion," said the American author. Random House received or was otherwise made aware of a number of complaints from Arab and Muslim groups including such disparate locations as South Africa, America, and Great Britain. Jones, however, maintains that "there were no terrorist threats against Random House. They never received any terrorist threat," she told FOX News.[17] It is noteworthy that eventually *The Jewel of Medina* was published by Beaufort Books in October 2008, and no reported threats or attacks of any kind were perpetrated as a result of its publication. It seems that although soft Jihad played some role in the pulling of this book by Random House, so did the internal, self-censoring Islamist appeasement, which is so prevalent in Western media.

• The American mainstream media is hugely culpable in this dangerous and misguided effort to defang the image of radical Islam out of misplaced political correctness. It has frequently promulgated antiseptic and overly benign portraits of fundamentalist Muslim life. A classic example is Ms. Andrea Elliott's gracious multi-part profile of a New York imam, Reda Shata, which was published in the *New York*

Times in March 2006. Mr. Shata is a Pulitzer Prize winner for an article about Islam. This series portrayed Reda Shata as a laudable interlocutor or mediator between Islam and America. According to a number of Islamic historians and experts, however, this is far from the truth. As it turns out, Shata didn't speak English, sought to forbid music, refused to even shake a woman's hand, and supported Hamas, and more specifically, suicide bombing. The *Times* minimized these and other such disagreeable details. When Middle East scholar Daniel Pipes pointed out that Shata was obviously an Islamist, in prototypical form a writer for the *Columbia Journalism Review* dismissed Pipes as "right-wing" and insisted that Shata was "very moderate."[18]

- Theo van Gogh was murdered in Amsterdam in 2004 in retaliation for his movie that spotlighted Islam's oppression of women. Western media failed to fairly and honestly report these events. The radical Islamic basis for his murder on a street in broad daylight by an Islamic terrorist was largely ignored.

- In 2005 when a Danish newspaper, *Jyllands-Posten*, published a series of 12 cartoons that satirized Muhammad. The Danish author of a book could find no artists to illustrate his book, so the newspaper asked 12 illustrators to draw the prophet for them. The paper's editor, Carsten Juste, said the cartoon was a test to determine if the threat of Islamic terrorism has limited the freedom of expression in Denmark. The resulting *worldwide* Muslim riots, violence, and murders pretty much served as a positive answer to his question. My point here, however, is that the entire incident was seriously underreported and "sanitized" so as not to offend Muslims. The West is "motivated variously, and doubtless sometimes simultaneously, by fear, misguided sympathy, and multicultural ideology—which teaches us to belittle our freedoms and to genuflect to non-Western cultures,"

according to best-selling author and expert in Middle Eastern politics, Bruce Bawer. "These Westerners have begun,
in other words, to internalize the strictures of Shari'a, and
thus implicitly to accept the deferential status of *dhimmis*
[infidels] living in Muslim societies."[19]

- The mainstream American media chronically fails to report
  radical Muslim misbehavior and events. When they do
  report them, they often conceal the Islamic nature of the
  perpetrators. When Salman Rushdie was knighted in June
  2007, the Islamists began another wave of international pan-
  demonium as they decried the West's anti-Muslim bigotry.
  Iran Foreign Ministry spokesman Mohammad Ali Hosseini
  called his knighting "a manifestation of Islamophobia" and
  said: "Giving a medal to someone who is among the most
  detested figures in the Islamic community is... a blatant example of the anti-Islamism of senior British officials." The
  Organization to Commemorate Martyrs of the Muslim
  World was reported to have offered a substantial reward to
  any successful assassin. The group's secretary general said,
  "The British and the supporters of the anti-Islam Salman
  Rushdie could rest assured that the writer's nightmare will
  not end until the moment of his death and we will bestow
  kisses on the hands of whosoever is able to execute this apos-
  tate." This worldwide invitation (if not provocation) to murder Mr. Rushdie was all but ignored by worldwide media.
  Tim Rutten wrote in the *Los Angeles Times*: "If you're won-
  dering why you haven't been able to follow all the columns
  and editorials in the American press denouncing all this
  homicidal nonsense, it's because there haven't been any."

- Another recent example is the Islamic uprising that befell
  the suburbs in France in the fall of 2005. The perpetrators
  of these riots were referred to as "young hoodlums" and occasionally as "immigrants," but the American press rarely
  referred to the Islamic extremism or Jihadist behavior that

it was. Rather they described the uprising as an "outburst of frustration over economic injustice."

• Harvard Law School professor, Noah Feldman, writing in the *New York Times Magazine* in 2007, actually praised Shari'a. He contrasted it favorably with English common law, and described "the Islamists' aspiration to renew old ideas of the rule of law" as "bold and noble."

• In November 2008, Islamist terrorists with links to Pakistan attacked civilians in Mumbai (formerly Bombay), India and murdered nearly 200 people. According to Mark Steyn, a well-known Canadian commentator and bestselling author, "You'd be hard pressed from most news reports to figure out the bloodshed [in Mumbai] was 'linked' to any religion, least of all one beginning with 'I' and ending in 'slam.'" In recent years the media have more or less entirely abandoned the offending formulations—"Islamic terrorists," "Muslim extremists"—and by the time of the assault on Mumbai found it easier just to call the alleged perpetrators "militants" or "gunmen" or "teenage gunmen," as in the opening line of this report in *The Australian*: "An Adelaide woman in India for her wedding is lucky to be alive after teenage gunmen ran amok," said Steyn.[20] This media deception is discussed in *The Jewish World Review* in December 2008: "Greater Mumbai forms one of the world's five biggest cities. It has a population of nearly 20 million. But only one Jewish center located in a building that gives no external clue as to the bounty waiting therein. An "accidental hostage scene" that one of the "practitioners" [terrorists] just happened to stumble upon? "I must be the luckiest Jihadist in town. What are the odds?"[21] Another ridiculous example of refusing to illuminate the anti-Semitic [religious] nature of this event is a piece from Tom Gross writing for the *Wall Street Journal*. He reports: "The discovery that, for the first time in an Indian terrorist atrocity, Jews had been attacked, tortured and killed produced from the *New York Times* a serene befuddlement: 'It is not known if the Jewish center was strategically chosen, or if it was an accidental hostage scene.'"[22] Really, "not known"?

Some of these on their own might appear fairly innocuous. However, when viewed as a global pattern by radical Islam to wear away the freedoms that have been bought and paid for over hundreds of years of societal evolution, these incidents and the failure of America and the West to honestly report and combat them have a far darker connotation.[23] These events reveal an ongoing insidious nonviolent Islamization globally and in America. This exists largely because of our nation's lack of response due a dangerous combination of ignorance, appeasement, and political correctness that is out of control.

COMMON SENSE MESSAGE

Radical Islamists choose to hate and attack modern civilization in a pathological attempt to eliminate the gap between the West and Islam. They use terror and legal (nonviolent) means in their great battle to defeat the modern world of the West, Christians, Jews, and even Asia. A large minority (Pew, CNN, and other polls) of all Muslims tolerate if not encourage Muslim extremism. In them resides the key to defeating Islamic extremism.

AMERICA, A POLITICALLY DIVIDED NATION

Many things need to happen before America and the world can turn the tide on this existential threat. Perhaps the most important first step is for America to wake up and recognize both the serious nature of radical Islam and how our current state of political division renders us impotent to counter the evil intentions of Islamic extremists. We must come to recognize that the extraordinary danger that Islamism poses leaves us no room for petty political squabbles, yet we find ourselves stuck in neutral on this and many other important current issues. America and Americans have made many mistakes with respect to radical Islam. One of the most devastating is the blunder of confusing what many believe to be commendable "tolerance" with dangerous acceptance of wholly unacceptable behavior, actions, and intentions on the part of Islamists today. Both so-called radical Islam and mainstream Islam are culpable; the violent extremists for perpetrating crimes against humanity and mainstream Islam for its curious silence in the face of horrific actions carried out in the name of Islam in recent years. As a nation, we need to more acutely perceive the threat. We then need to understand the extent and nature of our political divisions and that this lack of unity cripples our response to that threat. Only then as a nation can we, with eyes wide open, take the steps necessary to peel back the blinders that have clouded our vision as we react to the Islamist threat to our nation and our way of life.

POLITICAL CORRECTNESS AND APPEASEMENT: THE KISS OF DEATH

Americans pride themselves, as they should, on being a tolerant society and one that promotes a "live and let live" approach to global relations. After all, our nation was born out of the desire to abandon the aristocratic and intolerant repressive rule of Europe. In recent years, however, we have dangerously confused tolerance for others with an obsession with accepting the most heinous and hateful behaviors and actions on the part of Islamic extremists, both at home and abroad. This misguided attempt at staying true to our "tolerance dictum" has enabled and encouraged militant and radicalized Islam to grow and gain worldwide strength. By not vigorously rejecting radical Islam's vitriolic hate speech and call to arms, both literally (terrorism) and figuratively (nonviolent Jihad) at home and abroad, we have grown this modern plague. The result is that scarcely a corner in the world has not been victim to Islamic fundamentalism and terror. Only by honestly reporting and studying this phenomenon of Islamism (Islamic extremism) can we recognize its true threat and finally begin to unite both nationally and globally to fight and eventually expunge this present-day evil that threatens modern civilization.

From the English "Great Charter of Freedoms," better known as the Magna Carta (1215 A.D.), to the U.S. Constitution and Bill of Rights (1787 A.D.), achieving the West's liberty has been a long and arduous journey. Shouldn't we fight as hard to preserve it as our forefathers did to create it? Radical Islam is a horse of another color, intentionally blurring the line between the religion of Islam and its politics. This allows extremists to relentlessly attack the foundation of America and the West with impunity. Neither American leaders nor the press seriously challenge the political treason the Islamists promote, lest they be accused of denying Islam religious protection. The American press plays heavily into the hands of these extremists by failing to properly identify and confront the threats these radicals pose. Counterterrorismblog.org's Jeffrey Imm in his article, "Jihad, Islamism, and the American Free Press," delves into the issue in greater detail.[24] Mr. Imm's point is that in combating the anti-freedom ideology of Islamism, our free press should be our greatest ally. Due to a number of problems including a lack of the precise definition of the Islamist enemy, our leaders and press have created their own foreign policy decision on defining that enemy. Too often, they have concluded that America's conservatives, the Bush administration, and others have exaggerated Islamic enemies.[25] American writer and political commentator Daniel Pipes writes: "Quietly, lawfully, peacefully Islamists do their work throughout the West to impose aspects of Islamic law, win special privileges for themselves, shut down criticism of Islam, create Muslim-only zones, and deprive women and non-Muslims of their full civil rights." So pervasive is the fear of appearing intolerant of Islam that many in the mainstream media prohibit the word Islamism, yet even Al Jazeera has no problem using it.

Cinnamon Stillwell, writing about this global political correctness as exemplified by the 2008 Mumbai, India terror event (mentioned earlier) puts it this way: "Perhaps they [the media] were taking a cue from America's 2007 Departments of State and Homeland Security internal memorandum forbidding employees from using Islam-specific terminology to discuss Islamic terrorism.[26] Stillwell goes on to comment on how the hate-driven savageness and the radical Islamic fanaticism responsible for this tragedy were almost completely ignored for fear of appearing "intolerant." Similarly unexamined were the implications of the terrorists' barbarism. Witnesses described victims being lined up and shot execution-style and terrorists spraying bullets indiscriminately into crowds of men, women, and children. Some survived by feigning death for hours under the weight of countless dead bodies. If not for the heroism of the hotel and restaurant staff, as well as others who rose to the occasion, more lives would have been lost. But lacking analysis, these horrific details were soon forgotten. Is it any wonder that the world no longer grasps the utter depravity and cruelty of the formidable opponent it's facing? This is the same enemy who held hostage and slaughtered Russian children in Beslan; the one who lobs rockets at schools, uses women and children as human shields, preys upon the weakest in their own societies to mold them into suicide bombers, targets mosques and plans attacks on Muslim holidays, murders school teachers and aid workers, commits beheadings, hangings, stonings, and honor killings, puts children and pregnant women into car bombs so they can more easily pass through checkpoints, indiscriminately targets civilians the world over, and who seeks to squelch all human achievement and progress. Not a single example that she uses in this analysis is inaccurate, controversial, or in any way not ordinary *modus operadi* for Islamists, yet why do we cringe when reading it—almost feeling guilty of "stereotyping" or "bigotry"?[27] Where is the outrage? Where are the activists? Is this not at least as important as the trapping of dolphins in tuna nets, whaling off the coast of Iceland, nuclear testing, nudity in films and television, or Danish cartoons that poke fun at the Prophet Muhammad? What about those who advocate free speech to keep in check the world's evils—should they not decry the curious silence that only enables yet further growth of this barbarism? These questions will be carefully examined throughout this book and their answers comprise a major element of the solutions that we will discuss in the final chapter, "The Way Out."

WHY THE APPEASEMENT AND WHEN DID IT START?

The exact causes of this worldwide appeasement of radical Islam are a complicated and sometimes academic subject. When it started may be a bit easier to question although the answer will surprise you.

Vincent Gioia, a retired patent attorney from California, prolifically writes articles (at www.vincentgioia.com) about Islamism and appeasement in particular. He believes that political Islam's pervasive and impious 1,000-year-old desire to replace the world's faiths and cultures with its own is simply not understood by most Americans. It runs counter to the benevolent nature that most believe people harbor.[28] Gioia believes it is a chronic American misunderstanding that began with the inception of America in the 18th and early 19th centuries. President Thomas Jefferson sent the U.S. Navy to destroy the so-called "Barbary pirates" who were raiding ships in the seas of northern Africa headed to and from America. They were based in an area known as the Barbary Coast. Their primary business, however, was capturing Christians and selling them as slaves.

These raids were known as Razzias. Actually these "Barbary" pirates, who called themselves "ghazis" or sacred raiders, were practicing political Islamic doctrine, argues Gioia. They were attacking the infidels not simply for thievery or financial gain but for political purposes.[29] Although this argument is novel, it does have merit. Author Christopher Hitchens, who writes for *Vanity Fair, The Atlantic Monthly, World Affairs, The Nation*, and other publications, discussed this in a 2007 piece for *City* magazine. He writes: "Jefferson would perhaps have been just as eager to send a squadron to put down any Christian piracy that was restraining commerce. But one cannot get around what Jefferson heard when he accompanied John Adams to visit Tripoli's ambassador to London in March 1785. When they inquired by what right the Barbary states preyed upon American shipping, enslaving both crews and passengers, America's two foremost envoys were informed: 'It was written in the Koran, that all Nations who should not have acknowledged their [Islamic] authority were sinners, that it was their right and duty to make war upon whoever they could find and to make Slaves of all they could take as prisoners, and that every Mussulman who should be slain in battle was sure to go to Paradise.'"[30] Gioia believes that despite all of the history that clearly depicts a war declared by radical Islam upon the West and America; we simply do not understand the depth of their commitment to substitute our culture and religion with a superior one: Islam.

I believe that he is spot-on correct in this assessment. Jefferson didn't appreciate the enormity and depth of the Islamists fanatical dream to overcome the world's infidels in 1785, and most of us don't "get it" today. It stands to reason that the brand new American nation, founded upon a bedrock principle that no religious intolerance shall reign within its borders simply did not wish to be embroiled in an age-old religious war. Therefore, the underlying Islamist nature of the conflict between the brand new United States and these holy warriors or ghazis was "overlooked" in a classic act of appeasement. I suggest, therefore, that this decision by Jefferson to ignore the religious component in the Barbary conflict may well be the beginning of American appeasement of radical Islam.

As to why Americans appease Islamic extremism, an interesting theory is put forth by Serge Trifkovic, a European historian writing for *FrontPage* magazine. He says, "Our political and intellectual elite is remarkably inflexible in its secular liberal ideological assumptions. Having no serious religious faith of its own, its members refuse to take seriously the faith of others. Instead of pondering the complex problem of the relationship between the world's great religions—the West and the rest—they assure us that no religious problem exists."[31] He then explains that the West has attempted to co-opt and manipulate Islam for its political and financial gain. "Decades of covert and overt support for 'moderate' Islamic movements, countries, and regimes, whenever they were deemed useful to Western foreign policy objectives—and especially if they have lots of oil, or prove willing to make peace with Israel, or both—have been an unmitigated moral and political disaster."[32] Trifkovic believes that decades of Western and American appeasement (based upon an unwillingness to accept a religious cause for the conflict) has spawned the likes of Osama bin Laden, radicalized Iran, and other "co-religionists" all over the world. The naïve belief that we can wage "war on terror," while maintaining dependence on Arab oil, allowing mass immigration of Muslims into the West, and failing to comprehend the core Islamist overriding goal of ridding the world of infidels is the stuff of a great Greek tragedy waiting to unfold.[33] Other theories include the simple fact that idealistic Americans simply do not believe that evil exists. They will always seek another explanation for depraved acts of terrorism and even horrific wars, anything other than an inherent ill will on the part of some group of people or another. They point to the fact that as late as 1939, 50 percent of Americans refused to believe that Adolph Hitler posed a risk to the world despite mounting and irrefutable evidence to the contrary. Similarly, many refuse to admit the inherent evil in Islamic extremism. This is despite its being responsible for some 275 million deaths over recorded history. That is almost the equivalent of every man, woman, and child in America today.

I believe that while each of these theories has merit, they alone do not explain the pervasive unwillingness to address Islamism except in an oblique and almost apologetic fashion. Only a small number of politicians, historians, and/or pundits clearly promulgate the fact that radical Islam is a dangerous and malevolent movement that must be addressed in an honest and deliberate fashion. Most worry about being labeled as racists. In America, there are few accusations more detrimental to one's career than being labeled a bigot. I believe that fear is the underlying emotion behind our officious appeasement. We simply are not sure how to react to the frightening display of radical Islamic hatred toward us. So far rather than react aggressively to Jihad, be it violent or nonviolent, we retract and hope it all just blows over. We fear that if we respond fiercely, we might further anger these radical killers. Too many Americans simply want to believe that if we behave they will behave and all will be right in the world. Many of our leaders also fear the political ramifications of (mainstream) media criticism of our military actions. In my estimation, stubborn elitism, naïve hope that all people are inherently good, and fear are the ingredients that have brewed for years creating the soup of Islamist appeasement in which we find ourselves. A few of the most recent examples of governmental appeasement and political correctness would be funny if they weren't so sad—and in my estimation, frightening.

As reported by Mark Steyn (Canadian political commentator), Daniel Pipes (Harvard historian), and others, beginning late in the George W. Bush administration there has been a determined effort within the U.S. government to ban candid discussion about the nature of Islamic extremism.[34] The Obama administration has taken an accelerated approach to appease radical Islam so as not to offend them, apparently. Consider these two examples: The first is a new dictum from the Voice of America and the second an Obama administration policy banning certain terms when describing captured terrorists.

A leaked memo dated March 2, 2009 from the head of the Urdu Service at Voice of America (VOA), Jennifer Janin, sheds light on this. It also confirms that it is not a random event but rather a concerted government policy that placates the Islamists. VOA first went on the air in 1942 as a way for the Office of War Information to disseminate via short-wave radio. "News about America and the war that may be good or bad ... [but] we shall always tell the truth." It remains one of the world's most respected international broadcasters. Funded by the American taxpayer and speaking on behalf of the U.S. Government, the Urdu Service of the VOA is broadcast in Pakistan and reaches between 70 and 100 million Muslims in Pakistan, Afghanistan, India, and the Middle East. Janin's memo outlining language and words that are now "forbidden" shockingly reveals a tone of mollification to Islamists that is almost beyond belief. From the memo:

Islamic terrorists: DO NOT USE. Instead use simply: terrorist.

Islamic Fundamentalism / Muslim Fundamentalists: AVOID.

Islamist: NOT NECESSARY.

Muslim Extremists: NOT NECESSARY. Extremist serves well.

As Pipes puts it: "And while we're at it, could someone remind VOA employees that there's a lively debate in the United States about radical Islam; for a change, how about VOA covering this rather than smothering it under the Islamist line."[35]

In one clearer example of how the Obama administration is going to "respect" Islam, it announced its new policy on the term "enemy combatant" when referring to captured Islamist terrorists; it is disallowed.[36] Although enemy combatant is a lawful term for a prisoner of war (POW), also outlawed, it leaves only "detainee" as an acceptable designation. What is most disconcerting is that Obama has already suspended military tribunals and under current military commission law, only "alien unlawful enemy combatants can be tried at the Guantanamo war court."[37] Of course, Guantanamo itself will be closed by the president, so one must wonder whether this is the death knell for the military commissions established by Congress. There has been great apprehension by Americans of all political stripes regarding the disallowance of the term "enemy combatant," the suspension of military tribunals, and the Voice of America dictum to avoid offending Muslims.[38] Hopefully, once the Obama administration reconsiders all of these issues, they will conclude that it is only an aggressive (while just and lawful) offensive against Islamic extremism that will protect us from all forms of Jihad. This subject is carefully examined in a later chapter because it is so poignant an example of the quandary posed by intelligent but opposing perspectives.

This is perhaps the most absurd example of recent governmental appeasement to Islamists. In February 2009, FBI director Robert Mueller, while speaking to the Council on Foreign Relations, warned of Mumbai-type terrorist activity, saying a similar attack could come about in a U.S. city. He discussed the danger of domestic terrorists who become "radicalized," and eventually recruited to perpetrate terrorism on behalf of radical Islam. The point is that Mr. Mueller remains very concerned about the ever-present threat Islamic terrorism poses to America. Although hard to believe, our new homeland security chief, Janet Napolitano, seems to have a different perspective—certainly a different approach. Ms. Napolitano in recent interviews, speeches, and testimony to Congress (the same week as Mr. Mueller's remarks) did not mention the word terrorism once. In early March 2009 in an interview with the German magazine, *Der Spiegel*, she was pressed: "Does Islamist terrorism suddenly no longer pose a threat to your country?" Her reply: "I presume there is always a threat from terrorism." She then went on to refer to terrorism as "man-caused" disasters. "This is perhaps only a nuance, but it demonstrates that we want to move away from the politics of fear." Can you imagine Franklin Delano Roosevelt or Winston Churchill referring to the Nazi bombing of London or the horror of concentration camps as man-caused disasters so as not to offend these perpetrators? I think not. I hope not. If they had, would we have responded to the Nazi fascist threat with the force necessary to prevail? I fear not and yet that is where we seem to be today.

Shortly before publication of this work, what is arguably the worst terrorism event since 9/11 took place at the Fort Hood military installation in Texas. While all of the facts have not been yet established at the time of this writing, this may be the best example of politically correct accession. Major Nidal Malik Hasan, a Palestinian-American and an U.S. Army psychiatrist, reportedly opened fire at Texas' Fort Hood without obvious provocation, killing 13 and wounding at least 31. Hasan was seriously wounded during the attack. The reporting of this tragic event is interesting to say the least. The leftist websites, *The New York Times*, and other media outlets are currently reporting that they have serious doubts that terrorism played a role in this shooting.[39] The *Times* reported this: "investigators, working with behavioral experts, suggested that he may have long suffered from emotional problems that were exacerbated by the tensions of his work with veterans of the wars in Iraq and Afghanistan who returned home with serious psychiatric problems."[40] Following the shooting, the *Sunday New York Times* ran three articles discussing the Post Traumatic Stress Syndrome (Major Hasan never experienced battle) and the dreadful stress that military psychiatrists are subjected to. I suggest that while these topics are valid and important, they are offered on this day only to deflect readers' attention from the more apposite but politically incorrect issue of the day, Islamism. There were, of course, no articles in the *Times* about Islamic extremism.

The president himself cautioned the nation not to "jump to conclusions" and that "we cannot fully know what leads a man to do such a thing." President Obama, extending condolences to the community at Fort Hood, Texas, reminded Americans that people of "every race, faith, and station" serve in the military as he apparently attempted to prevent repercussion against Muslims after the attack.[41]

Now let's consider the following facts as we know them at this time:

- Major Hasan "confessed to his mosque elder months ago that he was conflicted between his devotion to Islam and his allegiance to the U.S. military." (*USA Today*, November 7, 2009)

- Major Nidal Malik Hasan, a Palestinian-American and an Army psychiatrist, reportedly shouted, "Allahu akbar!", which is Arabic for "God is great!" when he opened fire. (FOXNews.com, November 7, 2009)

- Coworkers allegedly complained to the army in the past year that Major Hasan was unusually critical of America fighting in Muslim lands and that he often argued with both colleagues and patients about the legitimacy of America's war against Islamic extremists. (Reported by Sean Hannity, November 6, 2009)

- "Hasan had visited websites that supported radical Islamic ideas and had e-mailed people with similar views and may have written postings, under his name that indicated a favorable view of suicide attacks." (*U.S. News*, November 7, 2009)

"Clearly I think it was a terrorist act. Whether he was connected to another group or not or a formal group is question we'll find an answer to over the next couple of days," said Michael Scheuer, the former leader of the CIA's bin Laden division. Another terrorism expert, Walid Phares, who is a senior fellow at the Foundation for Defense of Democracies, believes this shooting represents "the largest single terror act in America since 9/11. The murders at Fort Hood are about the radicalization of individuals by an extremist ideology, Jihadism, which fuels acts of terror," he said during a statement to FOXNews.com's FOX Forum. He further said that he doesn't expect the shooting to be considered an act of terrorism because the Obama administration has made a major political decision to not fight a war on terror. He cited the administration's decision to substitute the term "Overseas Contingency Operation" for the "global war on terror" as an example. I have to agree with Mr. Phares based upon the facts as we now know them. The imprudent way that the Obama administration and the mainstream media are preemptively trying to avert the terrorism allegation from gaining traction is disappointing. Whatever the final disposition of Major Hasan's motive turns out to be, this may well be one of the most illuminating examples of dangerous and misguided politically correct appeasement.

I will end this section with a series of quotes from all sides of the political landscape. The wisdom gleaned from great history is expressed in these quotes on appeasement and political correctness from liberals and conservatives of various eras.

SIR WINSTON CHURCHILL (PRIME MINISTER OF GREAT BRITAIN) ON APPEASEMENT:

"My good friends, this is the second time in our history that there has come back from Germany to Downing Street peace with honor... I believe it is peace for our time," said British Prime Minister Neville Chamberlain. To which Winston Churchill (then First Lord of the Admiralty) responded: "He [Chamberlain] was given a choice between

war and dishonor. He chose dishonor and he will have war anyway."
(On appeasing Adolf Hitler) *Author's note: This is the quintessential example of weakness and appeasement cloaked as "sensible compromise." Neville Chamberlain sacrificed part of Europe to Hitler in the hopes that Hitler would have mercy. This contrasts with the strength of Churchill who successfully forecast the greatest political error of appeasement in recent history.

"An appeaser is one who feeds a crocodile—hoping it will eat him last."

"There is no greater mistake than to suppose that platitudes, smooth words, and timid policies offer a path to safety."

"Victory will never be found by taking the line of least resistance."

VARIOUS STATESMEN AND PUNDITS ON APPEASEMENT:

"Every lesson in history tells us that the greater risk lies in appeasement, and this is the specter our well-meaning liberal friends refuse to face—that their policy of accommodation is appeasement, and it gives no choice between peace and war, only between fight and surrender."

– President Ronald Reagan, Republican

"There is no calamity which a great nation can invite which equals that which follows a supine submission to wrong and injustice and the consequent loss of national self-respect and honor, beneath which are shielded and defended a people's safety and greatness."

– President Grover Cleveland, Democrat

"No people in history have ever survived who thought they could protect their freedom by making themselves inoffensive to their enemies."

– Dean Acheson, American statesman, Democrat

"I trust that a graduate student someday will write a doctoral essay on the influence of the Munich [Islamist terrorists attacking the Israeli

Olympic athletes in 1972] analogy on the subsequent history of the
20th century. Perhaps in the end he will conclude that the multitude
of errors [appeasing radical Islam] committed in the name of "Munich" may exceed the original error of 1938."

> – Arthur M. Schlesinger Jr., U.S. historian

"Any appeasement of tyranny is treason to this republic and to
the democratic ideal."

> – William Allen White, newspaper editor and author

"Appeasement does not always lead to war; sometimes it leads
to surrender."

> – William Safire, New York Times columnist

"No man can tame a tiger into a kitten by stroking it. There can be
no appeasement with ruthlessness. There can be no reasoning with
an incendiary bomb."

> – President Franklin D. Roosevelt, Democrat

"You may gain temporary appeasement by a policy of concession to
violence, but you do not gain lasting peace that way."

> – Anthony Eden, British Prime Minister

"If all printers were determined not to print anything till they were
sure it would offend nobody, there would be very little printed."

> – Benjamin Franklin

"Being Politically Correct means always having to say you're sorry."

> – Charles Osgood, CBS radio and television commentator

COMMON SENSE MESSAGE

Americans and the West, often with good intentions, have confused "tolerance" of insufferable behavior by Islamic extremists with broadmindedness consistent with the "live and let live" attitude expected of a good American citizen. This misguided attempt to be the ever-tolerant American neighbor has permitted militant and radicalized Islam to grow and gain worldwide strength. In other words, our appeasement and politically correct silence has grown this epidemic. Americans must reevaluate the proper response to this threat. Reconciling our morality with a practical approach to radicalized Islam will unite us both nationally and globally to fight and eventually expunge this present-day evil that threatens modern civilization.

IS AMERICA AN INTOLERANT NATION?

I find it interesting that it has become popular to accuse America of Islamic intolerance and xenophobia. In Europe, the Middle East, and most significantly here in America the drum beat of America's bigotry pervades the print and news media. This is largely due to the fact that criticism of any aspect of Islam has become synonymous with shameful intolerance. Somehow America has lost the "moral high ground" in its attempt to fend off Islamic extremism. I find this fascinating because America is the birthplace and still the best example of the world's most successful experiment in multiculturalism, by far.

Our nation was founded by immigrants from a multitude of ethnic and religious backgrounds who willingly came together to forge a New World—one based upon tolerance and mutual respect. After all, they fled the tyrannical and intolerant regimes that we are now accused of having become. One can certainly argue that the American Indians and African slaves weren't invited to the party, at least early in America's history, but these are an aberration rather than the rule in America, past and present.

Let's briefly review the history of the Africans in America at its founding because this issue is often used as the quintessential example of America's inherent evil and intolerance. Many Africans, soon to become African-Americans, fought willingly in the war of independence even after earning their freedom while fighting for the Continental army. In other words, many African-Americans voluntarily contributed to the formation of this nation, adding their ilk to the fabric of multiculturalism in the hope that true equality and freedom within the American New World would materialize for them as well. The colonies in these pre-American years allowed slavery but did not invent it. Regretfully, due to the colonial South's economic system, slavery was impossible to eradicate in 1776 and again in 1787 when the Constitutional Convention was held in Philadelphia, Pennsylvania.[42] Many founding fathers including John Adams, James Madison, and even Thomas Jefferson (who owned some 200 slaves) knew that slavery was morally wrong and in direct conflict with the very spirit of what America was all about—yet America would never have come together as a nation if slavery was outlawed at that time.[43] The most that could be achieved in those early years was the prohibition of slavery in the "new lands" beyond the original 13 colonies—leaving the issue of slavery to finally be resolved in a bloody Civil War some 80 years later. The marvelous book, *Miracle in Philadelphia*, by Catherine Drinker Bowen, masterfully covers this and every other contentious issue during the fitful birth of early America through the prism of the Continental Convention in 1787.[44] It is at least an honorable mention that on November 6, 2008 America elected an African-American, Barack Obama, president.

American Indians are another story and one whose final chapter is not yet written. Suffice it to say that painful corollaries still plague this proud but displaced people from unethical and self-serving decisions on the part of an early American government. These two examples of bigotry and intolerance serve as deviations that flout the "Golden Rule" that is the core of America's soul: treat others as you would like to be treated. In recent years, many would have us believe that rather than aberrations, these examples are the epitome of America's value system—a shameful and unfounded charge that all Americans should unabashedly reject.

In our day, when America combats the cruel and primitive intolerance of ancient and radical Islamic extremism, it is too often accused of being "prejudiced" of all Muslims, presumably because they are somehow different than most of us. Is it not self evident that we MUST be intolerant of the world's most prevalent and oppressive form of intolerance (radical Islam) if we are to overcome it? What would the world be like today if during the 1940s America was consumed with the obsession of appearing "peaceful" and "tolerant" of all peoples, even a Nazi Germany? Would we have marshaled the strength to create from scratch the war machine that eventually delivered the world (with the help of allies, of course) from the wickedness of Nazism? Was not our "intolerance" of the Nazis not only justified, but necessary? If so, is not our "intolerance" of Islamic extremism similarly justified?

Herein lies the most poignant and central issue to America's current division on this most important topic—one that is literally splitting our nation in two. While we hope that all decent people desire peace, is there peace other than through strength? In the utopia that exists only in the hopeful minds of too many complacent, too comfortable, and idealistic members of the Western world, the answer is yes. To others (including this author) who subscribe to the belief that there is still evil in the world the answer is no. We prefer to apply Ronald Reagan's famous adages "peace through strength" and "trust but verify." It is only through the just application of moral and military strength that peace can be won and preserved. In other words freedom isn't free; it must be hard fought for. With one eye on the elusive prize of peace and the other on the moral and ethical standards that define us as a people, we must find the common ground and come together as a single nation as we did in World War II.

COMMON SENSE MESSAGE

For too long too many Americans, Europeans, and others have incessantly accused America of being a racist, intolerant, and immoral nation. One example often used to support that claim is that of the history of African-Americans. While there is no doubt that our history confirms that the journey of Africans in America has been a difficult one, the real story confirms the greatness, morality, and decency of America and Americans. Slavery and therefore racism existed here before the founding of our nation. As far back as during the tumultuous birth of America, great national debates and altercations over slavery marked the Colonial period. It took a while, but we got it right, proving the integrity of our nation and its people. In this regard, America is the antithesis of our Islamic extremist enemy: the most racist, intolerant, and hatemongering people on Earth.

CHAPTER TWO

Who Is The Enemy?

ISLAM DEFINED

Islam is a religion with well over one billion adherents, and that number continues to grow rapidly. In America alone, there are nearly two million Muslims (in layman's terms, any who follow Islam). Islam was founded by the Prophet Muhammad in or around the year 622 A.D. According to the historians Bernard Lewis and Daniel Pipes (with numerous other scholars supporting their position), Muslims believe in Allah, the *One God* that most believe is the same God as Yehuda, the Jewish *One God*. Muslims believe that Islam improves upon Christianity and Judaism, and is therefore a more perfect and superior religion than its predecessors. As stated in the opening paragraph, it is imperative to distinguish between Islam and Islamic extremism. It is equally important to distinguish between violent and nonviolent Islamic extremism. I have no desire to indict one-fifth of the world's population as hate-mongers. Islam, according to all reputable historians and scholars, is a perfectly legitimate religion grounded in the same mores and ethics as Christianity, Judaism, and other major religions of the modern world. There is one fundamental difference, however. It is that Islam is often incorrectly defined as a religion or faith alone. Islam is actually a universal system including religious, civic, and socio-political system. *The Mosque Exposed* by S. Solomon describes Islam as "a universal religion with a universal mission, a message to all of mankind."[45] This is a hugely important concept that is foreign to most non-Muslims with the exception of the most devout and pious Christians, Jews, Buddhists, Hindus, and others. A prevailing and universal theme taught by Islamic leaders and Imams the world over is that "Islam is Life and Life is Islam." It is also critical that we understand that, according to Muslim tradition and scriptures, it is incumbent upon Muslims to spread Islam to the world's infidels. This concept is central to the worldwide struggle by radical elements of Islam to overcome the nonbelievers and impose unto them the superior ways of Islam.[46]

There are two main sources for Islamic doctrine or law: they are the Qur'an and the Sunna. The Qur'an is believed by Muslims to be the word of Allah as presented to the Prophet Muhammad. The Sunna is the collective words, lessons, and deeds of Muhammad. Sunna literally interpreted means "way of the Prophet." Not to confuse the matter but another word, the Hadith also means "words and deeds" and is somewhat interchangeable with the word Sunna. Many Islamic scholars maintain that the Sunna is needed to interpret the Qur'an and it cannot be overstated how important it is for Muslims to obey the injunctions of Muhammad, the most venerated of any Muslim past or present.[47]

As in every religion, it is the manner in which religious leaders interpret the ancient writings and lessons that determines the current day complexion of that faith. In fairness, it should be noted that there are fundamentalist movements in Christianity and Judaism just as there is in Islam. However, Islam has struggled far greater with the concept of religious evolution and has therefore not undergone the reformation that the other major religions have. Islamic extremists, by inexorably obeying the ancient commands to convert infidels and impose Islam upon the nonbelievers through both violent and nonviolent means, are creating havoc in all quarters of the world today.

COMMON SENSE MESSAGE

Islam is a complex religion, born from a desire to "improve upon Christianity and Judaism." It, like the other major religions, has elements within it from a more primitive and brutal time. Islam, unlike its counterparts, has yet to undergo the evolution necessary to integrate or assimilate into the modern world.

ISLAMIC EXTREMISM DEFINED: "RADICALISM," "EXTREMISM," "FUNDAMENTALISM," AND "ISLAM<u>ISM</u>"

These terms and what they represent are somewhat more difficult to define. With the help of various scholars on the subject, this section should suffice our needs. First, let's clarify a few definitions; the distinction between the terms Islamism, Islamic extremism, Islamic radicalism, or fundamentalism can be quite erudite and voluminous enough to devote an entire book to. There are actually subtle distinctions between these terms, but for our purposes, they will all represent a deviation from Islam that is at the root of the current war between Islamic extremists and the West. In this book, we will generally use the term Islamic extremist to reduce this confusion. Whether you see the word radical, Islam<u>ist</u>, or Islamic extremist, interpret them here as synonyms. Lastly, the term Jihad generally means "holy war" and is always a term reserved for acting in the name of God. Jihad in this book generally refers to violent or terroristic Jihad unless "nonviolent Jihad" is used.

Many historians, including the esteemed Antony Black, G.E. von Grunebaum, and Bernard Lewis, believe that radicalization of Islam is at least in part due to the relative failure of Islam to maintain power and influence in the world after its early hegemony.[48] In other words, Islamic extremism is a response to the clear contrast between the medieval successes and worldwide influence that Islam once enjoyed and the modern-day marginalization of Islam.

Although the dominance of "Western society" (which is almost but not quite synonymous with Christianity) over Islam has been occurring for more than 1,000 years, there are factors in recent times that have rekindled the spirit of Islamic discontent. These include the oil wealth of Arabs who can now fund quasi-military attacks on Western influences, the envied American and Western European supremacy in terms of their wealth in the global economy, Western military, and technological capability, and the creation of the Jewish state of Israel (a prosperous "Western" nation in the heart of Arabia). This cultural hegemony of the West has resulted in a collective Islamic cultural humiliation. Islamic extremists react to this humiliation by focusing their shared anger onto one clear enemy: the West.[49] Another catalyst for extremist reaction is the revelation that the Great Powers are more vulnerable than previously believed. The 1979 Iranian revolution revealed a new type of susceptibility on the part of America, just as the Soviet military loss in Afghanistan did. Both of those events have taught extremists that giant military powers can be defeated by much weaker opponents through guerrilla warfare and terrorism. The world's acceptance of and relative silence toward Arab terrorism against Israeli civilians is likely to have encouraged Islamic terrorism against a broader enemy in the U.S., Europe, and elsewhere. The root causes of Islamic extremism is further explored in later chapters, but for now, let's look at the reaction of Muslims to these precipitants.

Daniel Pipes believes that Muslims have devised three identifiable political responses to modernity: *Secularism, Reformism,* and *Islamism.* Many permutations of these basic categories exist in Muslim and non-Muslim countries throughout the world.[50]

The Secularists believe that Islam must emulate the West, and that the Islamic Sacred Law of Shari'a should be largely abandoned for modernity's sake if Islam is to regain stature.

They reject Jihad and violence against non-Muslims, and they wish to fit into the modern world seamlessly while remaining Muslim. The best example of Secularism can be found in present-day Turkey. This is, however, a minority Islamic position, and even in Turkey this secularism has been under attack by fundamentalists—most seriously so in recent months.

The Reformists believe that Islam is actually compatible with Western society, culture, and invention, such as the advances in the sciences. In fact, Reformists believe that Islam is actually the true source behind most of the advances in the modern world, but the West has taken credit for it. Reformists, according to Mr. Pipes, fall back on revisionist history in pretending that Islam never lost ground to Christianity, save for "fictitious" Western history books and writings. Reformists practice the Muslim faith devotedly, and they only partially abandon traditional Islamic Law.

Islamism (Islamic extremism) are extremists devoted to Islamic Law or Shari'a. They tend to reject many, if not *most* Western influences, and believe that Islam lags behind the West because of ideological failings; namely that most of Islam's practitioners are not "good and true" Muslims. The extremists struggle to reject all things Western, but at the same time use the West's technology, weapons, strategies, and telecommunications to conduct their war against it. Extremists are contradictory in other ways. Some Muslim radicals such as the Taliban wish to revert back to the old way of life, though most are city dwellers who wish to somehow fuse the fundamentalist ways of past centuries with modernity and its trappings. Most notably, Islamic extremists embrace hatred and intolerance of the infidels (Christians, Jews, Americans, and the West), though that same hate is also directed at more moderate Muslims who are unwilling to participate in Jihad.[51]

COMMON SENSE MESSAGE

Radicalized Muslims come in many forms. Although they vary by sect, philosophy, degree of fanaticism, rejection of modernity, and hatred of infidels, they share a common belief. They share the belief that they must defeat, convert, or destroy infidels because integration and coexistence with non-Muslims is anathema to them.

WHICH IS MORE EFFECTIVE: VIOLENT JIHAD (TERRORISM) OR NONVIOLENT JIHAD?

Some say America is a melting pot where diverse peoples can come together to fulfill the "American Dream." This dream is remarkably idealistic, although we are closer to it than ever. The achievement of this dream, however, is predicated on one very clear and requisite tenet: each ethnicity, religion, or race must consider themselves Americans first and that we accept that the "whole" is inviolable and supersedes its parts.[47] Each group brings its culture, mores, and a unique ethos with them, but members of each group should not expect, and should certainly not demand that the whole must bend to their particular will or fit their singular notion of what our nation should be. Non-extremist American Muslims are just like the rest of us: grateful and patriotic believers that America is the greatest nation on Earth, a place where we can all celebrate our uniqueness and be encouraged to practice our particular faiths and beliefs, free from the tyranny and oppression that has plagued humankind since its inception. Islamic extremists, on the other hand, are a group of fundamentalists who attempt to bend the host nations they immigrate to toward their severe version of Islam. These Islamists use many tools and weapons to help them achieve this goal, and it is important to realize that terror is just one weapon that extremists employ. In this section we will address both violent Islamic extremism (terrorism) and nonviolent Islamic extremism.

VIOLENT ISLAMISM (TERRORISM)

Violent Jihad or Islamic terrorism is probably very familiar, so let's start here. Terrorism is often defined as "low-intensity warfare used against civilians by groups or individuals to achieve political or ideological goals."[52] Terrorism is a low-cost (but potentially high-yield) weapon used most often by weaker forces against stronger ones. Terrorism is not always successful, but there is no doubt that over the last century there have been many examples of terrorism that achieved the stated goal, including the retreat of whole armies. For example, the Beirut, Lebanon bombing which killed 241 U.S. Marines in 1984 resulted in early U.S. withdrawal. Similarly, the 1993 Muslim terrorist attack on U.S. Marines in Mogadishu, Somalia during Operation Hope resulted in an almost immediate departure of U.S. forces. Perhaps the best example is the 2004 train bombing that killed 200 people in Madrid, Spain, instigating a regime change to a candidate much more sympathetic to Muslim fundamentalism in the next election.[53]

The very word "terrorist" has a negative connotation, and is therefore a politically charged term. Terrorists often define themselves as freedom fighters, *fedayeen*, or guerrillas. I will define an Islamic terrorist as one that targets violence upon innocents for Islamist political purposes. Again, not all Islamic extremists are terrorists, some pursue nonviolent means, but those who attack civilians to advance radical Islam are terrorists.

I rely on many polls throughout the book as the most accurate way of assessing and reporting people's attitudes and dispositions. There are many types of polls and a number of organizations conducting them. They include the major news channels like CNN and FOX News. Other organizations include the Gallup organization, ABC News, *The New York Times*, *The Washington Post*, and the Pew group. While I utilize all of these and more, I mostly draw on Pew polls for two reasons. First, the Pew organization is widely respected for its integrity, neutrality, and methodology. Second, they study the subject of global Islam and radical Islam more completely than any other group in the world.

How many Islamic extremists are there, anyway? The actual number is very difficult to define. Most political researchers break this question down into five categories. These categories include those that *support, tolerate, appease, enable,* and actually *engage in* what we call terrorism. A Pew poll of 14,000 Muslims in 10 countries released several findings that were revealing. At least 15 to 20 percent of all Muslims fall into one of the first four categories, but the vast majority do not personally *engage* in acts of violence or Jihad. In other words, a large minority of Muslims harbor extremist views even if they do not actively engage in violent Jihad. Many other polls conducted post 9/11, including those from Civitas (British National Party News in 2008) and the Gallup organization (2006), place that number nearer to 25 percent depending on world circumstances at the time of polling. The June 2006 Pew Research Center poll sheds some light on this issue. These polls also concluded that Westerners and Muslims around the globe view one another across a wide divide of suspicion. It found that many Americans and Europeans view Muslims as fanatical and violent. Even greater numbers of Muslims in the Middle East and Asia see Westerners as "selfish, arrogant, and violent."[54] Many Westerners blame the violence around the world that resulted from Danish cartoons that depicted the Prophet Muhammad on "Muslim intolerance." But in that Pew poll, 90 percent of Muslims blamed it on Western disrespect of Islam and thereby found the Muslim reaction entirely justified. While this type of reactionary demonstration is generally not violent (and therefore not terrorism), it is representative of the temperament of Muslims that may lower the threshold for actual acts of terror.[55]

Muslims living in European countries have a more temperate view of Westerners than those in Asia and the Middle East, the poll also found. Even so, one out of every seven Muslims in France, Spain, and Great Britain feel that suicide bombings against civilian targets can be justified to "defend" the name and spirit of Islam. Consider the significance of this: 15 percent of Western Muslims support the suicide bombing of innocent civilians to avow a political statement!

A majority of those surveyed in Egypt, Indonesia, Turkey, and Jordan said that Arabs didn't carry out the 9/11 attacks on the United States. Most tribal Pakistanis agree. Andrew Kohut, director of the Pew Research Center, says, "Those attitudes reflect strong emotions [that] get in the way of rationality."[56]

Also noteworthy is that support for suicide bombing attacks against civilians declined sharply in Jordan, following a deadly terrorist attack on Jordanian soil in 2005. In 2006, 29 percent of Jordanians said suicide attacks are often justified, compared with 57 percent in 2005 prior to their terror attack. A repeat and somewhat smaller 2007 European poll suggests a continued trend away from this radicalism, although it is still very troubling given that a significant minority of Muslims still condones murder as fair retribution for political thought. The Associated Press on May 22, 2007 reported in another global poll that one in four younger U.S. Muslims say suicide bombing to "defend their religion" is acceptable under some circumstances even absent of any physical threat or violence. Consider these percentages: 17 percent of Turks, 14 percent of Pakistanis, and 28 percent of Egyptians believe that suicide bombings against civilian targets to defend the "honor of Islam" are often justified.[57] Twenty-five percent of American Muslims justify suicide bombings without physical provocation. These are some pretty chilling numbers. Many historians and politicians find the results both surprising and profoundly disturbing. Particularly so, since verbal expression of ideas pejorative toward Islam with no physical threat are justification for murdering innocent civilians for a significant percentage of the Islamic faith.

COMMON SENSE MESSAGE

Violent Jihad is Islamic terrorism. Nearly the entire world has felt its bite, including many Muslim countries. It is not only the actual perpetrators of violence that are responsible for their dreadful acts against innocents. So are the millions of Muslims that quietly condone, support, and/or justify terrorism against innocents as a legitimate political strategy.

WORLD MUSLIM POPULATION

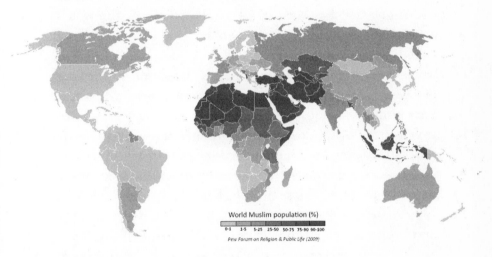

World Muslim population (%)

0-1   1-5   5-25   25-50   50-75   75-90   90-100

Pew Forum on Religion & Public Life (2009)

Source: The Muslim population of the world map by percentage of each country, according to the Pew Forum 2009 report on world Muslim populations. http://en.wikipedia.org/wiki/File:World_Muslim_Population_Pew_Forum.png

NONVIOLENT ISLAMISM (JIHAD)

It is important, particularly when reading this section, to remain mindful that Islam is not simply a faith. Islam is a universal belief system—a faith, a sociopolitical, an all-encompassing way of life—and therefore, it is not only reasonable but obligatory for many Muslims to transform any society in which they live toward the ways of Islam. This idea of conversion has been a pervasive force within Islam as it has been for the past 1,400 years. S. Solomon notes that throughout their history, moderate Muslims have not been able to successfully stray from the traditional, albeit radical, position that Islam is a superior faith and that it is the duty of all Muslims to convert or overcome infidels and nonbelievers in all lands. Islam is a comprehensive way of life rendering the very idea of "separation of church and state," or in this case, "mosque and state," anathema and entirely repugnant to Muslim fundamentalists.[58]

As discussed earlier, the issue on nonviolent Jihad and lawfare is one that has been largely unrecognized by the American public. Aside from a few individuals who have studied and written on the topic such as Brigitte Gabriel, Nonie Darwish, Steve Emerson, Dr. Zuhdi Jasser, and others, nonviolent Jihad receives very little public attention. Because this type of Islamic extremism is insidious it does not evoke as powerful a reaction as violent terrorism does. There is no military response to the slow Islamization of America; one court case at a time, one misguided media and government-driven capitulation of our freedom at a time, we lose the long war against religious intolerance by our over-tolerance. I believe that this is largely due to a misplaced fear of appearing bigoted on the part of many Americans. This fear prevents their willingness to acquaint themselves with, let alone reject, the slow Islamist creep that threatens our freedoms. This is curious because America is a nation founded by immigrants that has been at the forefront of promoting liberty throughout the world since its inception. In recent decades nearly any reaction to oppose Islamic extremism sets off the political correctness alarm and our Islamist foes fully exploit this as they march forward with their agenda. Groups such as CAIR are responsible for this so far successful tactic. CAIR, the Council on American-Islamic Relations, is one of the best known and most controversial organizations in America. CAIR likes to represent itself as the quintessential advocate for Muslims in America—they compare themselves to the NAACP. Many knowledgeable counterterrorism experts and congresspeople, including influential senators Charles Schumer (D-NY) and Dick Durbin (D-Ill), believe CAIR to be radical in nature with ties to terrorism. The Department of Homeland Security refuses to deal with them.

On April 6, 2009 the following Center for Islamic Pluralism advertisement appeared in *The Weekly Standard*, a popular American conservative magazine.

We, the undersigned American Muslims, have long known the true character of CAIR and its allies. Therefore:

• *We observe that they denounce "terrorism" in general terms but not the specific actions of Islamist groups like Hamas or Hezbollah. They denounce violence but not the ideologies behind it.*

• *We observe their commitment to radical aims, their attempts to chill free speech by calling critics of radical Islam "Islamophobes," and their false, ugly accusations against moderate American Muslims who disagree with their agenda.*

• *We reject any claim that CAIR and its supporters are legitimate civil liberties advocates or appropriate partners between the U.S. government and American Muslims.*

• *We congratulate the FBI for adopting a firmer attitude toward CAIR, as a defense of Americans of all faiths from the menace of radical Islam, including Muslims of all backgrounds—Sunni, Shia, Sufi, secular, etc.*

• *We call on the U.S. Department of Justice to affirm and continue this decision.*

• *We call on the entire United States government to follow suit in rejecting relations with the Council on American-Islamic Relations.*

(Signed:)

Dr. Kemal Silay, President, Center for Islamic Pluralism, www.islamicpluralism.org

Supna Zaidi, Assistant Director, Islamist Watch, www.islamist-watch.org

M. Zuhdi Jasser, American Islamic Forum for Democracy, www.aifdemocracy.org

Imaad Malik, Fellow, Center for Islamic Pluralism

Dr. Ahmed Subhy Mansour, International Quranic Center, www.ahl-alquran.com

Khalim Massoud, reformislam@gmail.com

Nawab Agha Mousavi, American Muslim Congress and Center for Islamic Pluralism

Kiran Sayyed, Council for Democracy and Tolerance, http://cfdnt.com

Stephen Suleyman Schwartz, Executive Director, Center for Islamic Pluralism, Shia.Protest@yahoo.com

Dr. Jalal Zuberi, Southern U.S. Director, Center for Islamic Pluralism [59]

This public memorandum is immensely important for two reasons. First, it clearly supports the validly of my basic premise; by summarily rejecting violent and stealth radical Islam, one is NOT exhibiting anti-Muslim bigotry. Second, that many moderate Muslim groups exist and are in desperate need of American independents and liberals to recognize their message. Only then, when all reasonable Americans can unite in understanding the truth about Islamic Jihad, will we turn the tide against Islamist fascism at home and abroad.

Virtually all of the Islamic groups in America that reject Islamism, radicalism, anti-American, and anti-Semitism, regard

CAIR as an Islamist (slow Jihad) group. These are *devout Muslims* who are not only in agreement that nonviolent Jihad is a threat to America and the agenda of these Islamist groups, they are in the forefront of combating it. We must appreciate that nonviolent Jihad's goal is to insidiously replace Western societies with Islam—both as a religion and as a culture.

The Mosque Exposed carefully explores the concepts of Dar al-Islam, Dar al-Harb, and al-Takiyya (pronounced tark-ee-ya). These terms are foreign to most readers, but they are easy to understand. The glossary at the end of the book is also a quick reference tool if needed. It is critical to understand these Islamic teachings when conceptualizing the overall goal and methods used by radical Islam. Dar al-Harb are the rules Muslims follow in non-Islamic lands (Muslims in America, for instance) and Dar al-Islam are the rules non-Muslim infidels are subjected to when they live in Islamic lands (Americans in Saudi Arabia, for instance) and regards them as separate and generally unequal guests legally and socially. Dar al-Harb is literally translated as "House at War." Whether violent or nonviolent, the ultimate goal is the subjugation of the non-infidels into becoming followers of Islam as that nation surrenders to Islamic rule. Under the laws of subjugation in Islam, non-Muslims in Muslim lands are provided a choice to convert to Islam or pay a hefty tax and they have few political rights.[60] Such has been and currently is the case in virtually all Islamic lands since the inception of the Muslim faith. While Dar al-Islam certainly concerns non-Muslims living in Muslim nations, it is Dar al-Harb (House at War) that is of great importance to Western society since it wishes to transform our nations.[61]

According to the aforementioned author, S. Solomon, and many other Islamic scholars, the goal of a large minority of Muslims is ultimately to convert the host nations (Dar al-Harb) into Islamic ones (Dar al-Islam).[62] In other words, whittle away at the societies of nonbelievers until, eventually, the majority become "believers," is the final objective. Solomon goes on to describe a series of intermediate goals where ever-increasing Shari'a law is achieved in Western lands through relentless political and legal maneuvers by Islamic extremists through nonviolent means via soft Jihad. They take advantage of democratic liberties while exploiting the West's obsession with political correctness, to slowly Islamize Western nations. In support of the Islamic extremist desire to convert the world to Islam, consider this statement by the former Turkish Prime Minister Necmettin Erbakan (1996-1999) to a German journalist—all the more disturbing when one considers that Turkey is a secular nation: "You think we Muslim Turks come here [to Europe] only for employment and to gather crumbs of your money. No, we are coming here to take control of your country and by being rooted here, and then building what we see as appropriate, and all that with your consent and according to your laws."[63]

Another example of this prevalent but extremist philosophy can be found in Khurram Murad's booklet, *Islamic Movement in the West: Reflections on Some Ideas*. In it, he quotes Sheikh Qaradawi, recently barred from Great Britain: "...it would be equally tragic if the tall and noble claims to the objective of a worldwide revolution and the ushering in of a new era was reduced to mere fulfillment of religious and educational needs... despite its seeming unattainability, the movement in the West should reaffirm and reemphasize the concept of total change and supremacy of Islam to Western society as its ultimate objective and allocate it to the highest priority."[64]

According to many authors and Middle Eastern experts, radical Islam is a revolutionary ideology, an ideology fixed on altering the social order of the whole world, and rebuilding it in conformity with its own tenets and ideals. As S. Solomon describes it, "The Islamic movement is an organized struggle to change the existing society into an Islamic society."[65]

The Investigative Project on Terrorism reported on July 20,

2009 in Oak Lawn, Illinois on an Islamist convention in the U.S.[66] The self-declared nonviolent international movement to reestablish an international Islamic state, Hizb ut-Tahrir, held a conference intended to recruit adherents to their cause. Their cause is to hasten the fall of America and the West in favor of a new caliphate to lead the world in a Muslim revolution. Some 300 people crowded into the Grand Ballroom of the Hilton Hotel. Woman were relegated to the back to "prevent people behaving like animals," consistent with the misogynistic tenets of fundamentalist Islam. Many of the speakers were so bizarre that it is difficult to take them seriously with statements like capitalism is a form of economic "terrorism" and "it causes us to be sent to mental hospitals" and the "CIA is to blame for [the behavior of despotic Muslim regimes and terrorists]." Of note is that Hizb ut-Tahrir is not considered a terrorist group by the U.S. Government because it insists its approach is one of nonviolent Jihad.[67]

The ever-vigilant Muslim activist and president of the American-Islamic Forum for Democracy, Dr. Zuhdi Jasser, stated, "Hizb ut-Tahrir preaches an ideology that calls for the destruction of the principles that America is founded on." He added, "While their words are protected by our First Amendment, their actions and movement must not be allowed to take hold. The silence of American Islamist organizations like [the Council on American-Islamic Relations] CAIR and [the Islamic Society of North America] ISNA in condemning the ideologies of Hizb ut-Tahrir and their agenda of insurgency in America speaks volumes to their own, albeit more camouflaged, Islamist agenda."[68]

Consider these comments by speakers and conference organizers:

> "[If we continue to push for change] the modern industrial powers could fall to Muslims the way Mecca fell to Muhammad nearly 1,400 years ago."

"If they offer us the sun, or the moon, or a nice raise, or a passport, or a house in the suburbs or even a place to pray at the job, on the condition that we stop calling for Islam as a complete way of life—we should never do that, ever do that—unless and until Islam becomes victorious or we die in the attempt."

"If the United States was in the Muslim world, the Muslims who are here would be calling and happy to see the Shari'a applied, yes we would and the Constitution gone. That's all."[69]

This attempt to force the West to yield to the customs and laws of Islam (a few of which are mentioned above)—are in contradistinction to other minorities who acclimate to the nations they choose to migrate to or reside in. At the forefront of combating this goal of transforming America into a more Islamic-like culture are a number of progressive and activist American Muslims, including Muslims Against Shari'a president, Khalim Massoud, FreeMuslims.org president, Kamal Nawash, and American Islamic Forum for Democracy president, Dr. Zuhdi Jasser. I have personally spoken to each of these individuals regarding this and related issues. These groups and their leaders celebrate the great promise of America and are working hard within the American Muslim community to convince them to reject the covet that is globally indoctrinated into Muslims to extend Islam (Dar al-Harb) throughout all lands.

According to Dr. Jasser, the American Muslim community is torn between enjoying the freedom that America provides them and the age-old mission to Islamize of the world's infidels. Other minority immigrants have no such ambition. Jews celebrate the Sabbath on Saturday but do not lobby America to recognize or adopt this tradition. Hindus revere cows and consider them sacred yet most American Hindus, while retaining their consecration of cows, do not rebel against the American "hamburger culture." Most Japanese Americans believe in "syncretism," a blending of Buddhism and Shinto. This form of syncretism is quite different from Christianity as exemplified by Shinto's global and polytheistic worship of various spirits believed to live within humans, animals, and plants and Buddhism's emphasis on the afterlife. Japanese Americans, however, do not use our legal systems or our liberalism in an attempt to transform America into something that resembles the Japanese faith or culture.

Almost daily, however, new examples of this attempted Islamization of the West are published on the Act For America (www.actforamerica.org/news) and Islamist-Watch (www.islamist-watch.org) websites.

DECEPTION

Another concept, al-Takiyya, must also be appreciated if one is to understand the nature of nonviolent Jihad. Al-Takiyya is the Muslim version of an age-old method often described as tradecraft or deception. Generally these tactics are employed by spies and military personal during times of war, so that they may assimilate and blend in while operating "behind enemy lines." In centuries past, Muslims practiced al-Takiyya as a means of defense and subterfuge against enemies, such as during the Spanish Inquisition.[70] Today, radical Islam uses this as a necessary tool that extremists living in non-Muslim lands (Dar al-Harb) utilize to deceive their unsuspecting compatriots into believing they are assimilating while they are actually engaging in nonviolent Jihad against their host societies. Islamic jurisprudence has sanctioned this in modern times and confiscated al-Qaeda training manuals clearly describing this tactic. It is said that al-Takiyya is "in tongue only, not the heart."[71] It is rooted in the Qur'an itself:

Sura 16:106: *Anyone who after accepting faith in Allah utters unbelief/kuffer except under compulsion, his heart remaining firm in faith but such as open their breast to unbelief, on them is wrath from Allah.*

Sura 3:28: *...let not the believer take for friends unbelievers... except by way of precaution that ye may guard yourselves from them...*

These commands are widely interpreted by promoters of Jihad as Allah's sanction of deception and dishonesty allowing Muslim radicals to work in the lands of infidels. This is evident when known radical imams deny their own quotes and actions of misogyny, calls for violent and nonviolent Jihad, and anti-Christian and anti-Semitic comments. They deceive Western cameras and reporters in with perfect ease, knowing that Allah supports their deception as a necessary tool to be used as they impose Islam upon the world. A believer can make any statement as long as the "heart is comfortable." The 9/11 terrorists lived and visited in the United States for two years before the 9/11 attacks. Takiyya is how they did this.[72]

In his article "The Real Danger Awaiting Turkey is Not Takiyya," appearing in the very popular *Turkish Daily News* on September 1, 2007, Mr. Orhan Kemal Cengiz describes a simple and seemingly banal story that depicts the issue of Takiyya very well. Turkey, it should be remembered, is the only secular Muslim nation, currently headed by a "reformed" Islamic extremist, Mr. Abdullah Gül. Since 1929, Turkey has been struggling in its effort to create a Muslim nation where the faith of Islam is separated from the secular law of the land—and the election of President Gül was wrought with turbulent debate due to his now recanted but quite radical past.[73]

A female member of a foreign delegation, Mr. Cengiz reports in this article, is on a fact-finding visit from the U.N.

when she "extended her hand for a goodbye handshake." Her Turkish counterpart from a Turkish human rights NGO raised his hands and said, "I do not shake hands with women," with a bashful smile on his face. The foreign delegate was offended and abruptly became suspicious about the man with whom she had been speaking to in a very friendly way just a few minutes earlier. Prior to this, the lady and the man had a friendly visit in which the man presented a "comprehensive account of the human rights problems in Turkey and in his region using an international human [and gender] rights perspective."[74]

Mr. Cengiz asked, "How should the lady see this incident? How should we evaluate it? Was this man doing Takiyya (pretending) about his identity as a human rights defender? Does this last incident erase all his hard work? Does it render his efforts in the human rights field useless, nonsense?" The concept of Takiyya is real, known to Muslims the world over and not some Western invention to exaggerate Muslim extremism.[75]

It is revealing that so many prominent American Muslim activists agree with this assessment and caution America and the West to wise up to this Islamist strategy. This issue of nonviolent Islamic extremism is relevant, broad, and important. Many experts on radical Islam have been increasingly addressing this issue in their blogs and media appearances in an effort to shine light on this insidious danger to our collective freedom. The universality of Islam—religious, civic, and political—is deeply ingrained in the fabric of Islam. This does not suggest that all Muslims subscribe to it, but this is not some small, radicalized faction of extremists either. Nonviolent Islamic extremism is a serious threat, made more serious because it is so poorly appreciated in the West.

COMMON SENSE MESSAGE

Takiyya is the intentional deception that radical Muslims employ as they pretend to be integrated citizens into Western (non-Muslim) nations. In actuality, they are "seeds" of a greater purpose: defeating their host nation and, in time, converting that Christian society (Dar al-Harb) into and Islamic one (Dar al-Islam). This is condoned by the Qu'ran, the Sunna, and supported by imams around the world. Despite being openly discussed and written about throughout the Muslim world, the West is largely unaware of this dangerous tactic.

INDOCTRINATION

Imran Raza is a California-born Muslim of Pakistani descent. While living and working in London in 2007, Raza narrowly escaped the July 7, 2005 four terrorist bombing attacks.[76] Mr. Raza learned that two of the four terrorists received their education at madrassas. Madrassas are educational facilities in the Muslim world, many of which are subsidized by Wahabbi Saudis and are suspect for teaching radicalism. This is not to say that most madrassas are havens for Islamist teachings, but many are, particularly in Pakistan. Curious as to what prompted these men from Leeds, England to murder their fellow countrymen, Mr. Raza decided to make a documentary film about his visit to the madrassas in Pakistan. When Raza arrived at the Jamia Binoria madrassa, he didn't expect to find two brothers from Atlanta, Georgia, Mahboob and Noor Khan, there. "As I walked into the madrassa, the big surprise happened when I suddenly heard two voices that were, you know, perfect American English," Raza told co-anchor Harry Smith at CBS's *Early Show* interview in 2007.[77] "The environment is just so different. Nobody really speaks English. And then suddenly you hear two kids saying, 'Are you American?' There was this immediate sort of bond because at that time they really wanted to get out of the madrassa. And so we connected on that level." As it turned out, these boys were sent to this madrassa by their father, a cab driver in Atlanta, Georgia who is working in America on a green card.[78] Raza says that the radical nature of what he saw caused him to change the purpose of the film as he created a documentary called *The Karachi Kids*. The children, 13-year-old Noor Kahn and 12-year-old Mehoob Kahn were serially interviewed over the next few years as Raza made trips back to the madrassa. Each time he recorded the rather striking transformation in the boys' attitudes.

Raza's film takes us behind the scenes of the madrassa Jamia Binoria over a four-year time period, showing the progression of indoctrination that occurs at these schools. At the outset the boys are very lonesome and loath to be away from home. By the end, they want to go back to America, but for a different reason—to spread the radical Islam and presumably anti-American teachings they learned at the Jamia Binoria. If one takes the time to view this video there can be no doubt that radical disinformation was instilled into these children. At least one goal taught to them by the headmaster, in his own words, is to spread their "teachings" back in America. According to the U.S. State Department as well as the film's executive producer, Dan Perrin, many madrassas "want to engineer the view and beliefs of children."[79] The Jamia Binoria currently enrolls 80 American students, hoping to indoctrinate them and send them back to America. Mr. Perrin goes on to tell Harry Smith, "Unlike other educational institutions, madrassas such as the Jamia Binoria do not teach math, science, or art. They focus solely on the Koran."[80]

Mufti Muhammad Naeem founded the Jamia Binoria and is a supporter of Deobandism, an extreme branch of Islam that is the religion of the Taliban.[81]

I wish to make clear that there is great controversy about

this film, as there seems to be about every book, film, or documentary about radical Islam. There are several claims made, including the one that Osama bin Laden visited this particular madrassa (Jamia Binoria), that are likely inaccurate. Nonetheless, the documentary is powerful and revealing. The statements from the children and the headmaster are in their own words and all captured on video.

"They went from obviously really, really, you know, just fervently wanting to leave to now where they feel it was a great thing that has improved themselves," Raza told Harry Smith in the *Early Show* interview. "So there is a dramatic change that's taken place. Obviously, it's an environment they've been in for nearly four years."[82] It is not too surprising that four years at an Islamic religious school would profoundly affect two American-raised teenagers. So far this story doesn't sound too "radical," but as you will see in the chronology that follows, radicalized Islam is not some mythical reality that only exists in the minds of "intolerant" Westerners. I will try to capture the spirit of the transformation of these children, in their own words. The video of these interviews are shocking, disturbing, and despite the charge of critics, clearly radical, and extremist in nature.

During year one, Noor Khan was missing home greatly: "I came here, I am not with my family... all these kids are sleeping in the room with me... I miss my family so much, I am never going to send my kids off to a madrassa." The following year Noor says, "There are disgusting smells, you get sick too much here (a panoramic view is shown of a filthy room with dirty inground toilets near a slaughtered animal)... The teachers here hit everybody with man-punches.... you don't know how badly I want to go back home to America." Later in year two, when Raza's interviewer asked Noor whether or not he wished to go back to the U.S., he replied, "Yeah, kind of. I am like a robot with no feeling. You try to live here for like, three years or something and let's see how you act." As time progressed Noor's attitude and opinions are obviously replaced with a progressively radical perspective on America, 9/11, and Jews. A similar change is seen in his younger brother Mehoob who was rather subdued and quiet in his first interviews. In year two when asked by the interviewer what he now believes (about America), Mehoob replies, "You are the terrorists, the American people are the terrorist, we are not the terrorists... we are trying to save our family, trying to have a mom and dad, we wish we had a mom and dad, until you guys came and killed them..." This apparent reference relates to America's murder of Muslims that permeates Islamist doctrine. When the boys were asked what they believe about 9/11, Mehoob replied, "The Muslim people didn't do it." To which Noor retorted, "Behind the 9/11 attacks there was no Muslim people involved." He also stated, "I'm glad my father sent me here...not one Jewish person died in the 9/11 attack." This reference is consistent with the well-known propaganda throughout the Muslim world that blames Israel, not Muslims, for the actual attacks on 9/11. Their version of reality is that the Israelis told all the Jews to stay home that fateful Monday and that is why no Jews died in the attacks. This is, of course, absurd, but it is quite clearly what was "taught" to these boys. Raza also interviewed the headmaster, Principal Mufti Muhammad Naeem, who stated that the Jamia Binoria currently has 70 to 80 Americans studying at it. During the year three interview, Mr. Naeem had this to say, "We work on altering the mindsets of the students so when they return to their home countries, they will work on altering the minds of others... These children will be able to convert non-Muslims." He also denied teaching the kids extremism. However, in his year three interview, Mehoob said, "When you are in an environment where it is Islam 24/7, you have to learn what it's all about... my main goal is to go back and spread Islam all over USA."[83]

Eventually, Rep. Mike McCaul (R-Tx) became aware of this issue and began lobbying for the return of these boys to America.[84] It must be noted that another controversial part of this story is whether or not these boys required "rescuing" at all. According to their father (as reported by CNN), they did not. A more salient issue may be whether or not America should tolerate the subversion of American students in foreign madrassas at all, regardless of the sentiments of their parents.

The following CNN story is a rather fascinating twist to *The Karachi Kids* documentary. It is an excellent example of Islamist appeasement so prevalent in our mainstream media. Although CNN is nowhere near as guilty of this as MSNBC, it too crosses the line of political correctness and bias to avoid the image of bigotry or intolerance. On July 31, 2008, CNN ran a segment called "Terror School Turns Out to Be Moderate Madrassa." Since I had seen the original documentary I found this very curious, which prompted me to further investigate this contradiction. The CNN article claims that the "films producers may have confused the madrassa with one with a similar name tied to Islamic extremists.[85] The madrassa the boys attended isn't linked to bin Laden or Muslim radicals; instead, it's one the U.S. State Department says is preferred by Pakistani-Americans for its moderate Islamic teachings and one recently visited by a top U.S. diplomat in Pakistan." As I stated earlier, bin Laden and other Taliban leaders actually visited nearby madrasses but not Jamia Binoria and the film's producers contritely admitted the mistake. Raza apologized for the error in this statement: "I do need to take responsibility for [bin Laden and Taliban leaders visits to Jamia Binoria]... these were errors that sort of spun out of control."[86]

CNN states that their reporters were welcomed in the school and spoke to its head, who denied the allegations made in the documentary. "This is a madrassa, not some jail," said Mr. Naeem, the headmaster of the school. Naeem told CNN that the school denies "any ties to militant groups, saying that if students or teachers were ever tied to extremists groups, they would be removed from the school immediately. "How could the film-maker have gotten it so wrong?" asks CNN, clearly implying that Raza's film is at best a mistake and at worst an agenda driven propaganda film.[87]

Alex Alexiiev writing for *FrontPage* magazine claims that CNN essentially accuses both Raza and Senator McCaul of lying. Alexiiev: "The most interesting purported 'gotcha' moment in the CNN report came when it cited an analysis of Karachi madrassas by the highly respected International Crisis Group (ICG) think tank to the effect that many [including Raza] confused Jamia Binoria with the better known, and openly Jihadist, Binori Town madrassa."[88] Alexiiev further claims that CNN undermines its entire premise that Raza "got it all wrong" when the ICG report they cite states in *the very next sentence* that the leaders of Jamia Binoria "have publicly adopted a pro-jihadi, anti-Western stance."[89] This was curiously missing from the CNN report. Furthermore, the ICG report states, "Even those [madrassas] without direct links to violence promote an ideology that provides religious justification for such attacks [against America]."[90] Moreover, the CNN piece is "silent about Jamia Binoria's role as a key member of an organization of Deobandi madrassas called Wafaq ul-Madaris al-Arabiya," whose leadership publicly advocates forcing Pakistanis to follow Shari'a law by "violent means if necessary."[91]

In summary, while there were admittedly some erroneous claims in *The Karachi Kids* documentary, there is no question that these kids were programmed with pro-Jihad and anti-American "education." There is also no question that CNN went out of its way to discredit the film's producers and to diminish the radical teachings of the Jamia Binoria madrassa as it "sanitized" this story about radical Islam into one that is politically acceptable.

This next topic, Muslim demographics, is by its very nature

contentious. I am reluctant to even include this subject, but it is too noteworthy to omit. Even I am reticent to breach the political correctness barrier, further proving how pervasive is our desire to be viewed as fair and open-minded. Nonetheless, we must allow ourselves to recognize the fact that there is an urgency that must be considered, as we motivate ourselves to repair our divisions and move forward in combating Islamic extremism. Muslim birth rates far exceed that of most Western nations. Islam is growing and Christianity is shrinking. Even within Western nations, Islamic birth rates far exceed that of their Christian and Jewish compatriots. If Islamic extremists weren't actively trying to annihilate Christians and Jews, who would care? Given the situation described in these pages, all of the world's "infidels" should care; in fact we *must* care.

MUSLIM DEMOGRAPHICS

For a culture to sustain itself, the reproduction ratio of children to parents must be 2.11 to survive for 25 years. In other words, each set of two parents must produce just over two kids (statistically, of course) to preserve. As population shrinks, so does its culture. A ratio of 1.9 has never been reversed.

The reproductive ratios for various nations are as follows: France 1.8, England 1.6, Greece 1.3, Germany 1.3, Italy 1.2. Spain 1.1, EU 1.38, and Canada 1.6. In all of these nations Islam will soon overcome the native religious and cultural populations. In the United States the ratio is 1.6 and if you include the immigration of Latinos, this increases to 2.1, the bare minimum for a culture to survive.

In Europe, since 1990, 90 percent of all immigration is Islamic. The Islamic reproductive ratio in France is 8.1 as compared to 1.8 for the non-Islamic population. In Southern France today there are more mosques than churches and 30 percent of all births in France are to Muslims. Based upon this trend, in 39 years the majority of France will be Muslim.

In England, the population of Muslims was 82,000 in 1977, today it is nearly three million. In the Netherlands and Belgium, 50 percent all newborns are Muslim. In just 15 years, these will both be Muslim majority nations. In Russia, one in every five people are Muslim. The Vatican has recently reported that the population of Muslims has surpassed the population of Catholics.

German government official statement (German Federal Statistics Office): "The fall in the [German] population can no longer be stopped. Its downward spiral is no longer reversible... Germany will be a Muslim state by the year 2050."

What this suggests is that we need to fix this problem soon, because in just a couple of generations the growth of Islam will render the predicament much larger and more difficult to resolve.

COMMON SENSE MESSAGE

The indoctrination of children by hateful and dishonest propaganda to ensure future generations that hate Christians, Jews, Americans, and infidels is a worldwide epidemic. Secretaries of state Colin Powell and Hillary Clinton are amongst hundreds of Western leaders, priests, rabbis, and Imams who have vociferously decried this abomination and pollution of young minds. *The Karachi Kids* provides us a window into this sordid world of polluting the minds of children to inculcate a hateful ideology. The "Solutions" section addresses this at great length.

CHAPTER THREE

America

WHY HATE AMERICA?

The wholesome, religious, simple lifestyle of the devout Muslim culture contrasts sharply to the progressively more modern and secular society of much of Europe and, to a somewhat lesser degree, America. Most people in both Western *and* Muslim nations seem to believe that progress in science and medicine is desirable. This is evident by the fact that many Muslim leaders educate their children in the West—even the radical regimes. Satellite TV (Iran boasts of the world's highest ratios of television satellite dishes per person), Internet access, and modernization of many major Muslim cities all speak toward the acceptance by many Muslims of Western technologies. Currently, there are nearly 10,000 Saudi students being educated in the West, mostly in America but also in Britain and France. Western medicine, it seems, is also desirable to much of radical Islam. The current president of Syria, Bashar al-Assad, is no friend of the West, as he is a major supporter of both Hamas and Hezbollah, and the head of the nation responsible (according to the United Nations) for the recent assassination of billionaire Christian Rafik Hariri in Lebanon. Yet, al-Assad trained as an ophthalmologist in Britain. When Yasser Arafat became seriously ill, he was flown to Paris, France. King Hussein of Jordan treated his cancer at the Mayo Clinic in Rochester, New York. Many Kuwaiti and Dubai businessmen have trained in Europe and America, and thousands of Muslim physicians train in the West although in recent years a trend toward educating in Asia is on the rise. When it comes to areas of social decorum such as law and societal freedoms, particularly in the area of gender equality and religious liberalism, there is a much greater distinction between the West and many Muslim nations.

Islamic extremists believe that the world as it was in Muhammad's time, or a modern-day revival of that time, is preferable to the world today. Islamic extremism does not afford "infidels" (non-Muslims) or moderate Muslims the privilege to deny living their lives by their rigid fundamentalist version of Islam. In other words they are not content with the adage that most of the world's civilized peoples subscribe to "live and let live." Quite literally their code is "live our way or no way."[92] What is behind this draconian behavior? Is it because Islam has failed to technologically and socially evolve as a society and as a religion? Is it because the modern world is almost the exclusive creation of non-Muslims? Many theorize that they collectively suffer from global disenfranchisement. This may be linked to the widespread lack of education and the misfortune of having thousands of national and religious leaders promulgate a message of intolerance and violence in the Muslim world.

We have established that the West represents a technologically and socially advanced (modern) civilization relative to fundamentalist Islam. No country embodies and represents the West better than America. No country has invented more of the modern world than America. No country has more military might and capacity. America, more than any other nation, lends support to Israel, which is the nemesis of many Arabs and Muslims. The U.S., more than any other nation, threatens the success of the Islamic extremist dream of Islam reconquering Europe and then the rest of world.[93] These are but a few reasons why America is referred to as the "Great Satan" by Muslim fanatics.

COMMON SENSE MESSAGE

It is quite germane to our topic to understand why Islamic extremists hate America. Simply put, America is the most powerful detriment to the Islamists' dream: a world where the severest brand of fundamentalist Islam reigns over the entire globe. Our threats to them run deep and include rule of law (secular, not Shari'a), powerful Christian values, respect for ALL religious worship except ANY religious worship that precludes others their faiths, respect for women, and the economic and military might to resist and retaliate against radical Islam.

AMERICANS

Now that we have some background into the root causes of the current situation, let's switch gears and take a more careful look at America.

Throughout its history, the United States, as a nation, has been widely recognized for its restraint of power and steadfast commitment to the rule of law. Despite the unpopularity the United States has garnered on the world stage during the George W. Bush administration, America remains, in the eyes of billions of people around the globe, the world's guarantor of freedom and liberty.[94] This worldwide esteem perseveres even in the face of the seemingly endless criticism we receive from European and Middle Eastern countries, as well as much of our own press.[95] All nations are governed by people, and all people are subject to both the good and bad sides of human nature. Our forefathers, having been victimized by the cruelty of tyranny, forged a country in a fashion that minimized the inevitable temptation of corruption and greed that all people will perpetrate if given the opportunity. The very nature of radical Islam's intolerance and disrespect of non-Muslims is anathema and incongruent with these core values that are the very essence of the America our forefathers created.

It is due to our founders' courage, brilliance, and sacrifices that our system of government limits corruption, resulting in what many consider the "profound decency of America." This is nothing short of magical (if you are, as I am, a believer). It is what separates us from all previous superpowers. Before those of you more skeptical patriots react badly to that statement, I am not implying that America is anywhere near perfect or corruption-free. That said, America has its fair share of imperfections and abuses, both past and present. Examples include America's treatment of the Native North American Indians, its tolerance of African slavery in the 17th, 18th, and 19th centuries, and its occasional support of ruthless but pro-American dictators. These examples are but a few that serve as a testament to our vulnerability to "human nature." Nonetheless, never in history has a nation enjoying so powerful a hegemony in terms of economics, military power, and culture behaved so well. It is interesting that despite the truth in this statement, the world's second favorite sport (the first being soccer) is "America bashing" as it is referred to in England. One needs only to read the headlines around the world or listen to what many consider to be the anti-U.S. ravings of the United Nations to see America under fire from all sides. Fundamentally, our forefathers created a country out of a desire to promote and preserve individual freedoms whose "inalienable rights" would protect them from the abuse of power and tyranny of government. Largely, though certainly not perfectly, billions of people the world over would agree that they succeeded, although the experiment of America remains a work in progress. There are boundless examples depicting America's successes and beneficial contributions to the world. Here are just a few: The U.S. rescued the world from evil regimes, once in Japan and twice in Germany, and from a fascist dictator in Moscow in just the past 100 years. America rebuilt Europe after it won a war that it did not start. The U.S. has delivered more people into freedom than any other nation on Earth. It is responsible for more inventions and discoveries since its birth than any other five nations combined throughout the totality of recorded history. America has provided more charitable relief per capita in the world than any other nation. It is the first nation to reach the moon and Mars. America is the first to discover the power of splitting the atom. Americans discovered electricity and innovated the automobile, the airplane, the telephone, and the Internet, just to name a few. It is the wealthiest nation humanity has ever created. And so on. Despite all of these successes, America is in a serious predicament today on several levels, including increasing global competition, the relative strength of the Euro, and, of course, Islamic extremism and terror. [96] Might this be a good time for us all to step up and lend her a hand in her time of need?

COMMON SENSE MESSAGE

Americans, simply put, are the most successful people who have ever graced this planet. A self-aggrandizing statement perhaps, but an accurate one. We have discovered more, accomplished more, helped more people attain freedom, and invented more of Modernity than any other people or groups of people, ever. The reasons for this are many, but certainly include our respect for each other's freedom to worship, live, and work free of the encumbrances of restrictive and controlling government—the antithesis of the Islamists' dream.

AMERICA, A HOUSE DIVIDED?

In the next few chapters, a close examination of America and its political divisions, real or imagined, is undertaken to provide a framework for understanding the political state of our nation. In recent years, there has been a great deal of national repartee on the subject of an alleged "great division" in America. The concept of an increasing polarity in America is very important because a pathologic division (as in *divide and conquer*) is a dangerous liability. Although most of our divisions are self-induced, Islamic extremists do exploit the West's liberalism in pursuit of their goal to Islamize America and also to affect our retreat from the Middle East. They consider our presence there intolerable; they wish it to remain free from "Western, Christian, and Jewish" influence. As a growing segment of America and the West accede to Islamism's advances, a growing cultural division in the West and America appears. This division is between Americans who "get it" with respect to Jihad in all its forms and those who not only don't "get it" but consider those who do racists and bigots. This portends a grave danger to us all. It is not clear if this division is caused by an intentional strategy of Islamists. I believe that it is, but either way the result is the same. It has been said that there are "two Americas." Generally, the "two Americas" label refers to class warfare in the U.S. based upon the premise that there are two classes in America, one rich and one poor. This may be a legitimate debate, but the "two Americas" I am referring to is the alleged political and social division of Americans that many believe exists.

LIBERALISM AND CONSERVATISM IN AMERICA

In America, the meaning of liberalism and conservatism has undergone a significant change in the past 70 years or so. Liberal, in Greek, is defined as "free"; to be free in this sense is to be the opposite of a slave. The Founding Fathers created our nation in the spirit of "liberalism," or "freedom," in many crucial aspects of life. This included freedom of speech, freedom of politics, and economic and religious freedoms. President Roosevelt changed the concept of liberalism by adding that people who lacked life's necessities, be they financial, medical, or employment related, were not truly free. The "liberation movements" of the 1960s, exemplified by gay rights, the anti-war movement, feminism, and the "sexual revolution" further defined this concept of liberalism.

Today, liberalism can broadly be described as more government and less traditional religion, more acceptances of gay and other non-nuclear families as equal to the traditional nuclear (husband and wife) definition of marriage, a greater level of socialization and distribution of wealth, and more societal rules. For instance, liberals may support the access to health care for everyone (the issue is less about access and more about who pays for it) and support instituting laws to moderate certain behaviors. Examples include mandating the wearing of helmets and life jackets, dictating specific work schedules, controlling wages, imposing corporate restrictions, providing limits on citizens' access to guns and other weapons, limiting military spending and military deployments, and maximizing personal and corporate taxes. Liberals, in recent years, appear to be better protectors or "conservators" of the environment. This is ironic since conservancy, one would think, should be a characteristic of conservatives. These are generalizations and not everyone would necessarily agree with each of these examples. Nonetheless, they serve as fair representations of present-day liberalism in America.

Conservatism in America is very different from European conservatism. In Europe, conservatives believe in supporting royalties and kings and preserving the political power of religion (primarily Catholicism). Not so in America. Conservatives in America generally believe in limiting government power, preserving traditional family values, supporting Judeo-Christian religious values on a national basis, and opposing gay marriage (particularly when it is defined as "marriage" as opposed to the term "civil or gay union"). Conservatives are more likely to sustain a strong military and to project the use of military power to protect American interests. As stated above, conservatives seem to have difficulty balancing the protection of the environment versus the protection of "big business." Generally, they are more likely to "conserve," and therefore resist change. This applies, depending on one's perspective, to both good and desirable changes and also to changes that may prove regrettable. Suffice it to say that change is not the motto of conservatism.

POLLS: UNDERSTANDING LIBERALISM AND CONSERVATISM

While there certainly exists many matters that "divide" Americans and, at first glance, this division may be widening into a permanent schism, first impressions can be deceiving. Let's dissect this concept via a number of opinion polls and surveys followed by an interpretation of these studies.

The entire exercise of examining liberalism and conservatism in America isn't to indict one side or the other, or both. I include it to help us take a step back and understand what makes us tick so we can then successfully build upon the considerable commonality that we share. Most of us are not entirely liberal or entirely conservative; we are not two-dimensional. We harbor opinions and feelings that lean both left and right. Political independents are more or less balanced where conservatives fall toward the right and liberals the left. As individual people we have a superego that internally considers issues from all perspectives when we have tough choices to make. Ultimately, we weigh the options and, hopefully more often than not, make the right decision. When we make the wrong ones, we try to learn from our mistakes. Appeasement and political correctness toward Islamism almost always comes from a liberal source. Many liberals, it seems, either don't recognize the extent of the danger, mistakenly believe that if we placate radical Islam they will end their hostilities, or are ideologically programmed to protest nearly any form of defense that includes confrontation—verbal or militaristic. I therefore believe that liberalism via permissiveness cripples America's efforts to combat Islamic Jihad.

Now, as an academic exercise to prove a point, consider for a moment that America must choose ONLY one side to combat Islamism: conservative or liberal. If that side is conservative, we would pursue military tribunals, Patriot Act-like laws and permissions, aggressive military actions, and generally chase the bad guys wherever they reside. If we choose the liberal (permissive) position: military tribunals and many global, covert anti-terrorism initiatives would be eliminated as would most of the Patriot Act. Given the inveterate hate ideology of fanatical Islamists, which side would be more likely to keep us safer? The conservative approach would contain the Islamic threat, the liberal would not. Some problems just cannot be negotiated away. Strength is the only guarantor of national security. This is not to discount the importance of *some degree* of liberal counterbalance, which, in all fairness, probably facilitates diplomacy and helps keep us from trampling the very values we try to protect. Both liberalism and conservatism have merits, but when it comes to combating radical Islam, the tougher conservative approach is indispensible, where the liberal approach is not.

POLL #1: THE PULSE OF AMERICA

1. "How important will terrorism be to your vote for Congress in 2006?" (Pew 2007)

Extremely 49%	Very important 33%
Moderately important 14%	Not very important 5%

2. "Do you think Republicans or Democrats in Congress would do a better job in dealing with terrorism?" (Pew 2007)

Republicans 40%   Democrats 45%
No difference 8%   Unsure 6%

3. "Do you think the United States is winning or losing the war on terrorism?" (Pew 2007)

Winning 46%   Losing 33%
Neither 10%   Unsure 11%

4. "Who do you think can do a better job of handling national security and the war on terrorism: President Bush or the Democrats in Congress?" (Pew 2007)

President Bush 43%   Democrats in Congress 38%

5. "How would you rate the way things are going for the United States in the War on Terrorism? Would you say they are going very well, somewhat well, somewhat poorly or very poorly?" (Pew 2007)

Very well 13%   Somewhat well 47%
Somewhat poorly 22%   Very poorly 17%

6. "In order to curb terrorism in this country, do you think it will be necessary for the average person to give up some civil liberties, or not?" (Pew 2007)

Yes 40%
No 54%

7. "Freedom of speech should not extend to groups that are sympathetic to terrorists?" (Pew 2007)

Agree 45%
Disagree 50%

9. "In the Middle East situation, are your sympathies more with the Israelis or more with the Palestinian Arabs?" (Pew 2007)

Israel 58%
Palestinians 20%

10. "There should be investigations that the Bush team used torture to interrogate terrorism suspects." (*USA Today* 2009)

Agree 64%
Disagree 36%

11. "Do you think the United States should not close the prison at the Guantanamo Bay military base in Cuba?" (Gallup 2009)

Should close 35%
Should NOT close 45%

(Note, in July 2009 53 percent of Americans re-polled believe that Guantanamo should NOT be closed.)

12. "Do you think the Guantanamo Bay detainees should not be able to challenge their detentions in the civilian court system [should they remain in the military tribunal system]?" (ABC News/*Washington Post* 2009)

Should be able to challenge in civilian court 35%
Should NOT be able to challenge in civilian court 45%

It is not very difficult to guess which responders are liberal and which are conservative by the way they answered these various poll questions. It is plain to see that in many of these "current issues of the day," the country is fairly evenly split. Does this actually support that there is a problem of division in America today? At first glance, it might, although upon further inspection, perhaps not.

POLL # 2: TYPOLOGY OF AMERICANS

Preamble: This Pew research typology poll provides further insights into who we are and why we feel the way we do. This political study named "Beyond Red Versus Blue" was published in May of 2005.[97] This survey primarily addresses the political party affiliation of Americans, and secondarily, the nation's conservative versus liberal character. The basic "types" identified in the poll are durable over time but minor changes are likely to have occurred. More recent polling information is also presented below. Let's dissect this poll with the stated purpose of shedding light on this question of the actual division amongst Americans.[98] The events of 9/11 and worldwide terrorism, along with the overall importance of national security issues, have had a major impact on this typology. Over the past 20 years foreign affairs assertiveness almost completely distinguishes Republican-oriented voters from Democratic-oriented voters. Most recently, however, concern over the badly damaged economy supersedes foreign policy concerns and until the economy stabilizes this will continue.

In contrast, attitudes relating to religion and social issues are not nearly as important to most people in determining party and political affiliation. Still, these less pressing issues do emphasize differences within parties, particularly among the Democrats. Democratic voters are much more divided than their Republican counterparts with respect to their religious disposition.

The divisions within the GOP are, perhaps surprisingly, greatest with respect to the role of government. Government regulation to protect the environment is an issue with particular potential to divide Republicans, where "wide divisions exist both within the GOP and among right-of-center voters more generally."

Voters inclined toward the Republican Party are further distinguished from Democrats by their personal optimism and belief in the power of the individual, the poll found. It also clearly revealed that Republicans tend to be generally more hopeful and positive in their outlook for the country than their more fatalistic counterparts in the Democratic Party.

Democrats overwhelmingly prefer effective diplomacy over military strength as the basis for U.S. security policy. They support the concept that the adverse life circumstances of our enemies should be considered before military engagements against them. In other words, while Islamist terrorists may be barbaric, the poor socioeconomic and harsh political conditions that fashioned them should serve as a mitigating factor in our response to them. The notion of personal responsibility is often muted by Democrats. Domestically, Democrats remain committed to a stronger social safety net than Republicans. Again, the placing of less emphasis on the individual and more emphasis on the government is characteristic of Democratic-leaning voters.

Of particular importance, and consistent with the basic premise of this book, is that this Pew poll finds "numerous opportunities for building coalitions across party lines on many issues currently facing the nation." These coalitions, in many cases, include some strange political bedfellows. When the topic of America's polarity is more carefully examined, it becomes clear that there are many additional colors in the American political landscape than the simplistic red and blue states we have seen on television news screens on election days.[99]

During the 1990s, the typology groups in the center were not particularly partisan, but in 2005 they leaned decidedly to the GOP. By 2008, the winds shifted left, toward the Democratic Party. The languishing nature of the Iraqi war, along with the unpopularity of the George W. Bush administration and the severe economic distress (that is always blamed on the party in power, the Republicans in this case) are responsible. There are three groups described for each of three categories: the political middle, left, and right.

TYPOLOGY: THE POLITICAL MIDDLE (INDEPENDENTS)

Upbeats are relatively moderate with positive views of their financial situation, government performance, business, and the state of the nation in general. They are typically well educated and are engaged in political news. Upbeats do not generally identify with either political party. They harbor a strong sense of personal responsibility and reject victimization. They hold themselves and others accountable, on foreign and domestic matters.

Disaffecteds are much less affluent and educated than the Upbeats. They are deeply cynical about government and unsatisfied with their financial situation. Disaffecteds lean toward the Republican Party.

Bystanders are largely consigned to the political sidelines. This category is composed of mostly young people. They lean toward the Democratic Party, particularly so since the war in Iraq.

TYPOLOGY: THE POLITICAL RIGHT (TYPICALLY, REPUBLICANS)

The Republican Party's 2002 and 2004 advantage with the political center made up for the fact that the GOP-oriented groups, when taken together, account for only 29 percent of the public. By contrast, the three Democratic groups constituted 41 percent of the public in 2005 but approximately 50 percent in 2008. There are also three GOP groups and they are highly diverse. The political right generally believes in strong personal responsibility and accountability—they reject the idea of blaming the system, the government, or someone else for their problems.

Enterprisers are stalwart conservatives. They are the most homogenously consistent ideologues of any group in the typology. Highly patriotic and pro-business, they oppose social welfare and overwhelmingly support a firm foreign policy. This group is largely white, well educated, male, and relatively affluent. They are socially conservative.

Social Conservatives are similar to Enterprisers except they tend to be critical of business and more supportive of government regulation to protect the public good. They are also more protective of the environment. They strongly support immigration control. Most are females and many live in the south. Like most conservatives, they support an aggressive stand against foreign enemies such as terrorists and anarchists.

Pro-Government Conservatives are decidedly religious and socially conservative. They are differentiated by their backing for government involvement in a wide range of policy areas including business oversight, generous assistance to the poor and protection of the environment. They too are mostly female and relatively young. This group is also highly concentrated in the South.

TYPOLOGY: THE POLITICAL LEFT (TYPICALLY, DEMOCRATS)

Liberals are generally opponents of an assertive foreign policy, strong supporters of environmental protection, and solid backers of government assistance to the poor. Liberals have swelled to become the largest voting bloc in recent years. This well-educated, affluent, and very secular group is consistently liberal on social issues, ranging from freedom of expression to abortion. Many tend to reside in the coastal Northeast and California.

Conservative Democrats are quite religious, socially conservative, and assume more moderate positions on several key foreign policy questions. This group is older, and includes many minorities, primarily blacks and Hispanics. Of all the core Democratic categories, the Conservative Democrats have the strongest sense of personal empowerment and personal responsibility, which is the feeling that they, the individual control his or her own destiny as opposed to abrogating this to government)—similar to Republicans.

Disadvantaged Democrats also include many minority voters, and they are the least affluent group. Members of this heavily female, poorly educated group are highly pessimistic about their opportunities in life. They are inclined to mistrust both business and government. They do, not surprisingly, strongly support government programs to help the underprivileged.

While the Republican Party is divided by what the role of government should be, the Democrats are divided by social and personal values. Most Liberals live in a world far removed from Disadvantaged Democrats and Conservative Democrats.

According to these Pew Research Center categorizations, there are clearly many subtypes of Democrats and Republicans (and by extension, liberals and conservatives), reflecting an America that is more aligned than many would have us believe.[100]

COMMON SENSE MESSAGE

The "use of force" issue remains a major dividing point among Americans. On other foreign policy issues, even contentious questions such as the ways in which we interact with allies, the partisan pattern is not as clear. Republicans tend to hold Islamists more accountable for their actions where Democrats are more likely to excuse them based upon unfortunate political or historical realities. On social issues, while real differences of opinion exist, we are in the same ballpark even if not on the same team. Generally, Republicans are more optimistic and self-reliant than Democrats. Democrats are more inclined to look to the government for support and guidance where Republicans prefer smaller government.

POLL #3: THE REAL AMERICA/ "LOCAL BAR" POLL

Imagine interviewing the teamster or truck driver patrons of a local, overwhelmingly Democratic blue-collar bar and asking these questions:

Do you fully support same-sex marriage?

Do you believe it is OK to burn the American flag?

Do you support welfare benefits for illegal immigrants?

Do you support allowing gay leaders in the local Boy Scouts troop?

The odds are the majority will answer no to all four questions. Although they may vote Democrat because of their union affiliation or for socioeconomic and other reasons, they will not blindly support the whole of the liberal Democratic platform.

Now, imagine interviewing the members of the local country club bar (in a Republican locale) and ask these questions:

Would you encourage your 18-year-old son or daughter to enlist for a tour in the military when there is an ongoing shooting war?

Considering at-risk children and others without other resources, do you oppose ALL Americans being guaranteed health care coverage?

Do you object to the government providing free access to higher education to economically challenged children who are without other resources?

Would you support the deportation of all illegal immigrants by Homeland Security, even if you employ one in your own home?

Once again, although they may vote Republican for a number of reasons, often economic and security related, they are not automatons and most will likely answer no to all four questions.

They, too, will not unconditionally support the entire conservative Republican platform.

As you can see in the polls (and more importantly, in the interpretation of these polls), there is less division amongst most Americans than we as a nation have been led to believe. The further we break down the categories of Democratic liberal and Republican conservative into smaller groups and individuals, the more we see that the lines are blurred and that much less polarization actually exists, particularly on core values. This bodes well, since logic dictates that when more common ground exists between people, they are more likely to mend fences for the common good.

Throughout our history, nearly every presidential election in the nation has involved campaign issues that fairly evenly split the nation. In our first presidential election in 1789, before the Electoral College was devised, George Washington received nearly 93 percent of the popular vote; John Adams received the remaining 7 percent. The next presidential election was in 1792, where President Washington received 70 percent of the popular vote. Four years later, George Washington refused to run for a third term, and John Adams received 54 percent over Thomas Jefferson's 46 percent of the popular vote. Since the 1792 election, with rare exceptions, our presidential election results have hovered around a 50-50 split, give or take about 10 percentile points. The fact is our system of government, freedom of speech, celebration of partisan-style politics, and America's (predominantly) two-party political design has resulted in Americans' 50-50 divide on issues since our inception. Despite the fact that current-day debate rhetoric runs high and we seem to be "split" on the important national topics, this is not necessarily as atypical, or for that matter as undesirable, as many lead us to believe. This does not suggest that Americans must compromise our vigorously held positions to "standardize" our national positions. Being a representative democracy does not suppose that Americans must homogenize our opinions by end-less compromise, but rhetoric and division alone will only fur-ther strengthen those who would do us great harm. We ought to, however, recognize that when America is faced with grave threats, particularly during times of war, we must come together through the process of honest, didactic, and productive debate. So it isn't Americans' differing views that pose a danger to us, it is the ill-natured spirit in which we seem to be interacting and the lack of respect for each other that poisons this otherwise healthy and necessary process. We are entitled to our varied po-sitions on a multitude of subjects. Americans shall remain true to our heritage by remaining thoughtful and passionate about our societal issues of the day. It is only through this type of na-tional dialogue that we, as a united nation, will solve our major problems including the vexing challenge of Islamic terrorism.

WHY DOES AMERICA *APPEAR* TO BE SO DIVIDED?

If one were to ask the casual observer whether or not America is divided as a nation, the answer would most likely be yes. We can verify by some of the poll responses above, as well as by the headlines of nearly every newspaper in the country, that clear battle lines have been drawn by liberals and conservatives, by Democrats and Republicans, and by the spirit of so-called red and blue states. Surprisingly though, as I have demonstrated above, as one studies this phenomena more carefully, it be-comes apparent that the topic of a national division is a much more complex.

America is synonymous with freedom: freedom from tyr-anny, freedom of religion, and freedom of speech. The *sine qua non*, or essential element, of freedom of speech is the very con-cept of debate. Debate can be defined as the taking of positions on varying subjects of the day in social discourse, whether by individuals, deliberative bodies, politicians, or the press. Debate presupposes differences of opinion, or what one may call "division," without which there can be no meaningful deliberation. Debate is woven into the fabric of America, even prior to the birth of this nation. In fact, the subject of whether or not there shall be an American Revolution was our first great debate. President Bill Clinton, when asked about the "polarization" of America, points out that in the 1796 John Adams-versus-Thomas Jefferson presidential election, the vitriolic exchange of accusations between voters was great enough to "blister the hairs off a dog's back." His point is that today we are, in the political sense, relatively calm and actually less polarized than we were at many points in our colorful past. Is he correct in this statement? In recent years, our nation has been inundated with pundits, politicians, historians, and the media who have decried the "division of America." As is so often true in life, what seems obviously correct may not actually be correct. As you read on, I think many of you will agree with President Clinton's analysis that diminishes these divisions in America. A differentiating factor, however, is that Americans in the Jefferson era were not subjected to dozens of news broadcasts and scores of pundits screaming their biases at us on television, radio, print media, and the Internet at light speed, 24 hours a day. The net effect of this is to slowly nudge Americans into their respective corners. There is nothing wrong with Americans maintaining strong opinions on a host of subjects; after all, independent, not blended thought, is the American way. There is a great danger, however, when increasingly hostile division causes rhetoric to replace constructive debate, thereby crippling our national response to serious threats. Islamic extremism and the terrorism it breeds is one such threat.

Jonathan Rauch, in his February 2005 article for *The Atlantic Monthly* named "Bipolar Disorder," discusses what he refers to as America's "bipolar disease." As a practicing physician, I define bipolar disease (formerly named manic-depression) in layman's terms as episodic and extreme mood swings.

Mr. Rauch is using this term to describe a nation of people who harbor extreme and diametrically opposed opinions, or to describe the taking of sides on nationally important topics. His premise is that while America is indeed divided, it is not divided in the way that most people believe it to be. It is mostly politicians and partisans who are divided and not so much the people; at least no more so than has been typical of America since its inception. Portions of our nation, however, are increasingly divided and partisan, and successfully drive a wedge between *we the people,* by moving us increasingly toward a dangerous and self-fulfilling prophecy. Let's explore this question of a real versus imagined division a little more carefully.

In the early 1990s, James Davison Hunter, a sociologist at the University of Virginia, wrote a landmark book named *Culture Wars: The Struggle to Define America.* Hunter described a deeply divided America. One culture, he noted, is conservative or "orthodox," the other, liberal or "progressive." This division, he documented, transcended particular issues to address different perceptions of moral authority, with one side anchored to traditional religion and the other side more relativistic. Not only does this incongruity of core values permeate throughout both politics and everyday life, Hunter said, but *"each side of the cultural divide can only talk past the other."* The concept of a country that is fundamentally divided over core moral and political issues quickly caught on. This was evidenced by a 1996 dissenting opinion by Supreme Court Justice Antonin Scalia who, in several high-profile cases including *Romer v. Evans* (homosexuality issue) and *U.S. v. Virginia* (female exclusion in a state college issue), stated that the Court could be accused of "choosing sides in the culture wars," and the country understood exactly what he was referring to. In the past decade, there have been countless articles and many books describing this great division of America. To name a few: *Party Wars* by

Barbara Sinclair, *Divided America* by Earl Black, and *Building Red America* by Thomas Byrne Edsall.

In 2002, political scientist John Kenneth White took this polarity of America a little further in his book, *The Values Divide*. He refers to the "value divide" based upon a different set of ethics between the conservative faction and the liberal one. These partisan authors and pundits make their observations regarding culture and values and categorize them into classic examples of what Rauch refers to as archetypes.

While placing people into categories or archetypes facilitates our understanding of disparate political *types*, it can also skew reality and create false divisions that do not apply to *individuals*. My assertion is that it is not the division of *Americans* but of *America* as reflected in the often-provocative words of our politicians and pundits that we need to appreciate. Common sense tells us that most people don't align themselves with either extreme, but probably reside somewhere in the middle. If this is so, doesn't this refute the very premise that we are so hopelessly divided?

Mr. Rauch goes on to point out that in April of 2006, *The Washington Post* ran a front-page Sunday article headlined "Political Split is Pervasive." It quoted various experts as saying, for example, "We have two parallel universes" and "people in these two countries don't even see each other." *The New York Times* took issue with the premise in that article, and subsequently ran a response piece titled "A Nation Divided? Who Says?" It quoted yet another set of pundits who claimed that the division among Americans is actually smaller than in the past, and continues to shrink; this is consistent with the aforementioned comments from President Clinton on this subject.

The rainbow of the American people spans far beyond red and blue or black and white.

In summary, although politicians, partisans, editorial writers, and television pundits are more polarized in recent years, *we the people* are still pretty well aligned on core values, desires, and ethos. There is a great danger, however, in average Americans being further drawn into believing this folly of an increasing division and segregation among Americans. This must not occur because from that inflexible position, constructive dialogue is stifled. This is the last thing we need in an age where unity is necessary if we are to act, as a nation, deliberately, carefully, and with purpose to fix what is obviously broken in our approach to many of our problems, including Islamic terrorism. The next section will examine liberalism and conservatism in a fresh light.

COMMON SENSE MESSAGE

How divided is America, really? As you can see above, this is a matter of perspective. In some areas we are roughly split down the middle, with a clear "left" and a clear "right." On the other hand, we sport a two-party political system so one should reasonably expect two viewpoints on key issues of the day. On many core issues, we aren't actually as divided as it appears from so many, books, articles, and television pundits who discuss this subject.

Most Americans believe in freedom, the sanctity of religious rights, the need for American might and influence, and a cultural compassion for less fortunate people at home and abroad, etc. It is how we achieve these goals that are the foundation for most of our polarity. As President Clinton has said, "we are less divided in many ways than in our colorful past." We are, however, in danger of allowing the unprecedented rhetoric of *media and politicians* in recent years to actually divide *Americans* further—a very dangerous and crippling prospect in the face of the perils we face in this age of Islamic terror and extremism.

THE TWO MAIN DILEMMAS OF LIBERALISM

Political correctness to the point of self-endangerment

Some argue that political correctness may be the epitaph on the tombstone of America if we don't wise up soon. It is certainly desirable to celebrate the differences among America's population, and when and where that is not possible, to at least tolerate those differences. Most Americans believe that our strength is in our diversity and harmony among different groups: black and white, Jew and gentile, Muslim and Hindu, etc. Have some confused socially desirable tolerance with blind tolerance? Do Islamic extremists who perpetrate sedition and traitorous behavior that seriously threatens our country deserve tolerance? A core question is: are we as a country (more so for liberals than conservatives) and as a world so concerned with being labeled as a "bigot" ourselves that we do not dissuade and react vigorously to subversive and hateful Islamic extremist speech and teaching? Is there such a thing as being politically correct to the point of extinction? Consider the following examples of situations that many believe require strong, unified, national condemnation, but liberal organizations do not agree, often based upon this idea that we should "tolerate" even subversive speech and actions. Clearly, this subject is hypersensitive because we Americans cherish our freedom of speech. As you read this, bear in mind that the issue may not be if such odious speech is *legal*, but whether or not we should rise up with a single, united, national voice rejecting this as abhorrent and inconsistent with the principles of our nation.

The Center for Religious Freedom is a division of the Hudson Institute, a non-partisan policy research organization that promotes global security, prosperity, and freedom. The Center for Religious Freedom was formerly known as the Freedom House and was originally founded by Eleanor Roosevelt and others in the 1950s. A Freedom House publication investigated Saudi hate ideology in the U.S. in May 2003. The publication revealed that hundreds of heinous religious edicts are taught to Muslims in American Mosques and schools that disparage Christians and Jews on a regular basis. Up to 80 percent of these mosques promote segregation from "the infidels" and forbid interaction with American Christians and Jews due to their "twisted beliefs and evil ways" (on page 39 of the report). Furthermore, their followers are advised to "only interact with Americans to convert them to Islam" (page 16 of the report).[101] A *Washington Post* article published October 2, 2003 written by Susan Schmidt also examined this Saudi Fundamentalism, called Wahhabiism, and the hundreds of American Mosques teaching this hatred. Her article confirmed the widespread vitriol taught in Muslim institutions throughout America.[102] More recently, on June 11, 2008 Ms. Viola Gienger writing for Bloomberg News reported that a Saudi government-controlled school near Washington, D.C. uses textbooks that explicitly endorse violence and intolerance of infidels.[103] This is according to a U.S. religious freedom panel that obtained some of the materials. The Saudi ambassador to the U.S. serves as chairman of the board at this school, the Islamic Saudi Academy, which is in a Washington, D.C. suburb located near Alexandria, Virginia. The State Department, it should be noted, designated Saudi Arabia in 2004 as a "country of particular concern" on religious freedom. The U.S. Commission on International Religious Freedom established by Congress the late 1990s acquired 17 textbooks utilized at an academy that is funded by the Saudi government and has more than 900 students enrolled. The books were obtained with the help of a congressional office and other unnamed sources.[104] "The most problematic texts involve passages that contain the Saudi government's particular interpretation of Koranic and other Islamic texts," the commission wrote in its statement. "Some passages clearly exhort the readers to commit acts of violence." The commission cites examples from two chapters that clearly encourage violence. The first, in a 12th grade textbook, says it is permissible for a Muslim to kill any convert from Islam, as well as an adulterer or someone who has murdered a believer intentionally." Another begins, "The cause of the discord: the Jews conspired against Islam and its people." Yet another says that "Muslims are permitted to take the lives and property of those deemed polytheists."[105] In 2008, even before seeing these texts, the commission advised the State Department to close the school, but since school officials denied these charges at that time, they declined to take action.

Political correctness and appeasement may have been at work here. Liberals generally support a more permissive interpretation of First Amendment rights than conservatives who typically promote a limitation of these rights for hate and seditious speech. Celebrating religious freedom versus tolerating political hatred cloaked in religion is further discussed later in this book. Not all liberals are inclined to tolerate behaviors, such as those mentioned above, but many do and this is perceived by many conservatives, independents, and libertarians as a blunder. Needless to say, political correctness will likely require some type of limitation if America is to succeed in defeating radical Islam.

Many liberals seem to harbor fear and disdain for the U.S. military

The problem with this is that we still live in a world that very much requires the military option, not only to maintain power but to survive. Good or bad, right or wrong—if it weren't for our military might, America would cease to exist. Consider these recent quotes, including ones from a current senator that exemplify the type of contempt that some, certainly not all, liberals harbor toward our military:

- Senator John Kerry was quoted in October 31, 2006 as saying, "Well you know... do your homework and you make an effort to be smart, you—you can do well. If you don't, you get stuck in Iraq." Senator Kerry, who served two voluntary terms in Vietnam during that war, is not likely to have intentionally insulted the troops. Nonetheless, comments such as these are not rare amongst liberals and it is the *perception*, not necessarily the *reality* of harboring anti-military sentiment that liberals must overcome.

• "Iraq is a rich man's war and it is a poor man's fight." This quote, originally describing the American Civil War, has been used by many liberals to portray the war in Iraq. The validity of this statement, however, is not well supported by the fact that in 2005, recruits from the poorest one-fifth of American neighborhoods decreased from 18 percent to 13.7 percent while the wealthiest one-fifth of American neighborhoods increased recruits to 22.5 percent. "The typical recruit in the all-volunteer force is wealthier, more educated and more rural than the average 18- to 24-year-old citizen. Indeed, for every two recruits coming from the poorest neighborhoods, there are three recruits coming from the wealthier neighborhoods."[106]

• *The New York Times*, the most popular left-leaning newspaper, ran the Abu Ghraib (Iraq prisoner abuse by U.S. guards) story on its front page for more than 50 days. Many in the (conservative) news media including Bernard Goldberg, Bill O'Reilly, and the *Free Republic*, have criticized the *Times* for this.[107] This alleged over-reporting of an atypical blemish in the behavior of our Armed Forces suggests a bias against either the military or, more likely, the George W. Bush administration. It seems that *The New York Times* and many left-leaning liberals harbored so much antipathy for former President George Bush that any embarrassment to the president and his administration was more important than the damage that over-enthusiastic anti-American reporting causes to America both at home and abroad. Hence, the apparent over-promotion of compromising stories regarding our military. This is particularly unfortunate, since by most accounts, including the embedded reporters in Iraq, most of our military forces are exemplary men and woman who proudly represent the United States.

These examples of anti-military statements and actions may prove problematic for liberal Democrats who now control both the Congress and the presidency. For example, the 2006 Congress (109th Congress) was elected on the promise they would quickly end the Iraq war. Despite the promises of that mid-term election, the issue proved to be more complex than a stay or leave dichotomy, and consequently, they have failed to deliver on their campaign pledge to immediately leave Iraq. This led to the lowest approval rating of any Congress in the history of America: 14 percent, even lower than President Bush at that time. Although the polls are mixed, this unpopularity is attributed to both their failure to end the war immediately as promised and for their naïve and allegedly insincere campaign promises, which denigrated the military simply to win the election and regain the majority position in Congress. The appropriate deployment and use of our military is still the "first responsibility" of government, vis a vis protecting its citizens. Consequently, campaign promises aside, both Congress and the president understand the need to act deliberately and carefully when contemplating the assignment of our young men and women into harm's way.

Lastly, there is a belief, regardless of whether it is real or imagined, that many liberal Americans do not have the stomach for war—even one where America is on the defense. There is no question that al-Qaeda has stated time and time again that Americans are weak, and when we are faced with television images of killed American soldiers, we will eventually throw in the towel. They refer to at least two good examples. The first was in Lebanon, in 1983, when a suicide truck bomber with

12,000 pounds of TNT killed 241 Americans. The second was in Somalia, in 1993, when Islamists attacked Americans who were in the country to distribute food to the needy, resulting in 18 American servicemen being killed. This story is told in the book and movie *Black Hawk Down*. Osama bin Laden himself is widely quoted as stating that this is when he first realized that the way to beat America was to avoid a head-on fight that his extremists could never win. Instead, the key to victory lay in attacking at the fringes until America gave in to "public pressure" and surrendered.[108] Most "public pressure" critical of American military action emanates from liberals, be they politicians, liberal print or broadcast news people, or Hollywood actors.

In both Lebanon and Somalia, America withdrew from the theater of operations against a much weaker Islamic extremist enemy very soon after successful attacks killed Americans. This created an image of defeatism and weakness that appears to be burned into the psyche of Islamic extremists throughout the world. It is important to note that the conservative, Republican President Reagan withdrew from Lebanon while the more liberal, Democratic President Clinton withdrew from Somalia. Nonetheless, liberals are perceived by many to be weaker in resolve and loathe to advocate the military option, which represents a serious dilemma for them.

THE TWO MAIN DILEMMAS OF CONSERVATISM

The use of force seems to contradict America's tolerance and values

Conservatives, on the other hand, have been accused of an overzealous use of American military force, lending credibility to the criticism that the U.S. and more specifically, conservatives are hawkish. It is a widely held belief that conservatives favor a militarily aggressive response to the war on terror and are generally more apt to choose a martial solution than liberals. While this may or may not be the correct approach, this propensity to use military force may frighten our allies as much as our enemies, particularly given that we are the only remaining superpower. Clearly, we need the cooperation of our allies if we are to successfully wage this war on terror, therefore alarming the very allies we need to work with represents a dilemma for conservatives.

I believe that part of the core controversy of our military forcefulness is the issue of collateral damage: unintentional injury to innocents. Interestingly, our previous typology review revealed a fundamental difference in interpretation of personal responsibility. Conservatives are more likely to blame our Islamist enemies rather than our military for much of the collateral damage that occurs as a result of our combating Islamic Jihadists. Conservatives believe that Jihadists, by placing their innocent population of women, children, and elders in the line of fire to protect themselves and to maximize camera coverage of casualties, thereby embarrassing the West's forces, are responsible, not us. In other words, conservatives are more likely to hold accountable the terrorists and the general population of Islamic nations that breed and tolerate radicalism. Conservatives say that while they lament injury and death to innocents, they accept this as a corollary to war—particularly this form of asymmetric war. Liberals are more likely to blame our failed policies and the poor socioeconomic conditions of these Muslim nations and their people for the rise of Jihadism; therefore, America caused their plight and only compounds it with collateral damage when trying to eradicate the very fanatics they helped create. Thus, liberals argue, America has a moral obligation to seek solutions that do not involve military actions.

Conservatives appear too quick to sacrifice freedom for the sake of security and the environment for the sake of "big business"

It is a popular thought, particularly amongst liberals, that conservatives are all too willing to sacrifice basic freedoms to make us more secure. The Patriot Act, for instance, is celebrated by conservatives as necessary, while at the same time reviled by many liberals as an overreaction, intended to allow the government to spy on anyone they like. Whether or not there is any truth to this charge, the allegation alone is challenging for conservatives. In February 2007, the Justice Department concluded that some abuses by the FBI of the "Patriot Act" have occurred, which further gives validity to this accusation.

Now that I have denigrated pretty much everyone, let's have a little fun with this. The following quotes are entertaining precisely because they contain at least a grain of truth.

Leo C. Rosten (scholar, author, and humorist): "A conservative is one who admires radical's centuries after they're dead."

Mort Sahl (comedian, speech writer for John F. Kennedy, and actor): "Liberals feel unworthy of their possessions. Conservatives feel they deserve everything they've stolen."

Ralph Waldo Emerson (author): "Conservatism makes no poetry, breathes no prayer, has no invention; it is all memory. Reform has no gratitude, no prudence, no husbandry."

West Wing (television show): "Somebody came along and said 'liberal' means 'soft on crime, soft on drugs, soft on Communism, soft on defense, and we're gonna tax you back to the Stone Age because people shouldn't have to go to work if they don't want to.' And instead of saying, 'Well, excuse me, you right-wing, reactionary, xenophobic, homophobic, anti-education, anti-choice, pro-gun, Leave it to Beaver trip back to the '50s,' we cowered in the corner and said, 'Please don't hurt me.'"

Abraham Lincoln (politician, U.S. President): "What is conservatism? Is it not the adherence to the old and tried against the new and untried?"

William Ralph Inge (author): "There are two kinds of fools: one says, 'This is old, therefore it is good;' the other says, 'This is new, therefore it is better.'"

Mark Twain (U.S. humorist, writer, and lecturer): "A conservative is a man who just sits and thinks; mostly sits."

Winston Churchill (politician, British Prime Minister): "Any man who is under 30 and is not a liberal has not heart; any man who is over 30 and is not a conservative has not brains."

Most Americans are a mix of both liberal and conservative predispositions. As I stated earlier, it isn't inappropriate or even undesirable for Americans to hold passionate views on whatever subjects they choose. After all, independent thought is what the War of Independence was fought for. When serious issues that threaten life and liberty, generate diametrically opposed views, and prevent America from protecting our interests, the issue of division becomes relevant. There is a time for debate and there is a time for action. If debate degenerates into ineffective rhetoric, thereby paralyzing the nation in endless idiom when action is needed to protect our nation, then we have a problem. When our politicians are more concerned with their party's winning than America's security, then we have a problem. Many believe that we are skirting dangerously close to this precipice.

Regrettably, many (if not most) Americans have been prodded toward a sort of partisanship on the issue of terrorism, as they are encouraged by the various national powers that be, to choose one side or the other to believe in and support at all costs. Many believe that Americans are either firmly in the (left-leaning) MSNBC camp or the (right-leaning) FOX News/conservative talk radio camp. This inflexible division of Americans into two groups, they maintain, has separated us into factions in recent years.

When serious security issues are looming, labels of liberal or conservative are not productive. "Labeled" people tend to dig their heels in and defend "group-think" positions with an almost herd-like mentality. This only serves to advance separation in the country. In times of war, America has historically come together to overcome great threats. Is it that we do not recognize the grave nature of this threat of Islamic terror? Is it that we have become pathologically political even to the point of placing the nation in a position of perilous vulnerability? Is it a little of both? It is important to understand the role this is playing in our current situation with respect to our national approach to Islamic terror.

Suffice it to say that the apparent segregation of America into "liberals" and "conservatives" is fostering a state of division when America desperately needs unity. There are doubtless times when the liberal approach is correct and others when the conservative approach is correct. The point is this: whatever one's primary ideological leanings, the time has come to stop defending a political party and start defending a nation. The key lies in identifying and modifying the potentially destructive behaviors of average Americans as well as our leaders in both the government and media. Only then will we discover how to work together to win the war being waged by radical Islam upon us, and the world. It will not be the first time that America has been forced by the aggression of others to rise up and rescue the world from evil. America has repeatedly demonstrated that once united, we can overcome any enemy. Time, however, may be running out to do so. The nihilistic nature of this enemy and the advent of a

WMD that can be squirreled away in something so small as a backpack by a single terrorist in an American city illustrate the urgent danger that exists for America, Western society, and the entire world.

COMMON SENSE MESSAGE

As reasonable people would predict, neither liberals nor conservatives are either all right or all wrong. The genius of our two-party political system and our three-branched government design is several-fold. First, it encourages each side to independently, through didactic debate, advance its philosophy for America both in general and with respect to current issues. Then, while following the civil rule of law, debate the other side until compromises that blend the best solutions from both parties are established. Debate is, as I stated elsewhere, as American as apple pie and hot dogs—vitriolic unconstructive rhetoric, on the other hand, must be resisted.

The time has come to retire this division, lest we fall prey to further attacks by our enemies who revel in the schism in present-day America. The Islamic extremists only hope for victory lies in promoting our divide—for in an America united, they haven't a chance to succeed.

POST-9/11: A CRACK IN AMERICA'S ARMOR?

Iraq

Immediately post-9/11, President George Bush seemed to have had an epiphany. He came to believe that the *great purpose* of his presidency was to reduce the threat of Islamic terrorism for America and the world. When Afghanistan was invaded to root out the Taliban, who were training and harboring al-Qaeda, most of the country (and the world) was united in support. With the invasion of Iraq, however, a great schism was created both at home and abroad. As the Iraqi war slowly degenerated into a drawn-out occupation, even greater fissures appeared between America's politicos, liberals and conservatives, and America and Europe. Even the conservative base began to crack apart during the waning months of the Bush administration. This increasing tension with many of our allies around the world further paralyzed America. There is no doubt that the Iraq war became an enormously polarizing event. Let's review America's stated reasons for invading Iraq.

For more than a quarter-century, Saddam Hussein sought to acquire chemical, biological, and nuclear weapons, and has, in several documented cases, succeeded. He supported Middle Eastern terrorists, including suicide bombers, to the tune of $25,000 given to the family of each homicide bomber who attacked Israel's citizenry. Although ties of various types existed with other known terrorists, it is not clear how strong the connection was between Saddam Hussein and other Islamic radicals. He was known to have gassed 60,000 of his own people in 1986 in northern Iraq.[109] William J. Bennett puts it this way in his book, *Why We Fight*, "Many leaders in the world are evil, and a handful possess weapons of mass destruction. But a toxic confluence of factors—malevolence, aggression, a fondness for terrorists, hatred for America and, of course, Israel, and an insatiable appetite for weapons of mass murder makes Saddam Hussein unique."[110] Hussein was repeatedly and urgently warned to disarm or face dire consequences. Prior to the invasion of Iraq, most of the world's intelligence agencies (including Great Britain, Egypt, Israel, Russia, America, and others) believed Saddam Hussein to still possess weapons of mass destruction (WMD). Interestingly, 50 percent of Americans as of July 25, 2006, continued to believe that Iraq possessed WMD when the coalition invaded Iraq in 2003.[111] The U.S. military released a comprehensive report on this subject in March 2009 that was based on 600,000 official Iraqi documents. The study found no "smoking gun" (direct connection) between Saddam's Iraq and al-Qaeda or the present-day existence of weapons of mass destruction. It is now widely known, however, that Saddam himself wished the world to believe he had these weapons for a variety of reasons, primarily to project power over his neighbors. His hatred for America was also undeniable and well documented. This, for many, was justification for military action. For others it was not and they maintain that we were likely all fooled into believing he possessed WMD, but so what? Who really cares that he flouted 16 United Nations resolutions that demanded him to give up these weapons and keep his nation open to inspections—he was a contained threat, so why bother to invade him? As you can see, both sides have validity, but hindsight being 20/20, the initial opponents of this war may well have the stronger argument. Whether or not it was correct to initiate this war, most agree that how it ends will likely have a much longer lasting impact on our nation and the world. As I have stated earlier, we must learn from the past. However, Iraq is still at this time an ongoing military conflict, and the long-term success or failure of the Iraqi invasion will be determined by future historians and later generations.

All of this does have relevancy, since one of the great debates of our era concerns what rights and responsibilities America and the West have to aggressively, and even preemptively, strike out at dangerous enemies before they strike. Most Americans, whatever their initial position was on the Iraq war, believe that the war was poorly executed for many years. Significant progress is finally being made and at the time of this writing it appears that the Iraqi people will soon assume sovereignty over their newly formed democracy. The final chapter on the Iraq war, however, is yet to be written. President Bush was widely regarded as politically vulnerable at least partially due to unprecedented media criticism that bordered on revulsion. This was compounded by abysmal approval ratings at home and abroad. The president's less than stellar oratory skills rendered him even more susceptible to censure which advanced his, America's, and the Iraq war's unpopularity. This national and worldwide disrespect of the president actually fueled division between Americans who respected either the man or at least the office and those who just loathed the lame duck president too much to care. All of this added to the progressive drumbeat of the Iraq wars unpopularity.

COMMON SENSE MESSAGE

The time has come to relegate this great debate—whether or not we should have engaged in the overthrow of Saddam Hussein's Iraq—to future historians. We should all agree that since we cannot change history, and we can only learn from it. It is how we exit Iraq not how we entered it that should be our focus moving forward. It appears that at the time of this writing we are starting to understand this. The Obama administration seems to have abandoned some of its campaign rhetoric (immediate, unconditional withdrawal) while remaining true to its overall pledge to unwind this conflict as quickly as possible while preserving the fragile new democracy there.

MILITARY TRIBUNALS

The controversy

The subject of military tribunals provides a very suitable example of the current political rift in our nation regarding the issue of radical Islam. Let's look at this controversial issue as a window into the practical aspects of the divisions in political America today. Before recapping the remote and recent history of these tribunals, I will outline the major contentious issues. Constitutional attorneys no doubt have a list of their own topics of contention, but for the average American, for whom this book is written, consider these subjects of debate as you read this section:

Should Islamist enemy prisoners—defined by any of several possible names which you will see is in itself a debate—be afforded all the rights and privileges of the U.S. Constitution?

Specifically, because radical Islam is generally not a specific nation-state but rather a dispersed group of enemies from dozens of nations, should we take advantage of them in unique ways that prisoners of war (POWs) and enemy combatants do not typically enjoy?

Is it more important to combat these religious fanatics with all the legal tools available to us, or is it more important to use the opportunity to show the world that America can be exceptionally "fair" in adjudicating the cases of these extremist killers who so detest us?

Perhaps the best way to view this issue is whether or not we *criminalize* terrorism. Do we treat it as the military attack against our nation and our people that I believe it is? Central to this debate is whether accused terrorists should have access to our civilian court systems or be subjected to military commissions or tribunals. Common criminals are prosecuted in our civilian judicial system, replete with all of our constitutional rights. Shall we recognize these foreign religious zealots who are so bent upon our destruction as mere criminals? The subject is a complex one, rooted in constitutional law, precedent, the sanctity of our constitutional rights, and the paramount importance of security. This is one of the most controversial issues we are facing, but it also provides us an unambiguous opportunity to decide on which side of this epic battle we, as individual Americans, wish to fall, irrespective of our usual political affiliations. In other words, although this is a flash point between liberals and conservatives, as liberals *generally* favor the civilian justice system over the military one and conservatives vice versa, it provides us an opportunity to move beyond these labels. As I see it the *real issue* is permissive behavior not liberalism, but most Americans who oppose tribunals are self-described liberals. In this age of terrorism where measures to enhance security can threaten personal rights, many Americans (generally conservatives) find themselves supporting the suspension of certain constitutional privileges, reasoning that doing so serves an even greater purpose: public safety. The key to this question is whether an individual's rights outweigh the government's. I take a hard view (my analysis follows the objective review on military courts) on this bellwether subject, which is at the heart of our national debate on the Islamic extremist threat and how we intend to meet it.

THE HISTORY OF MILITARY TRIBUNALS

According to Yale University alum and Stanford Law professor, William Taft IV, military commissions occupy a well-established place in international law and practice.[112] "The Third Geneva Convention on the Protection of Prisoners of War, for example, presumes that POWs "shall be tried only by a military court," he says. Often these courts are actually military commissions, although, in certain situations, they authorize trials in civilian courts. The United States has relied upon military commissions as far back as the American Revolutionary War in 1780, during and immediately following the Mexican-American War, and during the American Civil War. The most recent use was during World War II when the Allies relied rather heavily upon military commissions to prosecute war criminals largely because they were easily adapted to the unique circumstances of such cases.[113]

The authority for military commissions stems from Articles I and II of the Constitution: Article I, Section 8 grants Congress the power "to provide for the common good and to define and punish piracies on the high seas, and offenses against the Law of Nations." Article II confers on the president and makes him the commander in chief of the Army and Navy. In addition to the Constitutional articles above, Congress has also upheld the validity of military commissions in Article 21 of the Uniform Code of Military Justice (10 U.S.C. Sec. 821) with this language: "The provisions of this chapter conferring jurisdiction upon courts-martial do not deprive military commissions, provost courts, or other military tribunals." This has been substantially upheld in later years in the Articles of War 12, 13, 14, and 15. Before George W. Bush, the last president to use military commissions was Franklin Delano Roosevelt.

Proponents of military commissions to adjudicate terror suspects and enemy combatants do not believe that these individuals are entitled to all of the privileges that the Constitution provides. They cite the dangers associated with the accused being entitled to confront their accusers in the civilian justice system—many of whom are secret U.S. Special Forces or spies, both foreign and national. Foreign spies will be far less likely, detractors say, to cooperate with the U.S. if their undercover personnel have their identities placed in jeopardy. Even when genuine effort is made to seal "critically sensitive" secret information in the nonmilitary environment, leaks will occur due to the loose lips of defense attorneys, court administrators, and others who the government cannot absolutely control. Similarly, the often-secretive methods and processes used by the U.S. and allied governments in capturing these suspects are in jeopardy of discovery in a civilian court.

Opponents of military commissions believe that nothing trumps constitutional rights, and many even support offering non-U.S. citizens all the rights of U.S. citizenship, partly to broadcast to the world our commitment to the rule of law. They believe that allowing the government to suspend the rights of the people, even in the name of security, is a slippery and dangerous slope.

Islamic extremism is dynamic and decentralized. This type of power structure cannot be easily "decapitated" by a single attack to a central figure or institution, no matter how successful the assault. Instead, what is required is a protracted campaign against extremism, including intelligence gathering, domestic and global political coordination, military action, and law enforcement. Ironically, such an approach must utilize the tactics favored by many Islamic extremists themselves: the operations against extremism must be rooted locally but coordinated globally. Obviously, in this "war on terror," military action has a role to play. Equally obvious, however, is the fact that brute military action cannot succeed alone, as it cuts too wide a path of destruction, which only stokes the fire of anti-Western sentiment amongst the general Muslim population, and in turn, swells the ranks of new extremists. This conflict, therefore, requires a host of multinational and domestic activities, all of which generate prisoners of various stripes. It is therefore the nature of this type of war to produce nontraditional prisoners of war (POWs) and other detainees. The very definitions of "prisoners of war," "unlawful enemy combatants," and "terrorists" are subject to a large degree of interpretation, which poses several challenges to the U.S. and our allies with respect to the use of military courts rather than civilian ones. Further complicating this, the U.S. State Department has been critical of a number of other nations' abuse of military tribunals even as we reactivate our own in the wake of 9/11.

OTHER NATIONS STRUGGLE WITH MILITARY TRIBUNALS

According to the Human Rights Watch Briefing Paper in June 2003, China, Egypt, Kyrgyzstan, Malaysia, Nigeria, Peru, and Russia were just a few of the nations that had violated the rights of its citizens and others through the overzealous use of military courts. Consider these examples from the briefing: China's military tribunals, the United States maintains, is abusive "because defendants do not enjoy a presumption of innocence or its corollary rights, such as habeas corpus, standard of guilt, or the burden of proof necessary to ensure it." It goes on to state, "Trials involving national security, espionage, or state secrets are conducted in secret." The lack of procedural safeguards has resulted in crackdowns in predominantly Muslim areas, and that China has "failed to distinguish between those involved in legal religious activity and those involved in ethnic separatism or terrorist activities." In China, the police can monitor client-counsel meetings, and defendants are often not allowed to confront their accusers. The State Department states that in Kyrgyzstan, "the government frequently used the judicial process to eliminate key political opposition figures." Opposition leaders have been tried in closed military courts, although a civilian may also be tried in military courts if a codefendant is a member of the military. "In practice, there was considerable evidence of executive branch interference in verdicts involving prominent political opposition figures."

In contrast to these nations, supporters of military

commissions and tribunals say the U.S. system for military commissions differs from these nations. "The U.S. procedures offer essential guarantees of independence and impartiality and afford the accused the protections and means of defense recognized by international law. They provide, in particular, protections consistent with those set out in the 1949 Geneva Conventions, the customary principles found in Article 75 (Fundamental Guarantees) of Additional Protocol I to the Geneva Conventions, and the International Covenant on Civil and Political Rights," according to Professor William Taft IV in his March 2002 dissertation, *U.S. Military Commissions: Fair Trials and Justice.*[114] In Great Britain, the "Anti-Terrorism, Crime and Security Bill," introduced by the Home Office on November 13, 2003, allows foreigners to be held without a hearing if security officials have reason to believe them to be potential terrorists. France, New Zealand, Australia, and Canada all recognize that in times of war and other public emergencies, civil rights may necessarily be suspended but basic human rights should not. The fact that many nations are struggling to deal with the legalities of the Islamist threat is just one more example of the global nature of radical Islam and is important for not only American unity, but worldwide unity in responding to the threat it poses.

THE AMERICAN BAR ASSOCIATION'S TASK FORCE ON THE MILITARY TRIBUNALS

On January 4, 2002, the American Bar Association (ABA) weighed in on this subject in its "Task Force on Terrorism and the Law/Report and Recommendation on Military Commissions." The report starts out with this statement: "The [presidential] order provides that non-citizens whom the President deems to be, or to have been, members of the al Qaida [sic] organization or to have engaged in, aided or abetted, or conspired to commit acts of international terrorism that have caused, threaten to cause, or have as their aim to cause, injury to or adverse effects on the United States or its citizens, or to have knowingly harbored such individuals, are subject to detention by military authorities and trial before a military commission... it is the duty of the Government to bring those responsible to justice and to take all legal measures to prevent future attacks; it is also the duty of the Government to preserve and protect fundamental rights and liberties under the Constitution." The report states that this presidential order does, however, raise significant issues of constitutional and international law. Many constitutional scholars complain that "the language in the order makes its potential reach quite broad and raises questions for which there is no clear, controlling precedent." The Task Force paper disclosed and discussed the issues surrounding military commissions but was not designed to resolve them. Four years later, the Military Commissions Act of 2006 addressed some of these concerns, but others remain unresolved.

THE MILITARY COMMISSIONS ACT OF 2006

On November 14, 2001, President George W. Bush signed the order allowing for military tribunals. The U.S. Congress passed the Military Commissions Act of 2006 (MCA) in September of that year at the request of President Bush, who signed it into law. The Military Commissions Act's avowed purpose is to "facilitate bringing to justice terrorists and other unlawful enemy combatants through full and fair trials by military commissions, and for other purposes." The bill limits the right of habeas corpus, which is the mechanism by which a person can seek relief from unlawful detention.[115] The MCA protects detainees from blatant abuses during questioning—such as rape, torture, and "cruel and inhuman" treatment—but does not require that they be granted legal counsel. This bill was drafted after the Supreme Court ruled four months earlier that the military tribunal system the Bush administration had established to adjudicate detainees at Guantanamo Bay (Gitmo), Cuba violated Geneva Conventions to which the United States is a participant.[116] This case involves the first suspected terrorists to be put on trial by military commission. Salim Ahmed Hamdan was an Osama bin Laden bodyguard. *U.S. v. Hamden* became the first formal military trial in 50 years. His lawyers challenged the legality of the military commission process. The Court of Appeals for the District of Columbia Circuit upheld the military commissions system, but in June 2006 the Supreme Court overturned that decision. The Supreme Court ruled that military commissions are an "appropriate venue for trying terrorists, but ruled that military commissions needed to be explicitly authorized by the United States Congress."[117]

Legislation addressing detainees accused of terror also became necessary after the Bush administration acknowledged that the CIA had been secretly interrogating alleged terrorists overseas. The new law states that detainees will not be allowed to challenge their imprisonment in federal civilian courts. Human rights groups, many liberal organizations, and individuals, both civilian and elected, have voiced concern that the bill's language could result in a blurring of the lines between tough interrogation techniques and torture. A sizable minority of Democrats opposed the legislation because they claimed that it eliminated fundamental rights of defendants considered sacrosanct to American values, including a person's ability to protest their detention in a court of law. The American Civil Liberties Union (ACLU) executive director Anthony D. Romero said Bush was enacting a law that was "both unconstitutional and un-American." Officially, the ACLU in Washington, D.C. described the presidential order as "deeply disturbing and further evidence that the administration is totally unwilling to abide by the checks and balances that are so central to our democracy." In response, the White House communications director at that time, Dan Bartlett, countered by stating that "we have looked at this war very unconventionally, and the conventional way of bringing people to justice doesn't apply to these times." President Bush, at the bill's signing ceremony in the East Room stated, "The Military Commissions Act will save lives and give terror suspects a full and fair trial."[118]

THE FIRST CASES OF THE MILITARY COMMISSION ACT OF **2006**

The outcomes of the early uses of the Military Commission Act of 2006, supporters of the commissions say, prove that they are based upon rule of law—most of the detainees were either released or minimally punished. Of the first three cases brought against Guantanamo Bay detainees using the MCA, one resulted in a plea bargain and the next two were dismissed on jurisdictional grounds. The first case was David Matthew Hicks, an Australian who was captured by the Northern Alliance, handed over to the U.S. military, designated an unlawful combatant, and held at Guantanamo Bay. In March 2007, his prosecution ended with his plea of "guilty" and he was sentenced to nine months' imprisonment, to be served in Australia. On June 4, 2007, in two separate cases, military tribunals dismissed charges against the other two detainees. In both cases, the detainees had been designated as "enemy combatants" but not as "unlawful enemy combatants." Cases against Omar Khadr, a Canadian, and Salim Ahmed Hamdan, a Yemeni national, were dismissed without prejudice. It was ruled that "military tribunals, created to deal with 'unlawful enemy combatants' had no jurisdiction over detainees who had been designated only as 'enemy combatants,'" according to presiding judge Colonel Peter Brownback and later reaffirmed in the Hamdan case. Two of the first three cases prosecuted resulted in dismissals and the third was plea-bargained, and so the lobby against military commissions was somewhat dispirited.

On December 20, 2007, however, U.S. military judge Navy Captain Keith Allred decided that Hamdan is not a POW but rather an unlawful enemy combatant.[119] This conclusion was based upon a December 2007 hearing conducted in the presence of human rights monitors and journalists, in which Hamdan had six attorneys who confronted those who testified against him.[120] Judge Allred ruled that under the MCA law discussed above, a legal basis exists to try him in a war crimes tribunal. In yet another twist to this story, in June 2008, the U. S. Supreme Court dealt the Bush administration its worst legal blow regarding this issue since the September 11th attacks, ruling that terror suspects held at Guantanamo Bay can petition civilian courts to let them go.[121]

The five-to-four decision in the case *Boumediene et al v. Bush* caused upheaval in federal courts, where a number of lawsuits by Gitmo detainees had been suspended.[122] Attorneys for most of the military prisons' 270 detainees promptly filed renewed lawsuits and appeals. "It's going to cause chaos within Guantanamo and cause chaos here, in terms of how they're going to handle these hundreds of cases," according to Karen Greenberg, director of NYU's Center for Law and Security. "The court's decision today will deepen and complicate an already ridiculously complex and disordered morass of litigation brought by foreign terrorists against our government," said former Bush White House lawyer Bradford Berenson. The justices explained in great detail that prisoners have the right to challenge their detention, known as the writ of habeas corpus. This privilege, they argued, has existed since 1679 and is a right provided by the Constitution. Congress stripped captured terrorists of that right in the Military Commissions Act of 2006 because they felt it was outside civilian courts' jurisdiction. But that protection is fundamental, explained Justice Anthony Kennedy, a Reagan appointee, speaking for the majority of the court. Each of the generally liberal judges was in the majority.[123] "The laws and Constitution are designed to survive, and remain in force, in extraordinary times," Kennedy wrote. "Liberty and security can be reconciled." The conservative justice Antonin Scalia strongly disagreed: "It will almost certainly cause more Americans to be killed... the nation will live to regret what the court has done today," he wrote in the dissent. This ruling did not question the executive branch's ability to declare someone an "enemy combatant," an unprecedented power upheld by the Supreme Court in 2004.[124] Nor did it order any prisoners to be released. Nonetheless, even the Supreme Court is as evenly split as is possible over this issue, one more reflection of America's polarity at this juncture and over the way in which we are to grapple with Islamic extremism.

CONCLUSION OF THE HAMDAN CASE

Hamdan's defense team immediately challenged this new Supreme Court ruling in New York and lost—he was held for the first military trial in 50 years. In August 2008 after an eight-hour deliberation, a military jury found Hamdan guilty on five counts of supporting terrorism but not of conspiring in al-Qaeda's terrorist attacks on the United States, the most serious charge.[125] The jury consisted of five men and one woman. One conspiracy charge alleged that Hamdan knew that his work with bin Laden would be used to support terrorism, another that he provided surface-to-air missiles to al-Qaeda—both valid and perhaps even provable charges *since he was arrested with a surface-to-air missile in his car!* The military court was very lenient (typical of military tribunals) in sentencing Hamdan to just five months plus time already served, which turned out to be a total five and one half years. Hamdan thanked the jurors for their compassion upon receiving his lenient penalty and apologized for having served bin Laden.[126] I find this an interesting conclusion to such a contentious proceeding. The trial, as described above, was not without its controversies. Defense lawyers for Hamdan claim that the process was flawed in that certain rights were denied their client, particularly the civilian right to be warned against self-incrimination.

The George W. Bush administration, on the other hand, seized on the acquittal on the conspiracy charges and the light sentence to praise the tribunal system against accusations that it was politicized and unfair.[127] Tribunal advocates proclaimed the conviction a vindication of the process that has come under broad criticism since its inception. Army Colonel Lawrence Morris, the chief prosecutor, said that he was "wholly satisfied" with the verdict and that it "validated in its essence" the fairness and openness of the tribunal. "Hamdan's conviction on some but not all counts should dispel any speculation that this was a kangaroo court," said Jeff Addicott, director of the Center for Terrorism Law at St. Mary's University in San Antonio. So ended the first military trial in America in a half-century.[128]

NO "DECLARATION OF WAR"

Another challenge is the fact that Congress has not declared war on Islamic extremists. This is largely because Islamic extremists do not reside in a well-demarcated nation-state, but rather in dozens of countries as itinerants. This being the case, do these "Articles of War" still apply? Although many do question the legality of this, thankfully, the Supreme Court and Congress have recognized that a state of war may exist without a formal declaration. While a Declaration of War would provide the clearest authority in support of military commissions, martial courts have been used in many hostilities in which there was no formal declaration of war, including the Civil War and the Indian Wars. Nothing in Article 21 or elsewhere in the Uniform Code of Military Justice or other statutes explicitly limits the use of military commissions when war has not been declared. The courts have repeatedly supported the use of martial courts where no formal declaration of war has been enacted.

MIRANDA RIGHTS AND U.S. PROSECUTION FOR TERRORISTS?

According to a senior Republican on the House Intelligence

Committee, the Obama administration has decided to prosecute suspected terrorists captured on the battle field as criminals in American courts rather than by military adjudication.
"We capture them...and they're reading them their rights—
Mirandizing these foreign fighters," says Representative Mike
Rogers in an interview with Stephen F. Hayes from *The Weekly Standard* on June 10, 2009.[129] Rogers, a former FBI special
agent and U.S. Army officer who sits on the House Intelligence Committee, recently visited military, intelligence, and
law enforcement officials in Afghanistan said that he was "a
little surprised to find it taking place when we showed up
because we hadn't been briefed on it, I didn't know about it.
We're still trying to get to the bottom of it, but it is clearly a
part of this new initiative the White House calls 'Global Justice.'" As part of Global Justice, captured battlefield prisoners
will be read Miranda Rights by the FBI in their native tongue.
These rights include: "You have the right to remain silent.
Anything you say can and will be used against you in a court
of law. You have the right to speak to an attorney, and to have
an attorney present during any questioning. If you cannot
afford a lawyer, one will be provided for you at government
expense." A U.S. attorney experienced with detainee issues
supports Rogers' claim and says that the Obama administration's approach is reasonable because this administration anticipates that these suspects may eventually be tried in U.S.
courts.[130]

So well known are American Miranda protections that
when 9/11 mastermind Khalid Sheikh Mohammed was
apprehended in 2003, his first utterance was, "I'll talk to you
guys after I get to New York and see my lawyer," according
to former CIA Director George Tenet. "Had Khalid Sheikh
Mohammed had a lawyer," Tenet wrote, "I am confident that
we would have obtained none of the information he had in
his head about imminent threats against the American people.

Although Rogers and a cadre of other Republicans and some Democrats are alarmed at this apparent paradigm shift, others think it an overreaction.[131] In an interview on June 9, 2009, however, General David Petraeus, U.S. Central Command, reportedly denied that all detainees are automatically read Miranda Rights.[132]

At a July 7, 2009 Senate hearing regarding the use of military commissions to prosecute terrorists being held at Guantanamo Bay, a number of members of the Armed Services Committee rejected the Obama administration's apparent position that the detainees actually have American constitutional rights. The panel included ranking member Senator John McCain (R-Ariz.) and Senator Joe Lieberman (I-Conn.) and the interviewees included Assistant Attorney General David Kris and General Counsel for the Department of Defense Jeh C. Johnson.[133]

Assistant Attorney General David Kris stated, "It is the administration's view that there is a serious risk that courts would hold that admission of involuntary statements of the accused in military commission proceedings is unconstitutional." Senator McCain then asked Kris, "Does that infer that these individuals have constitutional rights?" Kris answered, "Ah, yes."

The following excerpts of that interview are a window into the thinking of the Obama administration's view of alleged Islamic terrorist's rights—and this view should give all of us pause.

> McCain: "What are those constitutional rights of people who are not citizens of the United States of America, who were captured on a battlefield committing acts of war against the United States?"
>
> Kris: "Our analysis, Senator, is that the due process clause applies to military commissions and imposes a constitutional floor on the procedures

that the government sets on such commissions..."

McCain: "So you are saying that these people who are at Guantanamo, who were part of 9/11, who committed acts of war against the United States, have constitutional rights under the Constitution of the United States of America?"

Kris: "Within the framework I just described, the answer is yes, the due process clause guarantees and imposes some requirements on the conduct of (military) commissions."

McCain: "The fact is they are entitled to protections under the Geneva Convention, which apply to the rules of war, I do not know of a time in American history where enemy combatants were given rights under the United States Constitution."

Later in the interview, Kris and Jeh C. Johnson stated that military commissions were a viable "alternative," but that the administration preferred to prosecute terror suspects as criminals in U.S. federal courts—a position Senator Lieberman clearly challenged.

Lieberman: "Why would anyone prefer to try people apprehended for violations of the law of war? ...The fact is that from the beginning of our country, from the Revolutionary War, we've used military tribunals to try war criminals, or people we have apprehended, captured for violations of the law of war."

Lieberman said (to Johnson): "Why would you say the administration prefers to bring before our federal court system instead of military commissions that are really today's version of the tribunals that we've used throughout our history to deal in a just way with prisoners of war?"

Johnson: "When you're dealing with terrorists whose, and I'm going to

*say this on behalf of the administration, one of their fundamental aims is
to kill innocent civilians, and so it is the administration's view that direct
violence on innocent civilians, let's say in the continental United States,
it might be appropriate that that person be brought to justice in a civilian
public forum in the continental United States," Johnson then added: "Because the act of violence that was committed here was a violation of Title
18 (federal criminal law), as well as the law of war, so we feel strongly
that both alternatives should exist."*

*Lieberman: "Again, I think the unique circumstances of this war on terror-
ists, against the people who attacked us on 9/11, have taken us down, including the Supreme Court, some roads that are not only to me ultimately
unjust but inconsistent with the long history of military commissions. Why
would you say the administration prefers to bring before our federal court
system instead of military commissions that are really today's version of
the tribunals that we've used throughout our history to deal in a just way
with prisoners of war?"*

*Johnson: "I applaud this committee's initiative to reform the military com-
mission act. I think the military commission should be a viable ready
alternative for national security reasons to deal with those who violate
the laws of war, and I'm glad we're having this discussion right now, and
I thank the committee."*

*Lieberman: "I respectfully disagree. These are people we believe are war
criminals; that's why we captured them. The greater legal protections of
the terrorists because they have chosen to do something that pretty much
has not been done before in our history to attack Americans, to kill people here in America, as they did on 9/11, civilians, innocents, it doesn't
matter, and to do it outside of uniform.[134]*

Therefore, it certainly appears that the Obama administration is actively pursuing the criminalization of captured alleged
terrorists although to what degree we do not yet know.

Another reason for concern, however, is the trial that is just beginning in New York at the time of this writing. Meet Ahmed Khalfan Ghailani, the first Guantanamo Bay detainee to face criminal trial in the United States. He faces charges relating to two U.S. Embassy bombings in Africa in August 1998. On the U.S. bank roll, Ghailani, a Tanzanian national, will enjoy all of the rights and benefits of an alleged U.S. citizen in a criminal trial. He was captured in 2004 and transferred to Guantanamo in 2006. His alleged crimes include scheming with Osama bin Laden and other members of al-Qaeda to murder Americans. His other charges include the murder of 224 people killed in the U.S. Embassy bombings in Tanzania and Kenya.

His prosecution in New York courts rather than a military tribunal in Guantanamo "sets a dangerous precedent for the more than 200 suspected terrorists currently held at Guantanamo Bay," says Judiciary Committee ranking member Lamar Smith (R-Tx), in a written statement in early June 2009.[135] He also warned that, "even if convicted, Ghailani could be released in the U.S. after serving his sentence." The trial will likely begin in the late summer or fall of 2009.

Based upon potential Mirandizing of suspected terrorists captured in theater and the undeniable current prosecution of Ghailani, it is not too difficult to see why many Americans fear that the Obama administration is flirting with an unprecedented criminalization of the war on terror—perhaps all the more disturbing since the term "war on terror" is itself no longer allowed by the Obama administration.

FINAL ANALYSIS OF MILITARY TRIBUNALS

Now that we have a little historical and legal background of military tribunals, here is my take. While there are many complicated legal scenarios regarding POWs and captured enemies, the core issues are clear—at least to me. For example, when a "combatant," by whatever name one chooses to use for him or her (soldier, POW, terrorist, legal or illegal enemy combatant) is weaponized and picked up on the field of battle, it is a "military" situation, not a civilian one. This isn't a two-bit criminal who robbed a 7-Eleven at gunpoint for a few dollars; this is a war circumstance. War is, by definition, a last-resort situation when civility and diplomacy have failed. Make no mistake; radical Islam is at war with America. Although there are certain "rules of war" that should be respected by all parties (but rarely are), what kind of tortured logic could possibly justify flying a captured enemy from a foreign battle field to New York to be hooked up with a defense attorney so we can further inundate our crowded civilian court system?

Solutions to other situations may be less obvious; for example, how should we define "enemy combatants"? Do they include foreign nationals on the battlefield of Afghanistan? What about foreigners accused of terrorism that have entered the U.S. illegally? Do we consider those who entered the U.S. legally but whose travel visas have expired as enemy combatants or illegal enemy combatants? Now for the toughest one of all: how about an American citizen accused of terrorist activity? Does this suspicion warrant a suspension of their constitutional rights to try them in a military court? It is fitting that our best legal minds sift through these scenarios as they occur but I hope that most Americans and most jurists err on the side of caution and fall on the side of protecting our homeland and our soldiers.

Military courts exist for good reason. They streamline the process of war-time justice. They greatly reduce the "gaming" of the system so prevalent in civilian American courts. They also reduce the expense and resources needed to dispense justice for combatants and terrorists. Finally, it is much easier to guard military secrets, processes, informants, and other covert strategies to protect both our men and women in uniform and our allies. Eliminating military courts is on its face absurd, dangerous, costly, and counterproductive. Why don't we just ban military courts altogether, use rubber bullets against the enemies' AK-47 machine guns, and provide our soldiers in the field with Ford Fiestas rather than fortified Hummers to protect them against the IEDs (Improvised Explosive Devices). After all, what kind of evil nation is America to actually use its many resources and assets to protect itself? That wouldn't be very sporting since our Islamist enemy is so primitive now would it? This twisted self-defeating reasoning will appease our permissive domestic and foreign critics, as well as our enemies overseas who believe that everything America does is wrong, but is that really the direction in which we wish to go? I think not and with the exception of the (often vocal) far left, I doubt that many Americans will support so feeble a stance on this issue once they understand it.

Americans enjoy the benefit of all the rights and liberties afforded us by the Constitution of the United States. These privileges are sacrosanct and must not cavalierly be ignored or eroded. At the same time, there exists the responsibility that our (and every accountable) government must provide for the security of its citizens. The sooner our national dialogue is freed from party rhetoric and the inane defense of our "liberal" or "conservative" dispositions the sooner will our leaders sort through the complexities mentioned here to form the national policies that will properly define the use of military commissions.

Military tribunals are a just, long-respected, and necessary approach to doling out justice during times of war. Protecting enemies' "rights" (notice how I do not use the term "constitutional rights" because I don't believe them to be entitled to these) must be balanced against protecting America and Americans. Criminalizing terror and Islamic extremism will only lead to catastrophic results and this must stop.

COMMON SENSE MESSAGE

The legal challenges regarding military courts are obviously complex. The rationale for using them, however, is not. Either we recognize that we are actually fighting a war against fanatical, religious zealots who are cold-blooded killers—or we don't. In other words, we either "get it" or we don't "get it." The conservative view on this, rooted in legal U.S. military history, is reasonable and necessary. The liberal perspective is frighteningly permissive and as emotional as it is dangerous for our nation, the civilized world, and the future that most Americans hope to have.

AMERICAN UNPOPULARITY

It is customary to harbor envy and suspicion toward the strongest and most successful, be it a person, a corporation, or a country. America is the only superpower today, and this generates an obligatory love-hate relationship with the rest of the world. Our 43rd president, George W. Bush, was particularly unpopular which increased his vulnerability for reasons described previously. This unpopularity and political susceptibility was a dangerous combination that fostered a progressively demonstrative and overt dislike for the U.S. by much of the world during his administration. Make no mistake: American unpopularity is a dangerous thing. One of President Abraham Lincoln's favorite axioms was both prophetic and accurate, "With public sentiment, nothing can fail; without it, nothing can succeed."[136] Although Lincoln was referring to his ability as president to achieve domestic goals, particularly the preservation of the union, it is equally applicable to the global stage.

The reasons for America and President Bush's disapproval were numerous. They include the charge that the Bush administration was arrogant and militarily overzealous. This, combined with the president's lack of public support, caused worldwide disapproval of America that has been unparalleled in recent decades. It is also true that France, China, Russia, Iran, and many other nations all gain economically and politically when American is whittled down a few notches. To be fair, this foreign national self-interest as a motivating factor in attacking America should also be considered when analyzing why we find ourselves isolated.

Even having said all that, the world is locked into an unbounded ambivalence toward America. The world loves our liberty, our wealth, our music, our movies, and our technological inventions, but it dislikes our fast-paced lifestyle and our perceived arrogance and isolationism. And it fears our power. Of course, when they require our power to bail them out of some disaster or another, they quickly lose their apprehension and appreciate it beyond measure. Hence, the quintessential, worldwide, seemingly never-ending confused relationship between the U.S. and the rest of the world.

Underestimating the dangers of American disapproval is unwise. Unpopularity is contagious and dangerous and we as Americans need to be careful in the way that we air our dirty laundry. Our Islamist enemies use our self-deprecation as evidence of our ill repute and use it to recruit new Jihadists and to turn world opinion against America—a classic self-fulfilling prophecy.

COMMON SENSE MESSAGE

Transparency and a free press are critically important to us Americans, as they should be. However, too much of a good thing becomes a bad thing. We must maintain respect for each other lest "outsiders" such as our Islamic extremist enemies exploit our self-criticisms as "proof" of our corruption, incompetence, or evil to their advantage. American unpopularity is indeed a dangerous sentiment that self-perpetuates and increases our vulnerability to enemies.

FUSION

America presents the world's greatest love-hate relationship—they love us *and* they hate us. Hopefully with a new president, the balance will swing toward the "loving us," which will aid us as we repair the rifts within our great nation and between America and the world. This harmony is requisite to our goal of focusing of our considerable talent, power, and attention towards defusing the Islamic extremist threat before an even greater tragedy than 9/11 is visited upon us. Whatever one's personal feelings are as to how we got here, it should be clear to all that when religious hatred results in the ever-escalating and global mass murder of innocents, the world must unite and react aggressively. Like it or not, in today's world, this means America must do something. Although perhaps clichéd, these words are apropos: if not us, who? If not now, when? We need to come to terms with what it is we are facing and what we are going to do about it.

The proverb that history repeats itself applies to recent as well as remote events. It is very likely that our current administration will enjoy greater world popularity than the last. Human behavior often reflects an overreaction to recent unsuccessful or unpopular events resulting in a sociological pendulum from one extreme to the other. Some in America exhibit a near obsession with America remaining popular to the world at large. America in this current age must avoid a radical swing in the direction of even greater political correctness in an attempt to garner greater world admiration. Nations, like people, have egos and reputations to protect. It is good to be popular but not so desirable that a nation or a person should sacrifice core values or security for short-term gains at the expense of long-term losses. We must resist the temptation to try to swing that pendulum too far to the left in a misguided effort to please the Europeans—lest we lose precious ground on securing our culture, our nation (and theirs, ironically) from the insidious creep toward an Islamization of the West.

II

Where Are We and How Did We Get Here?

CHAPTER FOUR

Where Are We?

In this chapter we will examine where we are and why we're here as it relates to the causes of Islamic extremism.

ISLAM: AT ODDS WITH MODERNITY

In the 9th century A.D., the Prophet Muhammad founded the religion known as Islam. Soon after his meteoric rise to power, Islam began to fade, over time becoming progressively less dominant in the world. This is in stark contrast to the rise of Christianity. In terms of military might, political power, and economic standing, Islam has largely fallen from history. If not for huge petroleum reserves under the Arab continent, Arabs and Muslims would be amongst the poorest people of the world.[137] Despite their oil wealth, most Muslims live in what the West would define as poverty. Socially and politically, Muslims have been plagued with one tyrannical autocrat or dictator after another. In terms of worldwide inventions, discoveries, and the advance of modern society as a whole, Islam has been largely absent from the global stage, aside from a brief period during the Middle Ages. There are many theories as to why this is so. While there are several books devoted to this subject, we will touch upon only the most obvious causes in this book.

Understand that it isn't my intention to harshly critique Islam or Arabs but rather to identify the root causes of the mindset which fuels Islamic extremism. Ignoring the undeniable reality that modernity is largely a Christian enterprise would be a classic example of the politically correct appeasement that has gotten us where we are today. Having said that, it is telling that I feel the desire and the need to tread carefully here to avoid being erroneously characterized as xenophobic or anti-Muslim.

When one considers telecommunications, travel, computerization, manufacturing, space exploration, advanced farming, medicine, or nearly any other advanced human endeavor, it is the largely Christian Europeans and their offspring who have created the modern world. America, more than any other country, is responsible for the ingenuity and creations that define modern society in the 21st century. This is one reason why there is such antipathy, envy, and hatred (in the case of the more radical elements) on the part of many Muslims toward America.[138]

As Princeton historian Bernard Lewis points out in his book, What Went Wrong, it is only natural when things are going badly for people to ask, "Who did this to us?" A good example of this can be found when Islam blamed the Mongol Wars in the 13th and 14th centuries for its early downfall. In more recent centuries, it has been the Christians who usurped the Mongols as the root cause of Muslim failures in the minds of most radical (and perhaps even moderate) Muslims, according to Professor Lewis. In the last 60 years, Jews have also been blamed as a result of their success as a state. All despite Israel's diminutive size relative to the hostile Muslim nations surrounding it.

The Muslim world has suffered dozens of disappointments over the last several decades. They include Israel's continued accomplishments. The high rate of poverty and primitivism in Muslim lands as contrasted to the West is also a source of humiliation for Muslims. Cumulatively, these failures and missteps on the part of Islam have been skillfully exploited by the extremists to fuel the hatred of the West on the so-called "Arab Street." Arab Street is a reference to the average Arab in the average Arab city as opposed to Arab pundits or politicians. As *Washington Post* journalist Amr Hamzway puts it in his February 2005 article, "The Real 'Arab Street,'" "Arab writers normally see themselves as embodying an imaginary 'Arab Street,' and they had no trouble, in the absence of independent public opinion surveys, in representing their own quite ideological views as those of the Iraqi majority and those of Arabs generally."[139] Arab national ambitions were frustrated by the Western control over of the Middle East after World War I. This, in the eyes of many Arabs, prevented the goal of worldwide Arab nationalism from being realized. Much of the Arab and Muslim world is troubled by huge population growth, which is partly due to the advent of modern medicine into the Middle East. The relative lack of an Arab and Muslim middle class ensures a lower standard of living than the West, which, by way of envy, further stokes the fires of hate. Literacy rates are low and infant mortality is high in most of the Arab and Muslim world. Additionally, Islamic extremists propagate the claim that the oil-hungry West boosts the wealthy, repressive Arab regimes that pilfer oil revenue for the leaders of these nations, thereby leaving the masses poor.[140] All of this furthers the populist, radical, and violent reactionary philosophy on the Arab Street, swelling the ranks of young and angry Islamic extremists.[141]

The major groups of these Islamic extremists include the Shiite followers of the late Ayatollah Khomeini of Iran, the extremist Wahhabi Muslims in Saudi Arabia, the Muslim Brotherhood in Egypt, the Hamas in Palestine, the Iranian-backed Hezbollah, Islamic Jihad, the followers of Osama bin Laden, and the infamous al-Qaeda. These Islamic extremists all share a belief that Islamic Law or Shari'a must apply to both religious and state life, an intolerance of the West, and antipathy for the State of Israel. Generally, they possess an ideology of emancipation, in which the economically challenged Arab and Islamic peoples play the part of the oppressed and poor. They blame the decline of Islamic society on the lack of discipline in religious observance, and support a return to strict observance of the Qur'an.[142] Most extremist groups advocate reestablishment of the caliphate (supreme ruler of Islam) and Jihad (holy war) against infidels, exemplified best by America and the West. They typically reject democracy as a Western invention.

ISRAEL

The Arab-Israeli conflict plays a significant role in the creation and propagation of Islamic extremists. To many Muslims and Arabs, Israel is seen as an extension of America into their "neighborhood." The Arab/Muslim hatred of Israel runs wide and deep, and the entry of America into the Middle East as an ally of Israel is reason enough for many Muslims to hate us. This conflagration spans more than 100 years of regional and global tensions, in addition to many open conflicts. The Arab-Israeli conflict, which has valid arguments on both sides, is an open wound that fuels the wider Islamic extremist war with all things Western.

On May 14, 1948, the State of Israel was established as a Jewish nation, based upon the United Nations Partition Plan. This was the defining event in the history of the clash between Arabs and Jews. Following the Holocaust of World War II, the United Nations decreed a tiny strip of mostly desert land for the Jewish people to develop a country. Israel accounts for less than 1 percent of the Middle East. Perhaps the most common justification used by Arabs for their hatred of Israel's very existence is that Israel forced into exile some 800,000 Arabs for no reason whatsoever. There is controversy regarding how many Arabs left the newly founded Israel and under what circumstances they left. Most experts believe that the vast majority of Arabs underwent a voluntarily (and very transient, or so they thought) exile in order to get out of the way of the invading united Arab armies in 1948, when Israel was granted its independence by the United Nations. The armies of Egypt, Transjordan, Syria, Lebanon, and Iraq attacked Israel in the first 24 hours of her birth, and to avoid being caught in the crossfire, many Arabs left. It is certainly possible that some were actually ejected forcefully by Israelis, but little proof of this exists. In fact, even Libyan President Muammar Qaddafi (self-described "reformed terrorist" extraordinaire) states in his January 22, 2009 *New York Times* op-ed article that, "It is important to note that the Jews did not forcibly expel the Palestinians."[143] Nonetheless, many Arabs and Muslims keep this myth alive to feed the continuing condemnation of Israel. Further enraging and embarrassing many Arabs is that Israel succeeded in converting this seemingly desolate area into one of the Middle East's wealthiest and most successful countries, and the only democracy in the region. The undeniable achievements of Israel, which ironically sits in the middle of Arabia, rubs salt in the 1,000-year-old wound of Islam's fall from power. For these and a host of other reasons there exists a deep-seated conflict between Arabs and Muslims and the State of Israel. By proxy, the West (and particularly America) is blamed by the Arabs for its continuing support of Israel, which has prevented Israel's obliteration by her Arab neighbors.

The importance of this, and the Middle East in general, cannot be overstated due to the fact that most of the world's population has a deep religious and/or emotional attachment to this region known as the "cradle of civilization."

NOBEL PRIZES

The Muslim resistance to modernity can be illustrated by looking at past achievements in scholarship. There are 1.3 billion Muslims, two billion Christians, and less than 14 million Jews on Earth. Yet there have been nine Nobel prizes awarded to Arabs and Muslims, 178 awarded to Jews, and most of the remaining 787 prizes awarded to Christians. This is not to suggest that these Nobel laureates are devoutly religious—only that they are members of these respective religions and that the absence of Muslims based upon their relative population is surprising. Sorted by country, America has the highest number of Nobel Prize winners.[144] This data is not exactly astonishing, but it does exemplify the premise that modernity is almost the exclusive result of societies that are predominantly Christian. There may be many reasons for this discrepancy between Christian and Muslim Nobel Prize winners. Perhaps it is because Muslim scholars are more apt to spend their lives studying the Qur'an rather than Western literature or the sciences. Regardless, the Nobel laureates are just further confirmation that the modern world is not accredited to Arabs and Muslims commensurate with their population, which is nearly 25 percent of all the people on Earth.

HINDUS/INDIA

Hindus have played a mostly separate role in their evolution, and like Muslims, Hinduism has not changed nearly as much as Christendom over the last millennium. This may be why there is less Muslim hatred for Hindus than for Judeo-Christians. Islamic-Hindu friction certainly does exist, however, as evidenced by the ongoing India-Pakistan conflict over the Kashmir region that is juxtaposed to both nations. India and Pakistan were one country until 1947 after some 20 years of Muslim clamoring for greater independence from the mostly Hindu Indian nation. At that time, Kashmir did not immediately decide which nation to join. A period of violent unrest followed, and India, in response to a request by the Maharaja of Kashmir (Indian ruler), signed the "Instrument of Accession." Kashmir, along with the province of Jammu, acceded to India, prompting the Indo-Pakistani War of 1947. Kashmir remained relatively quiet until 1989 when, India contends, a group of Afghan mujahideen (freedom fighters) immigrated to Kashmir and from within this contested province began suing for Kashmir's annexation from India. Pakistan also claims that Kashmir should be annexed from India. The chief minister of Kashmir denies the charge that the separatist movement is actually the Islamist/Taliban/ al-Qaeda/terrorist-instigated insurgency that U.S. intelligence, India, the Rand Corporation, and even Pakistan President Asif Ali Zardari, in 2008, claims it to be. This otherwise relatively small conflict is thrown onto the national stage because both India and Pakistan are nuclear-armed nations.

REFORM, OR LACK THEREOF

Another important distinction between Christians and Muslims is that Christianity has significantly reformed itself in the centuries following the crusades.[145] The Church's instigation of ancient and medieval wars, its literal interpretation of violent biblical passages to justify aggression upon enemies, its intolerance of other religions, and its state-sponsored corruption in the name of religion has been mostly purged from Christian society and no longer exists in modern times.

Islam, however, has yet to face its demons. Despite the existence of many Muslims who reject extremism and terror, Islam has largely refused to clean its own house and root out extremism. We, it seems, have little choice but to do so ourselves. Ironically, when it does, it only further deepens the hatred of the West and Christians by many Muslims, due to the radicals' ability to successfully spin the events as an example of Western aggression and intolerance not toward Islamic terror but against Islam itself. In fact, the extremists have quite successfully portrayed the West as waging an offensive anti-Islamic war rather than a defensive anti-extremist/anti-terrorist war. America and its allies have failed miserably in the public relations arena with respect to this issue. This has accelerated Muslim hatred and distrust of America and the West, further ensuring that the ranks of radical Muslim recruits increase.[146]

Although there are certainly other explanations, factors, and precipitants for Islam's hatred of the West, it stands to reason that Islam's relative failure to propel its civilization forward over the centuries is the most clear-cut answer to the question, "How did we get here?"[147]

Having said all that, perhaps the uncomplicated and unchanging simplicity of traditional Islamic life is actually more fulfilling than the endless hustle, competition, work schedule, and stress of Western society. In creating the modern world, it is often said that Muslims have been passengers, not drivers and deep in their psyche, they know it. The generational and collective Muslim humiliation that results from this realization is considered by many historians to be a critical cause of Islamic extremist hatred of the West.[148]

It is encouraging, however, that there are a number of Muslim groups, authors, and others who encourage Muslims to consider every aspect of their religion as it applies to modern times. One such organization that will be quoted throughout these pages is the Free Muslims Coalition, whose website (www.freemuslims. org) states, "The unwillingness of the Muslim religious establishment to consider modernizing the faith has relegated most Muslims to third-world status and often medieval existence."

Finally, it is notable that crude oil fuels worldwide Islamic extremist terrorism. So-called "petro-politics" plays a significant albeit difficult to define role in this region, since most of the world's known oil reserves reside in the Middle East.

So, where are we? We are in a world where Islam is both a religion *and* culture—unlike Christianity and Judaism whose religion is much more separated from its culture. Islam has followed a continually downward course in terms of worldwide influence ever since its meteoric rise to dominance in the 8th century. Muslims, as a people or culture, have played almost no role in the creation of the modern world. Yet, Islam as a faith is growing worldwide. Many experts believe that Islam has never reconciled its relative inconsequentiality. As a result, resentment, collective embarrassment, and other factors fuel Muslim extremists to hate the West and the entire modern world as they aspire for a reversion to how it was in ancient days when Islam ruled the world.

COMMON SENSE MESSAGE

Islam has suffered nearly 1,000 years of slow enervation, experienced a collection of failures, and drift into an inconsequentiality that fuels its chagrin and resentment of the more successful Western societies. Additionally, the birth of the amazingly successful albeit tiny Jewish state of Israel in the heart of Arabia is another source of embarrassment. America's status as Israel's greatest ally and the greatest democracy (the antithesis of Shari'a) on Earth puts us in the gun sights of Islamic extremists, both figuratively and literally.

HOW DID WE GET HERE?

Knowing where we've been helps guide us on where we wish to go. I have included the next short section as a brief but informative summary of the history of the Abrahamic religions: Islam, Christianity, and Judaism. While history can be somewhat banal to readers, it is necessary to know the past in order to understand the present and plan for the future. This section provides a foundation from which the reader will much better comprehend both the nature and the root causes of Islamic extremism in the world today. Accompanying the history of Islam is a running Islamic history timeline at the bottom of the page for those readers that prefer an even briefer history. Most readers have a much better understanding of Judeo-Christian history, so no timeline is present for these sections.

ISLAM: A TIMELINE

Before and around 570 A.D. On the Arabian Peninsula, two empires, the Christian Byzantines (remnants of the Roman Empire) and the Persian kingdom, struggled for dominance. The indigenous populations were nomads of Semitic decent.

570 A.D. Muhammad Ibn Abdallah is born in Mecca on the Arabian Peninsula. At this time, the only monotheistic religions are Judaism and Christianity. Most inhabitants in Arabia are idol worshipers.

595 A.D. Muhammad marries a 40-year-old wealthy widow named Khadija. They spend the next 15 years trading with caravans and living among the Hanefites, an Arab sect that rejected idol worship and longed for a true religion.

610 A.D. Muhammad has his first "vision," following which his wife's uncle declares him a prophet to the Arab people. Muhammad, in the city of Mecca, claims Allah as the one true god and slowly accrues a following of adherents, beginning with his wife. Islam's birth was turbulent, as it was rejected by Jewish and Arab inhabitants of Mecca.

612 A.D. During the Hajj (an annual religious pilgrimage to Mecca), tribes from the city later known as Medina met Muhammad and soon afterwards declare him the prophet they had been searching for.

622 A.D. The Muslims in Mecca, due to increasing hostility, leave Mecca for Medina.

622–627 A.D. The Muslims begin raiding caravans on their way to Mecca for their livelihood. Many attribute the Jihad's birth to these events. Medina's Muslims begin a three-year period of battling with Mecca.

630 A.D. The Muslims, after nullifying a treaty with Mecca, capture the city and the Meccans "submit" to Muhammad and to Islam.

632 A.D. Muhammad dies rather suddenly, leaving no clear orders of succession. Abu Bakr, Muhammad's father-in-law, expands the religious and political Islam.

632-644 A.D. The 2nd Caliph (Muslim ruler) expands Islam further into Persia and Jerusalem.

644 A.D. The 3rd Caliph, Uthman of the Umayyad family rejects Ali, Muhammad's cousin, and divides Islam.

644-750 A.D. Uthman's followers murder Ali and the Umayyad family rules Islam from the capital, Damascus, in present-day Syria. Islam spreads to Spain and northern Africa.

750-935 A.D. The Abbasid Caliphate rules all of Islam (except Spain, still under Umayyad rule) from present-day Bagdad, Iraq. The so-called "Golden Age" of Islam was under Abbasid rule. Islam prospered while Europe faltered under relatively illiterate monarchs. This was Islam's greatest period of advancement and cultural growth.

935-1300s A.D. Medieval Islamdom includes most of Arab and Persian lands. Invasions from outsiders, including the Christian response to Islam's invasion of Europe (the Crusades) and the Asian Mongols, weaken Islamic kingdoms. Although the Mongols easily defeat the Muslims militarily, within 150 years they convert to Islam.

1299-1922 A.D. Turkish tribes displace the Mongols and grow the great Ottoman Empire that rules Islam until the 20th century. The Ottomans invaded the Christian strongholds of Europe and very nearly exterminated Christendom twice.

Early 1900s Following WWI, the great partition replaces Islamic empires.

Mid 1900s The Americans and its allied Nation States win WWII, and the remnants of the Ottoman Empire (allies of Hitler's Germany) are further divided.

Present-Day Islam 1.2 billion adherent Muslims are the majority of nearly 60 nations and are present in most of the nations on Earth.

Note that this timeline excludes the history of Islam in Persia (Iran), Asia, and Russia, as they are succinctly covered in the last few pages of this section.

ISLAM: A BRIEF HISTORY

Many Americans are not very familiar with the religion or history of Islam. Its history spans more than 12 centuries, more than 10 empires, and a vast region, stretching from Spain to the islands of Indonesia. The evolution of Islam, as you will see, was a complex and tumultuous journey.

PRE-MUHAMMAD ERA

The Arabian Peninsula, the birthplace of Islam, consists mainly of desert. Originally, nomadic peoples populated the region. It is widely believed that the Semitic descendents of Noah's third son, Shem, migrated into the area known as the Fertile Crescent and there became assimilated into the indigenous civilizations.

In the 6th century A.D., in the northern Arabian Peninsula two great empires were engaged in a struggle for dominance. The Christian Byzantines, remnants of the Roman Empire, ruled the northern peninsula all the way to the Mediterranean Sea, north Africa, and the lands of the present-day Middle East. The Persian kingdom ruled the northeast. Neither of these powers included Arab citizens but each had Arab allies.

The Arabian Peninsula became a land of refuge for those

seeking escape from both of these empires. Heretic Christian sects like the Nestorians, traditional Christians, and Jews found refuge in the lands of the Arabian Peninsula.

In this era, the tribal people of Arabia were divided into cities. Each city had many gods and goddesses, totaling some 360. These Arabs coexisted uneasily. Once a year the various tribes of Arabia would meet in the city of Mecca, in present-day Saudi Arabia, during an event known as the Hajj. Here, all the warring tribes would put aside their differences during this five-day religious event.

THE MUHAMMAD ERA: THE BEGINNING OF ISLAM

Muhammad Ibn Abdallah was born in the year 570 A.D. in the city of Mecca. His father died before he was born and his mother, Amina, died when he was a young child. He was raised primarily by his uncle. At the age of 12, Muhammad accompanied family members on a caravan-trading venture and experienced the outside world for the first time. Muhammad at the age 25 married a 40-year-old widow named Khadijah who owned trading caravans. During the next 15 years of his life, he lived and worked among the Arabs known as the Hanefites, a sect who rejected idol worship and were searching for one true religion. They looked to the religion of the Jews and Christians as being close to the goal. The Hanefites would pray and seek haven in the caves of Mecca.

In the year 610 A.D., Muhammad had his first vision on Mount Hera and thought he was possessed by demons. He shared this fear with his wife, whereby she sought the council of her uncle, a Christian Hanefite who assured them Muhammad's vision was from God. He declared Muhammad the Prophet to the Arab peoples. Soon after this revelation, Muhammad proclaimed Allah as the one true god and rejected the idol worship so prevalent in Mecca and the Arabian Peninsula. Muhammad's wife, Khadijah, was his first convert to Islam.

There were few adherents early on, and Muhammad actually feared for his life as resentment of his self-proclamation as the Prophet grew. For a while his family protected him, but after the death of his wife and her uncle the new leaders refused to protect Muhammad. He sought refuge and protection in nearby cities from those after his life.

Two years later during the Hajj, Arab tribes from the city Yathrob, later to be known as Medina, met Muhammad during an annual pilgrimage. They invited him to their city to bring peace and settle disputes between the warring tribes. Yathrob was founded by three Jewish tribes. Jews were the world's first monotheistic people, believing in one god. They, too, were searching for the Messiah, and the Arabs of Medina wished to beat them to it. It was at this time that the Arabs of Yathrob, accustomed to the concept of monotheism from the Jews, declared Muhammad to be the Prophet they were searching for. As Islam grew from the first few Muslims in those years, so did opposition to them by the Jews and Arabs of Yathrob. Soon, the situation became intolerable for the Muslims, and in June 622 A.D., they made what has become known as the Hejira or flight. In small groups, the 150 Muslims of Mecca left for the more northern city of Medina.

In Medina the warring Arab sects submitted to Muhammad's claim to be their Prophet. The Muslims were without work and they resorted to caravan raiding. The Muslims in Medina began to rob the caravans heading toward Mecca. This is where the Muslim tenet of Jihad was born. With their caravan business being threatened, Mecca's leaders battled over the next few years with the Muslims and in 627 A.D., they surrendered to the mercy of Muhammad. A treaty was signed, but in January 630 A.D., the Muslims nullified the treaty and all of Mecca submitted to Muhammad and his warriors and accepted him as the Prophet.

Muhammad made his final Hajj in 632 A.D. and died of

unknown causes in the summer of that year. Muhammad's father-in-law, Abu Bakr, succeeded him as leader of the Muslims,
but Muhammad left no clear will or orders for succession, and
before long Islam was rife with power struggles, some of which
continue to this day.

Map of Early Islam

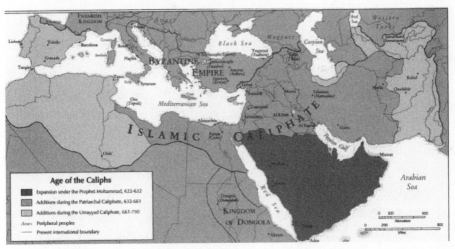

Source: http://www.gl.iit.edu/govdocs/maps/maps.htm

POST-MUHAMMAD ERA

Muhammad failed to leave any instructions or guidelines as to
succession, a colossal error that set the stage for a series of conflicts among the Muslims that spanned many hundreds of years.
Soon after Muhammad's death, under a series of rulers Islam's
power in the Arabian Peninsula was completed. So successful
was the rise of Islam that within 100 years Islam had spread to
all of Arabia and northern Africa. In Europe, Islam made deep
incursions into Spain and France, although a decisive battle for
Europe was lost by the Muslims in 732 A.D. at the Battle of
Tours. In spite of this defeat, their presence persisted in Spain

and resulted in a so-called "Arabization" of the Spanish culture, and soon Spain became an independent Muslim country. Parts of Spain remained in Muslim hands until it was conquered by the Christians at the end of the 15th century. Still, the Islamic army's expulsion from Spain is remembered with bitterness by many Muslims who consider Spain, known as Al-Andalus in Arabic, lost territory. Most present-day extremist groups demand the recapture of Spain and its conversion to a Muslim nation.[149]

THE ABBASID ERA

At about this time, Islam was subjected to various sectarian divisions and wars that eventually brought to power the Abbasid Caliphate, significant in the fact that it began what scholars refer to as the "Golden Age of Islam." The rise of the Abbasid Caliphate from so many disparate factions represented a true social revolution. In this Golden Age, the divisions of aristocracy were washed away. The distinction between Arab Muslims and converted Muslims (often those conquered) was similarly eliminated, and the basis was laid for a tolerant and progressive Muslim society. During this time, a great city was built as their capital, known as the "City of Peace." This is present-day Baghdad.[150]

The peak of Abbasid power came under the famous caliph, Haroun al-Rashid. The Arab-Muslim empire had grown from the Arabian Peninsula to cover all of northern Africa, Mesopotamia, and Central Asia in a very brief period. Baghdad became the cultural center of the world at a time when Europe was buried in the darkness of the Middle Ages. Iraq and the Arabian empire underwent an impressive cultural revolution. Advances in literature, science, and mathematics occurred; as did the preservation of the ancient classics, as literature from Europe was being translated into Arabic. Baghdad was one of the greatest cities in the world during this time.

The contrast of the achievement of Arab Islamic civilization with that of the troubled empires in Europe (ruled by relatively illiterate monarchs such as Charlemagne) is remarkable. Muslim activity had a profound effect, not only on Muslim civilization but also on the intellectual life of Western Europe. Much of the science and philosophy taught in universities in the Middle Ages was derived from Arabic translations that were rendered into Latin in Spain during the 12th century. Muslim Arabs became the brokers of a cultural revolution, transmitting advances of technology from the Far East, including "Arabic" numerals.

However, the Arab empire began to collapse soon after the Golden Age, and a period of independent caliphates and successive chaotic invasions followed. The Muslims were then challenged by the European Crusaders who finally responded to Islam's expansion and arrived in the Middle East in 1096 A.D. They captured Jerusalem in 1099 A.D. The Muslim world reacted slowly but eventually retook Jerusalem in 1187 A.D., having defeated the crusaders at the Battle of Hattin.

The following centuries were marked by Mongol invasions into Muslim territories. The Mongols are a group of peoples loosely defined as the ancient relatives of present-day Mongolia, China, Russia, Afghanistan, and Pakistan. The Mongols swept across the Middle East rather easily due to the collapse of the Arab empire. Although the Mongols were largely victorious in their expansion into Arab and Muslim lands, they eventually assimilated into Muslim culture. The remaining Mongols were eventually diffused and defeated in the early 15th century.[151]

THE OTTOMAN ERA

Turkish tribes in Anatolia, the forerunner of the great Ottoman Empire, eventually displaced the Mongols and grew into an empire spanning three continents. Socially, economically, and militarily, Turkey was largely unaffected by developments in the rest of Europe. Between 1299 and 1922 A.D., the ethnically diverse Ottomans were, however, the intersection between East and West. The Ottomans were noteworthy in that they were the only Islamic power to seriously challenge the rising power of Western Europe in that period. Between 1299 and 1683 A.D. the Ottoman Empire gained huge territorial control until its expansion into Europe was stopped by King John of Poland at the battle of Vienna in 1683 A.D.

The Ottoman Empire is widely remembered for its pervasive corruption and bribery but also for its religious tolerance of non-Muslims. The despotic rule was, to a degree, lessened by observance of (non-radical) Muslim law; without it, the suffering of common people would likely have been far greater. The Ottoman Empire slowly declined in power and importance. Following World War I, the Treaty of Sevres confirmed the dissolution of the Ottomans. A nationalist movement in 1922 that rejected the Treaty of Sevres began the era of modern Turkey.[152]

PERSIA (IRAN), IRAQ, AND THE BIRTH OF THE MODERN MIDDLE EAST

During the confusion that ensued with the weakening of the Abbasid Arabs and the withdrawal of the Mongols, the Persians were constantly fighting for their independence. Unlike many other Middle Eastern countries, Iran managed to remain independent throughout much of its history. The Persian Shiites began to consolidate their power and even retook Baghdad in present-day Iraq.

Today, Iran is 89 percent Shi'a, although the majority of the world's present-day Muslims are Sunni. In the course of history, Islam diverged into numerous schools and sects with different approaches and philosophies. These factions have had far-reaching ramifications in the present-day Middle East and the world. Although to most non-Muslims, these divisions seem trivial; to Muslims, they are not. Muslim sects range from fierce and puritanical schools, such as the Wahhabi of Saudi Arabia and the radical brand of Sunnis represented by the Taliban in Afghanistan, to tolerant and spiritualistic Sufi practitioners.[153]

The Iranian Constitutional Revolution took place between 1905 and 1911. The revolution marked the creation of a parliamentary system in Persia. Then World War I took place and the subsequent invasion of Iran by so many combatants weakened the government and threatened its independence. In 1925, Reza Shah Pahlavi succeeded the Qajar Dynasty as a new monarch of Iran. To a large degree, America's foreign policy with respect to Iran is at least partially responsible for the 1979 the Iranian Revolution. Iran's uprising spawned a larger "Islamic Revolution." It transformed Iran from a constitutional monarchy, under Shah Mohammad Reza Pahlavi, to a theocracy ruled by Ayatollah Ruhollah Khomeini, a Shia Muslim cleric. This momentous event is believed to be the key trigger for the increased acuity in the war between the West and radical Islam. At the same time, the U.S., U.S.S.R., and most of the Arab governments of the Middle East feared that their collective dominance in the region was challenged by the new Iranian Islamic ideology. Consequently, the U.S. encouraged and supported Iraq's Saddam Hussein in his invasion of Iran, which was at least partly to blame for the Iran-Iraqi war. Here again, the U.S., by supporting Iraq, another corrupt, autocratic, cruel, and despotic regime solely because they supported American interests, blundered. The nearsightedness of this misguided policy provides a good example of America's habit of taking actions incongruent with our own ethics for a short-term gain at the expense of a long-term loss; incurring the wrath of Iran and much of the Muslim world along with them.

In November 1917, before it had conquered Jerusalem and the area to be known as Palestine, Britain issued the Balfour Declaration, stating Britain's support for the creation of a Jewish national home in Palestine. Jews have existed in this region for more than 3,000 years. Following the events of World War II, the United Nations in 1948 issued a mandate for the creation of a Jewish homeland in Palestine. Immediately thereafter, five Arab armies attacked the Jews, and against all odds, the Jews eventually prevailed and formed the State of Israel. The advent of Israel quickly resulted in Arab-Israeli conflict, which has produced several wars and serves as a flash point for Western-Arab-Muslim conflicts.

ISLAM IN CENTRAL ASIA

In Central Asia, the history of Islam began just a few years after the death of Muhammad and its growth more or less parallels that of the Middle East. Central Asia is the home of the former Soviet Union, and its progeny: present-day Russia. China also shares both history and great challenges with Islam and Islamic extremism. Both Russia and China pose serious political challenges for America and the West; therefore, a brief history of Islam in Asia is presented below.

ISLAM IN RUSSIA

In Russia, Islam is the largest religious minority, encompassing 19 percent of the total religious population. The exact number of practicing Muslims is difficult to calculate since there is no national census or statistics available from the Russian federal government or any other governmental organization.

The first Muslims within the current Russian territory were the Dagestani people (from the region of Derbent) after the Arab conquests in the 8th century. The so-called Caucasus is a region of Eurasia at the southern boundary of present-day Russia. It is bordered by Russia to the north, Turkey to the southwest, the Black Sea to the west, and Iran to the south. Most of the European and Caucasian Turkic peoples also converted to Islam. The native Siberians were conquered by the Russian empire in 16th century. In the 18th and 19th centuries, Russian conquests in the North Caucasus brought the Muslim peoples of this region into the Russian empire. The conquest of various other Islamic peoples followed, and eventually the independent states of Central Asia and Azerbaijan were brought into the Russian state as part of the same expansion that integrated the North Caucasus. Most Muslims living in Russia were the indigenous people of lands long ago seized by the expanding Russian empire.

Under communist rule, Islam was oppressed and suppressed, as was virtually every other religion. Mosques were generally outlawed, along with most churches.[154] On February 7, 1990, under Soviet President Mikhail Gorbachev's administration, the Central Committee of the Communist Party of the Soviet Union, decided to surrender its monopoly of power. Most experts attribute this about-face from the Soviet president to President Ronald Reagan's strategy to militarily outspend and bankrupt the Soviet empire in their attempt to remain competitive. It apparently worked. Over the next few months, the 15 constituent republics of the U.S.S.R. held their first competitive elections. Many of the nations whose names end in "stan" were formed as relatively independent states. They include current-day Kazakhstan, Kyrgyzstan, Tajikistan, Turkmenistan, and Uzbekistan. These countries are largely Muslim and therefore Muslim influence (and Islamic extremism) has grown in Central Asia following the dissolution of the Soviet Union. In this power vacuum throughout the 1980s, Saudi and Iranian influence has grown in these newly independent countries, and continues to grow today.

After the collapse of the Soviet Union, governmental oppression of Islam eased considerably. Many Muslims were allowed to make pilgrimages to Mecca, for instance.[155] An organization named the Union of Muslims of Russia is the direct successor to the pre-World War I Union of Muslims, which had its own faction in the Russian Duma (government). There is an Islamic Cultural Center of Russia (which includes a madrassa) that opened in Moscow in 1991. Still, as is the case in much of the world, city-dwelling Muslims tend to segregate from non-Muslims in modern Russia. The majority of Muslims in Russia are Sunnis, and Moscow is home to the majority of these Muslims.

Chechnya deserves special note since this republic contains the fiercest Russian-Muslim tension. Chechnya is located in the North Caucasus Mountains, and there have been two major wars in this region since the mid-1990s. Chechnya's population is mostly Muslim. It wishes to be independent from Russia, but for a number of reasons including oil pipelines and a reserve of oil and natural gas, Russia is disinclined to grant that wish. The majority of Islamic terrorism on Russian soil has been due to the conflict in this region.

ISLAM IN CHINA

China's history of Islam dates back to as early as 650 A.D. An uncle of Muhammad was sent by the Third Caliph, Uthman, as an ambassador to then Emperor Gaozong. By the Sing Dynasty in 1000 A.D., Muslims dominated the import-export industry. By the middle of the Ming Dynasty (1368–1644 A.D.) several hundred years later, new immigration of Muslims to China was restricted. In these years Muslims began assimilating more and more in terms of Chinese dialect and even Mosque architecture. With the rise of the Qing Dynasty (1644–1911 A.D.), the relationship between Muslims and other Chinese became much more tenuous. During this time period, the Chinese government forbade the slaughtering of animals (an affront to Muslims) and the construction of new Mosques. At least five bloody rebellions ensued, and by the time the Republic of China replaced the Qing Dynasty, the government proclaimed that the nation belonged equally to all ethnic factions, including the Han, Hui (Muslim), Meng (Mongol), and the Tsang (Tibetan) peoples. Currently, there is, to some extent, a revival of Islam in China similar to what most of the world is experiencing. There are currently approximately 40 million Muslims in China, according to the Population Studies Center at the University of Michigan in 2004.[156] As it is in most of the world, in much of China, Muslims are segregated from the rest of Chinese society.[157] Islamic extremism has grown significantly in China, as it has in Russia and the former Soviet Union countries.

As discussed throughout this book, Islamic society (as we may observe it today in both Muslim and non-Muslim countries) has not undergone the same type of perpetual evolution and change as has Christian and other societies. As one can see even from this very brief history of Islam, countless battles and wars have resulted in an almost endless shifting of territorial military and political control of Islamic lands. Yet, the culture and day-to-day behavior of most Muslims has changed very little over the centuries. Those that have advanced have done so largely by adopting Western technologies and behaviors. This cultural divide results in a natural isolation of Muslims from other members of their host nations in much of the world. Many historians and political experts consider this to be a key source of friction and incompatibility between Muslims and both Western and Asian cultures that helps to fuel extremism.[158]

CHRISTIANITY: A BRIEF HISTORY

In stark contrast to Muslim societies, Christianity has been on the move for 2,000 years. Although history has frequently been tumultuous and violent for Christian countries and societies, they've reached a point of unparalleled prosperity in the modern world. In fact, as previously stated, Christianity's success is largely responsible for the modern world.

Jews have played a role disproportionate to their diminutive population, although it is not easy to distinguish their part from the much larger Christian population in the creation of modernity. Suffice it to say, Christendom and all that it entails is responsible for most of the inventions, institutions, and prosperous societies in today's world.

Christian history begins with Jesus of Nazareth, a Jew who was born in a largely Jewish but small corner of the Roman Empire. The world at that time was governed centrally by Rome under the rule of Augustus Caesar, the first Roman ruler called emperor. Some 60 years earlier, the Roman army invaded Palestine resulting in the expansion of the empire to more than 50 million subjects. Although Rome governed with a strong hand, many of Rome's local foot soldiers including the Huns, Syrians, Kurds, and other tribal chiefs were often at war with each other. Little is known of Jesus' early life, but we do know that at around the age of 30, Jesus was baptized (a religious act of purification by water) by John the Baptist. After experiencing a vision in which he received the blessing of God, he began a ministry of teaching, healing, and miracle-working. He began teaching about what he referred to as the "Kingdom of God," and criticizes those whom he felt were religious hypocrites. He spoke before large and ever-increasing crowds of people. He also chose the "12 disciples," whom he taught privately. His disciples and followers believed him to be the long-awaited Messiah who would usher in the Kingdom of God on Earth. As his popularity grew, so did opposition to him by the Jewish leaders, who thought him blasphemous, and the Romans, who feared his popularity. Ultimately, the Romans executed Jesus in Jerusalem by crucifixion. Most of Jesus' followers were distraught by such an unexpected outcome. Three days following his crucifixion, women who went to anoint his body reported that the tomb was empty and that an angel told them Jesus had risen from the dead. The disciples were initially skeptical, but later came to believe this series of events. They reported that Jesus appeared to them on several occasions and then ascended into heaven before their eyes.

For the remainder of the 1st century A.D., Jesus' followers grew significantly. It was at this point that they became known as "Christians." Influential in the expansion of Christianity was a man named Paul, a religious Jew who had persecuted Christians, then converted to the faith after experiencing a vision of the risen Jesus. Paul traveled on numerous missionary journeys throughout the Roman Empire. He founded churches and then remained in contact with them via mail once he had continued on his journey; the letters offered further counsel and encouragement to the Christians who stayed behind. Incidentally, many of these letters would become part of the Christian scriptures, or as we better know them, the "New Testament."

In the 2nd and 3rd century A.D., Christians fell victim to persecution throughout the Roman Empire. Christian leaders, known as the "church fathers," wrote defenses of the false claims made against Christians as well as arguments against the false teachings spreading within the church, which were called polemics. Policies were explored, developed, and solidified. Ultimately, the canon of the New Testament was formed and the notion of "apostolic succession" established a system of authority to prevent unsanctioned or counter wrong interpretations of Christian teachings.

In its first three centuries, the Christian church endured regular (although not universal) persecution at the hands of Roman authorities. To the early Romans, religion was a social custom whose intent was to promote loyalty to the state. Many considered Christianity more a dangerous "superstition" than a religion. Most Roman subjects at the time lacked any clear sense of religion beyond believing in a variety of gods and idols, the result of the assimilation of many conquered peoples. The Roman Empire was actually quite tolerant of most religions until the monotheistic Christianity was viewed as a threat to Roman authority. The imperial policy was generally one of incorporation and allowance of local gods, although they were often given Roman names. The Jews were the only monotheistic (one god or single deity) religion at the time. On a more social level, Christians were distrusted in part because of the secret and misunderstood nature of their worship. Words like "love feast" and talk of "eating Christ's flesh" sounded understandably suspicious to the pagans, and Christians were suspected of cannibalism and other sorts of immorality.

A major turning point in Christian history came in the early 4th century A.D., when Roman Emperor Constantine converted to Christianity. Under his rule, the Christian religion was legalized, and persecution all but ceased to exist. Supported by the Roman Empire, Christianity gradually rose in power and importance until it became the "Christendom" that would eventually encompass the entire Western world in the Middle Ages, the Renaissance, and beyond.

During Christianity's early years, not everyone agreed that Jesus was actually the Son of God; a number of councils were convened to work out the differences of opinion. Eventually, a united position was adopted that claimed Jesus to be the Son of God. Over the next 100 years or so, the church then turned to issues about Christ's divine and human natures, which were largely resolved in 451 A.D. at the Council of Chalcedon in Constantinople, or present-day Istanbul, Turkey.

In the meantime, an increasing cultural and religious schism between the Eastern and Western churches was becoming increasingly apparent. The two sects of Christendom had different views on topics such as the nature of the Holy

Spirit, and the date on which Easter should be celebrated. Culturally, the Greek East tended to be more philosophical and abstract while the Latin West advocated a more pragmatic and legal-minded approach. There is an applicable saying: "The Greeks built metaphysical systems; the Romans built roads." Upon the death of the Emperor Constantine, the empire was divided between his two sons, one of whom ruled the western half of the empire from Rome while the other ruled the eastern region from Constantinople.

In 1054 A.D., Pope Leo IX excommunicated the patriarch of Constantinople, the leader of the Eastern Church. The patriarch condemned the pope in return, and the Christian church was officially divided into West ("Roman Catholic") and East ("Greek Orthodox") ever since.

One cannot discuss the history of Christianity without mentioning the Crusades. The Crusades were a series of military conflicts during the years 1095 A.D. through 1291 A.D. Most of these were sanctioned by the pope in the name of Christendom. The proximate cause of the First Crusade was when Pope Urban II agreed to send mercenaries to resist the substantial Muslim military advances into the Byzantine Empire. Another stated goal was to recapture the Holy Land of Jerusalem from the Muslims. The First Crusade unleashed a wave of popular violence against Jews and Orthodox Christians throughout Europe. In total, there were more than 15 separate and distinct crusades, most of which were successful against the Muslims.

In the 1400s A.D., certain Western Christians publicly challenged aspects of the church. They spoke against the abuse of authority and corruption in Christian leadership. They called for a return to the gospel, with a reemergence of customs like purgatory and the withholding of the communion wine from non-clergy. They began to translate the Bible from Latin into the common languages of the people.

In 1517 A.D., a German monk named Martin Luther revisited these reforms with much greater success due to growing German nationalism and the invention of the printing press. Luther nailed his *95 Theses* to the doors of Castle Church in Wittenberg, Germany, criticizing the church and sparking the Reformation. His teachings spread quickly. He was excommunicated from the Roman Catholic Church, but Luther spent the remainder of his life spreading the Reformation and died of natural causes. His ideas spread throughout Germany and spawned similar reform movements in Switzerland and England. Lutheranism, today, is a major branch of Western Christianity. It is a denomination within Protestantism, which is one of the three principle traditions within Christianity; Roman Catholicism and Eastern Orthodoxy being the other two. In the most simplistic of terms, the major tenets of Protestantism are their belief that salvation is achieved through faith alone and that the Bible (not church tradition as in Catholicism) is the final source of Christian authority.

In the 17th century, Christians of many ideologies embarked on the hazardous journey across the Atlantic to the New World. Quakers, Catholics, and the Dutch were amongst the earliest travelers. With the exception of some Puritan communities, there was no attempt to impose religious uniformity in America.

The period from about 1648 to 1800 A.D. was an age in which reason and logic became increasingly important. Religion also prospered at the time of the American Revolution. At the same time that religious skepticism and adherence were growing in the West, so too were revivalist movements that sought to return the masses to a faith in Christ and the gospel of salvation. Jonathan Edwards was one such example of these revivalists. He famously described in detail the torments of those who do not have personal faith in Jesus

Christ. John Wesley was also a revivalist preacher, but he differed strongly from his Presbyterian friend when it came to the doctrine of predestination. Wesley founded a small group of preachers who focused on holy living; we know them today as the Methodists.

Today, Christianity is the largest religion in the world, totaling more than two billion adherents. There are Christian churches in almost every nation in the world. Virtually all Christians believe in the basic doctrines of the Church as they were laid down in the 4th century, but differ in matters of doctrine and practice. In recent years, there has been a growing movement among these denominations to work together in unity for the good of the world. In 1948, the World Council of Churches was founded with that in mind.

As described throughout this book, Christianity has played a central role in creating the world as we know it. Much of Western civilization is a product of Christendom, which currently claims one-third of the world's population. It is world's predominant religion. Although it has many sects, each with its own tenets and beliefs, Christianity today is an evolved and stable religion that has largely exorcised its demons, and its believers rarely, if ever, resort to armed conflict to resolve religious disputes.

JUDAISM: A BRIEF HISTORY

Judaism was founded in that part of world known the cradle of civilization in Mesopotamia by a local inhabitant named Abraham, circa 2,000 B.C. Many believe that the ancient Hebrews conquered the Canaanites and established their religion soon afterward. As we have already reported, the ancient world was beset with endless conflicts and wars. In these early years, Egypt absorbed the Hebrews into their culture as slaves. In the early 13th century B.C., Moses led the Jewish people from Egypt in the famous Exodus, a defining event in the history of Judaism.

Over the following 400 to 500 years, Judaism evolved into a wealthy nation beginning with the rule of King Solomon, who himself succeeded King David, known for establishing Jerusalem as the capital of ancient Israel. King Solomon housed the Ark of the Covenant in the great temple he built in Jerusalem. The Ark was a golden box that is reported to contain the tablets of Law (Torah) that the Jews believed Moses received from God himself on Mount Sinai during the legendary 40 years in the Sinai desert after their exodus from Egypt. These tablets are the most sacred symbol of the Jewish people. The Torah is defined by the *Columbia Encyclopedia* as "the Law of Moses, which are the first five books of the bible." In a wider sense, the Torah includes all the teachings of Judaism: the Hebrew Bible and the Talmud (rabbinical record of Jewish laws and ethics).

Centuries later, in the year 722 B.C., Assyrian Emperor Sargon II conquered the entire region, splitting the Jewish empire into Israel in the north and Judah in the south. The Assyrians were brutal rulers, and the Jewish people were subjected to many hardships. More than 100 years later during a war with Egypt, Babylonian King Nebuchadnezzar destroyed Solomon's temple and enslaved the Jews. Some 50 years later, the Persians, after conquering Babylonia, freed the Jews and brought about prosperous times for the Jewish people. The Persians also restored the Law of Moses.

In 332 B.C., Alexander the Great conquered Jerusalem. He is reported to have respected the Jews and their faith. Following his death, however, in the year 169 B.C., Greek King Antiochus Epiphanies "Hellenized" the Jews, attempting to destroy Judaism by forbidding studying the Torah, male circumcision, keeping kosher, etc. Ultimately, this resulted in what many historians consider the world's first religious war: the war of the Jewish Maccabees versus the Greeks. Following 25 years of conflict, the Jews were ultimately successful in restoring Jerusalem, and with it, Hebrew law in the land of Israel.

The next two centuries were wrought with various conflicts, although the Greeks ruled ancient Israel at that time. During this period, many different factions of Judaism rose and fell. After many conflicts between these different factions, the Romans invaded and were easily able to conquer Israel. In the 1st century A.D., Israel rebelled against Rome. For reference, the act of Israel attempting to overthrow the Roman Empire at this point in history would be roughly the equivalent of the relatively tiny modern-day Israel waging war with the whole of Europe. After some surprising early successes, the Romans dispatched their most experienced commander, Vespasian. The Romans then easily put down the rebellion and appointed Herod, so-called "King of the Jews," who many historians place as the ruler of Jerusalem in the year that Jesus was born.

After years of unrest, in 70 A.D., Roman Emperor Titus ordered the destruction of Solomon's Temple and that the Jews be dispersed. Titus then "recruited" 100,000 Jewish slaves to accompany him to Rome. Once there, they would build the Arch of Titus in 79 A.D., commemorating the fall of Jerusalem. The Arch of Titus currently resides adjacent to the Coliseum in present-day Rome. Israel fell under Roman rule until the empire fell, leading to the rise of the Byzantine Empire. Interestingly, many Romans were attracted to the monotheism of Judaism, but were put off by the restrictive Hebrew laws. The disciple Paul preached a variant of Judaism whereby he replaced the Torah (which many Romans found cumbersome and at odds with Roman culture) with a belief in Jesus, which resulted in a huge conversion of Romans to Christianity. As mentioned earlier, it was at this time that the Roman Emperor Constantine was himself converted to Christianity before becoming emperor of Rome.

From this time through the Crusades in 1100 A.D., which was a response to Islamic military aggression deep into Europe, the Jews stood as infidels to the Christian Crusaders and they were attacked and defeated along with the Muslims.

The infamous Spanish Inquisition in 1478 A.D. was yet another chapter in Jewish persecution. The result was that the Jews were expelled from Spain at just about the same time that Columbus discovered America, in 1492 A.D.

There were rare periods of good fortune for the Jews in Europe, exemplified best when King Boleslav of Poland invited the Jews into Poland in 1567 A.D., granting them unprecedented rights and privileges. Nearly all of the descendants of these Jews later died at the hands of the Nazis during the Holocaust of World War II.

Jews played a prominent role during the early years of America's birth. When America was founded by the Puritans, they themselves identified with the Jews as a persecuted people as they fled Europe and sought a safe haven in which to flourish. The Puritans literally incorporated part of the Jewish Bible in their Code of 1655 A.D. Jewish traditions and the Hebrew language were so popular at that time that both Harvard and Yale Universities taught Hebrew. The Yale seal still contains an open book with the Hebrew "Urim V'Timum." Dartmouth University uses a Hebrew word meaning "God Almighty" in its seal, as does Columbia University. Jews contributed both men and money to the American Revolution. Haym Salomon lent the first Continental Congress $200,000 and eventually died bankrupt. The first Georgian patriot killed in the war was a Jew, Francis Salvador. President George Washington remembered the Jewish contribution to America's founding when he visited the Touro Synagogue in Newport, Rhode Island in August of 1790. President Washington's famous letter to the Jewish Congregation at Touro includes these passages: "For happily the Government of the United States, which gives to bigotry no sanction, to persecution no assistance, requires only that they who live under its protection, should demean themselves as good citizens... May the children of the stock of Abraham, who dwell in this land, continue to merit and enjoy the good will of the other inhabitants."

The end of World War I heralded the First Zionist Congress in 1887 A.D. in Basal, Switzerland. This was a reaction to vehement European (mostly French) anti-Semitism of the day. In the summer of 1948, just three years following the Holocaust of World War II, the United Nations agreed to grant the Jews a homeland in the land of Palestine (Israel). This angered the other indigenous people of that land, the Arabs. The rest, as they say, is history. Following a number of wars and conflicts in the Middle East, today Israel stands a democracy that has few friends in the world, notwithstanding the United States.

Jews represent just 15 million people today, only one-quarter of 1 percent of the world's population and less than 1 percent of America's. To many, this is an irreconcilable statistic because it seems that Jews play so prominent a role in so many human endeavors. Their considerable contributions in the fields of science and medicine, television and movies, as well as literature and politics certainly play a role in anti-Semitism. Some resent the prominence and success of Jews; others respect and try to emulate them. There is great debate as to why they play so significant a role in the world both today and historically. The Jewish tradition of emphasizing, if not revering, education combined with their survival during 2,000 years of persecution are no doubt contributors. Israel, the only Jewish nation, situated at the birthplace of the world's great religions, remains the focus of irrational Islamist hatred, all of which keeps the Jewish nation front and center in the world's news.

TIMELINE OF ISLAM

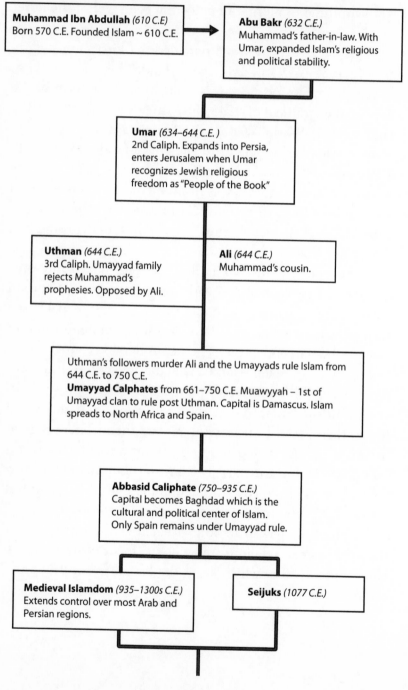

Muhammad Ibn Abdullah *(610 C.E)*
Born 570 C.E. Founded Islam ~ 610 C.E.

Abu Bakr *(632 C.E.)*
Muhammad's father-in-law. With Umar, expanded Islam's religious and political stability.

Umar *(634–644 C.E.)*
2nd Caliph. Expands into Persia, enters Jerusalem when Umar recognizes Jewish religious freedom as "People of the Book"

Uthman *(644 C.E.)*
3rd Caliph. Umayyad family rejects Muhammad's prophesies. Opposed by Ali.

Ali *(644 C.E.)*
Muhammad's cousin.

Uthman's followers murder Ali and the Umayyads rule Islam from 644 C.E. to 750 C.E.
Umayyad Calphates from 661–750 C.E. Muawyyah – 1st of Umayyad clan to rule post Uthman. Capital is Damascus. Islam spreads to North Africa and Spain.

Abbasid Caliphate *(750–935 C.E.)*
Capital becomes Baghdad which is the cultural and political center of Islam. Only Spain remains under Umayyad rule.

Medieval Islamdom *(935–1300s C.E.)*
Extends control over most Arab and Persian regions.

Seijuks *(1077 C.E.)*

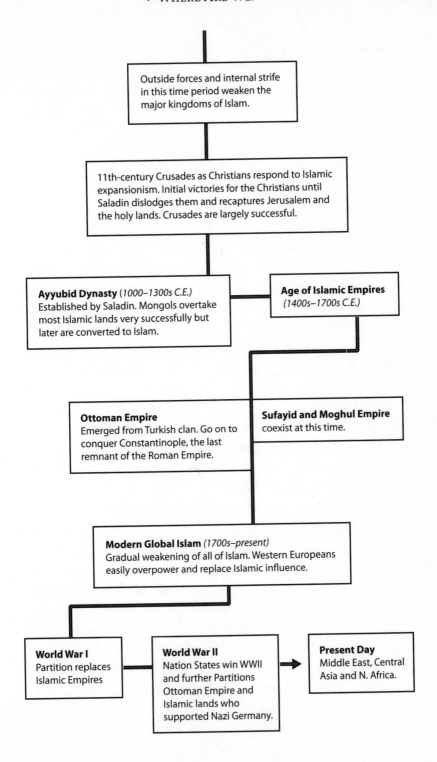

Outside forces and internal strife in this time period weaken the major kingdoms of Islam.

11th-century Crusades as Christians respond to Islamic expansionism. Initial victories for the Christians until Saladin dislodges them and recaptures Jerusalem and the holy lands. Crusades are largely successful.

Ayyubid Dynasty (*1000–1300s C.E.*) Established by Saladin. Mongols overtake most Islamic lands very successfully but later are converted to Islam.

Age of Islamic Empires (*1400s–1700s C.E.*)

Ottoman Empire Emerged from Turkish clan. Go on to conquer Constantinople, the last remnant of the Roman Empire.

Sufayid and Moghul Empire coexist at this time.

Modern Global Islam (*1700s–present*) Gradual weakening of all of Islam. Western Europeans easily overpower and replace Islamic influence.

World War I Partition replaces Islamic Empires

World War II Nation States win WWII and further Partitions Ottoman Empire and Islamic lands who supported Nazi Germany.

Present Day Middle East, Central Asia and N. Africa.

THE THOUSAND YEAR WAR

Are we experiencing the same Muslim-Christian war that has existed since long before the Crusades? Not exactly, although the Islamic extremists would like us to believe so. The current invocation of this conflict is actually one of Islamism versus Modernity. The explanation as to why much of Islam, in recent years, has become more radical and aggressive around the world is simpler than many may think. Let's interpret the history we have reviewed. We have covered the ongoing, simmering warfare between Christendom represented by the West and Islam over the past 1,000 years. Both religions inherited from Judaism a belief in the one God who created the world and performs divine intervention. Early on, approximately 1,300 years ago when the Prophet Muhammad founded Islam, Muslims exhibited considerable respect for Jews ("people of the book") and harbored at least some respect for Christians. As acknowledged earlier, when Islam widened its reach, it quickly conquered much of the Judeo-Christian lands, including the Holy Lands. The Christian reaction to this was the Crusades from the 11th through the 13th centuries. The Crusades were largely successful for the Christians, due to their superior weapons and their evolving culture that encouraged growth and change. In contrast, Islam did not encourage nor often tolerate change, and even today's Islam struggles with societal evolution.[159] In his book, *What Went Wrong*, Bernard Lewis explores the cultural differences that account for the superior weaponry and military strategy of the Europeans. Basically, the Europeans have (with the exception of the Middle Ages) habitually documented societal, scientific, and military advances so subsequent generations will benefit and advance from the former's discoveries. Islam, except during the "Golden Age" between 800 and 1100 A.D., has discouraged growth and change to a much greater degree, preferring a fundamentalist preference for the status quo.[160] Militarily, a less disciplined and hive-minded approach was (and many experts say still is) pervasive in Muslim armies, partially due to individuals practicing a silo approach in an attempt to remain indispensable to the army in the name of job preservation, according to Strategy.com's editor-in-chief, Jim Dunnigan. "Improvisation and innovation is generally discouraged in Muslim society where individualism gives way to conformity." Arab armies 'go by the book.' Western armies 'rewrite the book' and thus, usually win wars. Additionally, paranoia prevents adequate training. Arab tyrants have historically insisted that their military units have little contact with each other, thus ensuring that no single general can become powerful enough to overthrow his superior. Units are purposely kept from working together or training on a large scale. Arab generals often don't have as broad a knowledge of their armed forces as do their Western counterparts. Promotions are based more on political reliability than combat proficiency. Arab and Muslim leaders prefer to be feared (rather than respected) by their soldiers, according to Kenneth Pollack's exhaustive study called *Arabs at War* on Arab military effectiveness. Security trumps efficiency. Everything even vaguely militaristic is often kept top secret. While U.S. Army promotion lists are routinely published, this rarely happens in Arab armies. Officers are suddenly transferred without warning to keep them from forging alliances or networks. Team spirit among officers is discouraged, according to warfare historian John Keegan and others.[161]

Upon close examination, Western culture has been more conducive to military efficiency than that of its Arab and Muslim counterparts. If that were not so, the complexion of our world might look very different today. Is it possible that Islamic extremists, keenly aware of this, are trying to shift the balance of this reality with this new age of terrorism?

Ever since those ancient days, Christianity and Islam have rarely been harmonious. This is chiefly due to radical Islamic doctrine that demands that Muslims extend Islam throughout the world and that they convert infidels to Islam or die trying. As Christianity has flourished and Christian nations have advanced so greatly, an enormous gap between these two diverse ideologies has been created. So large is the disparity between the power of Christian nations and that of Muslim nations that only small skirmishes have been possible between them, despite their age-old feud. Radical Islam is using terrorism as a great equalizer in an attempt to balance the scales and bring the giant to its knees.

COMMON SENSE MESSAGE

The main reason why the world is ablaze with radical Islam is that it has discovered (rediscovered) a new weapon. Islamic guerilla warfare and terror against civilians has proven to be a godsend—no pun intended. Terrorism has succeeded to elevate the extremists' cause to the front burner of the world. Suddenly, Islam is relevant again—in the eyes of radical Islam. In the face of Islamic terror, the far more powerful West is brought to its knees because they so value life and the terrorists are so willing to sacrifice it. A new strategy is born and Islamists are maximally exploiting it.

DEMOGRAPHICS OF ISLAM AND ISLAMISM: ATTITUDES BY REGION

The first of the two tables presented in this section serves as a summary of the population of Muslims relative to non-Muslims, demarcated by nation. The second table is a summary of a recent Pew Poll on global attitudes, which is a barometer of the relative support of the Muslim population for terrorism around the world. Finally, a recent report from the United Kingdom serves as an example of the disturbing prevalence of radicalized attitudes in the Muslim population of Western nations.

VITAL SIGNS: THE PULSE OF ISLAM

MUSLIM POPULATION BY COUNTRY

Country	Population M=million K=thousand	Muslim (%)	Muslim M=million K=thousand	Shia Muslim (%)	Sunni Muslim (%)
Saudi Arabia	24.6 M	100	24.6 M	10	90
Turkey	72.9 M	99	72.7 M	20	80
Algeria	32.8 M	99	32.4 M	4	96
Morocco	30.7 M	99	32.4 M	2	98
Afghanistan	29.9 M	99	29.6 M	18	82
Yemen	20.7 M	99	20.6 M	42	55
Somalia	8.6 M	99	8.6 M	1	99
Mauritania	3.1 M	99	3.1 M	1	99
Kuwait	2.6 M	99	206 M	35	65
Oman	2.4 M	99	2.36 M	5	55
Bahrain	700 K	99	700 K	70	30
Maldives	300 K	99	300 K	5	95
Western Sahara	300 K	99	300 K	3	97
Iran	69.5 M	98	68.8 M	89	9
Tunisia	10 M	98	9.8 M	2	98
Comoros	700 K	99	6.8 K	1	99
Pakistan	165 M	98	160 M	20	80
Iraq	28 M	97	18 M	65	35
Niger	14 M	97	13.5 M	3	97
Libya	5.8 M	97	5.6 M	1	99
Azerbaijan	8.5 M	96	8.2 M	87	13
UAE	4.6 M	96	4.4 M	15	85
Gambia	1.6 M	95	1.5 M	2	98
Qatar	800 K	95	760 K	10	90
Egypt	74 M	94	69 M	1	99
Senegal	11.7 M	94	10.9 M	5	95
Jordan	5.8 M	94	5.4 M	2	98
Djibouti	800 K	94	752 K	1	99

Country	Population M=million K=thousand	Muslim (%)	Muslim M=million K=thousand	Shia Muslim (%)	Sunni Muslim (%)
Syria	18 M	90	6.1 M	15	85
Tajikistan	6.8 M	90	6.1 M	5	95
Turkmenistan	5.2 M	89	4.6 M	4	96
Indonesia	221 M	88	129 M	5	95
Bangladesh	147 M	88	129 M	5	95
Uzbekistan	26.4 M	88	23.2 M	6	94
Guinea	9.5 M	85	8 M	3	97
Kyrgyzstan	5.2 M	75	3.9 M	3	97
Sudan	40.2 M	73	29.3 M	2	98
Bosnia & Herze-govina	4.5 M	60	2.7 M	7	93
Ivory Coast	18.2 M	60	10.9 M	4	96
Lebanon	3.8 M	55	2.1 M	60	40
Nigeria	131 M	50	65.7 M	5	95
Tanzania	36.5 M	50	18.25 M	6	94
Burkina Faso	13.9 M	50	6.9 M	3	97
Eritrea	4.7 M	50	2.3 M	1	99
Kazakhstan	15.1 M	47	7.09 M	5	95
Ghana	22 M	45	9.9 M	12	88
Ethiopia	75 M	32	24.4 M	1	99
Macedonia	2 M	32	630 K	1	99
Kenya	33.8 M	24	8 M	7	93
Benin	8.4 M	20	1.6 M	3	97
Russia	143 M	19	27.6 M	15	85
Serbia/Kosovo	10.7 M	19	2 M	15	85
Uganda	26.9 M	16	4.3 M	7	93
Israel/Territories	10.8 M	46	5 M	2	98
India	1,200 M	14	154 M	20	80
Malaysia	23 M	61	14 M	2	98
Bulgaria	7.7 M	12	890 K	10	90
France	60.7 M	10	5.9 M	6	94
Albania	3.2 M	63	2.12 M	25	75

Country	Population M=million K=thousand	Muslim (%)	Muslim M=million K=thousand	Shia Muslim (%)	Sunni Muslim (%)
Mongolia	2.6 M	6	160 K	5	95
Germany	82.5 M	4	3 M	10	90
China	1,303 M	3	390 M	8	92
United Kingdom	59.6 M	3	1.6 M	10	90
United States	269 M	1	2.9 M	15	85
South Africa	46.9 M	2	938 K	10	90
Canada	32.2 M	2	620 K	10	90
Brazil	184 M	1	921 K	30	70
Argentina	38.6 M	1	500 K	10	90
Australia	20.4 M	1	280 K	10	90
Italy	58.7 M	0.51	50 K	5	95

*Sources: http://en.wikipedia.org/wiki/Demographics_of_Islam; Encyclopedia Britannica 1997 ed.; Registered religious communities in Finland (2003); *The World Almanac & Book of Facts*, 1998; http://islamicweb.com/?folder=beliefs/cults&file=shia_population

VITAL SIGNS: THE PULSE OF ISLAMIC TERRORISM

The Pew Global Attitudes Project. July 24, 2007

Muslim Tolerance for Terrorism, July 2007

Suicide Bombing as Justified Often/ Sometimes Justified	2002 (%)	2007 (%)	2002-2007 change (%)
Lebanon	74	34	-40
Bangladesh	44	20	-24
Pakistan	33	9	-24
Jordan	43	23	-20
Indonesia	26	10	-16
Tanzania	18	11	-7
Nigeria	47	42	-5
Turkey	13	16	+3

Suicide Bombing as Justified Often/ Sometimes Justified	2002 (%)	2007 (%)	2002-2007 change (%)
Palestinian Territories	-	70	-
Mali	-	39	-
Malaysia	-	26	-
Kuwait	-	21	-
Ethiopia	-	18	-
Senegal	-	18	-
Morocco	-	11	-
Egypt	-	8	-

The pervasiveness of Islamic radicalization in the West is well reflected in a recent report from the United Kingdom. In this report conducted by the Centre for Social Cohesion (CSC) in June 2008, one in three Muslim students in England approve killing for Islam.[162] The Centre for Social Cohesion is a conservative organization in England. This report also revealed a widespread desire on the part of young Muslims in Western nations to Islamicize their host nations. These findings echo similar ones released in 2007 by the Policy Exchange, which found 37 percent of all Muslims aged 16 to 24 would prefer to live under a Shari'a system in Western Europe. The CSC poll included 600 Muslim students at 12 universities in the United Kingdom.

Among its findings of Muslim beliefs:

• 40 percent support the introduction of Shari'a (Islamic law replacing the secular laws of England) into British law for Muslims.

• One-third back the idea of a worldwide Islamic caliphate (one worldwide Islamic leader) based on Shari'a law.

• 40 percent believe it is unacceptable for Muslim men and women to associate freely.

• 25 percent have little or no respect for homosexuals.

• 32 percent believe killing in the name of religion is justified.

• More than half favor an Islamic political party to support their views in Parliament.

• One-third doesn't think Islam is compatible with Western views of democracy.

Based upon these findings, the June 26, 2008 publication of the WorldNetDaily.com concludes that, "Significant numbers appear to hold beliefs which contravene democratic values." Hannah Stuart, one of the CSC report's authors, informed *The London Times*, "These results are deeply embarrassing for those who have said there is no extremism in British universities."[163] Equally disturbing is that the report notes radical Islamic preachers regularly deliver inflammatory speeches that target homosexuals and border on anti-Semitism. It should be noted that the wider Muslim community in England challenges these findings including that country's largest Muslim student body, the Federation of Student Islamic Societies. In the best light possible, where one concedes that these 600 Muslim students are for some reason not an accurate reflection of all Muslim students in England, it must still give us pause. In the worst light, a very significant minority of young Muslims are indeed radicalized and desirous of Islamicizing non-Muslim nations, by both violent and nonviolent means.

The authors of the CSC report remind us that campus Islamic societies have, historically, been the source of radicalization of Islamic terrorists. They cite Kafeel Ahmed, who rammed his truck engulfed in flames into a building at the Glasgow Airport in 2007. Investigators believe he formed his Jihadist beliefs while studying at Anglia Ruskin University, Cambridge.

"The finding that a large number of students think it is okay to kill in the name of religion is alarming," said Anthony Glees, professor of Security and Intelligence Studies at Buckingham University. "There is a wide cultural divide between Muslim and non-Muslim students." He suggests, and I agree, that the solution is to "stop talking about celebrating diversity and focus on integration and assimilation."[164]

Suffice it to say, any discerning reader should find it disingenuous when the popular media describes Islamic extremism as a "fringe and non-mainstream faction" or a "small and inconsequential minority." It may be comforting for us to believe this, but a surplus of objective data incontrovertibly contradicts it. The veil of political correctness that clouds our judgment and therefore our response to the threat must be lifted. If not, how are we to extricate ourselves from the hole we have dug in an effort to be "tolerant and fair" in the face of the intolerance and hatred of Muslim extremism?

COMMON SENSE MESSAGE

The bottom line on the prevalence of Islamic extremism, both violent and nonviolent Jihad, is rather inconvenient. It is far more widespread than most people wish to believe, for reasons ideological and practical—practical because if it is this widespread, we have much more to worry about.

Still, poll after poll, we see the same statistics and those data are consistent with worldwide frightening demonstrations (burning effigies, promises of death to America, Israel, Britain, and France) that involve literally millions of Muslims. We've seen celebrations of 9/11 in Muslim countries—often not covered by our media for reasons of political correctness. We are witness to brazen acts of violence in the Middle East, America, Asia, and South America. So, with our blinders off, it is rather obvious that Islamic extremism is a real, widespread, and dangerous movement that we need to dispatch.

IS IT WORSE NOW AND IF SO, WHY?

As discussed above, Islamic extremism is committed to the expansion of Islam, conversion of all infidels, and global implementation of Islamic law (Shari'a). It also engineers the most heinous violence upon its enemies, including civilians, while it promotes terrorism as its warfare of choice. It is intolerant of non-Muslims and only permits Muslim interaction with these infidels to eventually "seed" their lands and convert the world to Islam.[165] Islamic extremism has grown from its early roots and spread throughout the Middle East and the world.

Muslim radicalism is definitely provincial in nature. The drivers of Islamic extremism vary considerably from region to region. The West's dependence upon oil has forced America and all industrialized nations to greatly increase their dealings with Arab and Muslim countries. This is the primary reason for the intersection between Islam and the West. The "Why America" segment carefully explores the rationale behind the hatred that Islamic extremists harbor for America, which is broad and complex. It includes America's great wealth, its symbolic position as the world's greatest secular democracy (and therefore non-Shari'a or Islamic laws), its military strength, its cultural permissiveness (which many Muslims perceive as decadent), and its support for the state of Israel and the more moderate Arab countries. The next sections explore geopolitics beyond America.

GEOPOLITICS PRIMER:
THE ROLE OF ASIA

FORMER SOVIET REPUBLICS: RUSSIA AND CHINA

One last piece of the geopolitical puzzle should be mentioned: Asia. In the heart of Central Asia lies Russia and China. Each of these powerful nations exist somewhere between allies and enemies of the United States. Both are great powers, however. Russia longs to recapture its previous position as a true superpower, and many believe that China is desirous of replacing our position as the world's only superpower. In the wake of the terrorist attacks on the United States, it is not surprising to find that each of these major powers are increasing their focus on the potential domestic security threats posed by Islamic extremism as well. For these reasons and others, we will explore the rise of Islamic extremism in these nations next.

CENTRAL ASIA

Uzbek's ambassador to Iran, Abdusamat A. Khaydarov, delivered a lecture series to the students at UCLA a few years ago. In them, he pointed out that the principal Central Asian states are all former Soviet republics. As such, it was Soviet repression rather than anti-Americanism that was the main force prompting the Islamic reaction there.[166] The Soviets, pausing only during World War II, harshly repressed Islam within their borders. In the mid 1980s, there were only 129 official mosques in the whole of the U.S.S.R., Khaydarov said, compared to 5,000 in Kazakhstan alone when measured in 1999, just a few years after the nation gained its independence.[167]

Soviet leader Mikhail Gorbachev's liberalizing, glasnost policies in the late 1980s allowed for more Islamic freedom, even before the collapse of the U.S.S.R. Islam is the common denominator, and therefore the most important component of national identification in all the newly independent countries of the Central Asian region freed from the "Soviet" branding.

Ambassador Khaydarov discusses two streams within the Islamic revival. One is moderately radical and the other is "ultra radical." Both agree, he said, on working to establish Islamic states under Shari'a law. The former has chosen peaceful and political means to accomplish this aim; the latter has turned to terrorism. It is interesting that he is basically describing the violent versus the nonviolent Islamic extremism that is a major topic of this book—but in Central Asia—supporting my major premise that Islamic extremism is a serious and global phenomenon.

An unofficial clergy that is intolerant of secular law has arisen in many of the Central Asian nations that are supportive of Salafi doctrines and focused on the revival of early Islamic life. Numerous militant Islamic party-type organizations have formed over the last 20 years. A few of the larger such organizations are the Adolat, Islam Lashkarlari, and Hizb-ut Tahrir, a cross-border underground extremist Islamic organization that operates in Uzbekistan, Kyrgyzstan, and southern Kazakhstan.[168]

There are a number of causes of this Islamic and extremist revival. They include, in part, a remonstration against communism and the ideological vacuum that it created, as well as an economic drop in living standards and massive unemployment in the region. External influences include the 1978–1989 Afghan conflict, in which Islamic militants fought and ultimately defeated the Soviet supported government; this precipitated years of infighting that ended with the capture of power by the Taliban in 1996 and led to the formation of regional Islamic networks linked to the Taliban and al-Qaeda.

Another Islamic influence in Central Asia is the Saudi-supported and Saudi-financed building of mosques and support organizations, some of which promote the super radical brand of Islam known as Wahhabiism in the region. Additionally, the 1979 Islamic revolution in Iran created a Shiite theocratic government that the Saudis (Sunnis) responded to by propagandizing their version of Islam in rivalry with the Iranians. Many Sunnis throughout the world, representing the majority of Muslims, are threatened by the current Iranian government's aggressive brand of Islam. Currently, America and the West are trying to shore up support from predominantly Sunni nations such as Egypt, Jordan, and Saudi Arabia against Iran in their quest for nuclear capability, fearing their acquisition of nuclear weapons.

With the end of the U.S.S.R., the relative isolation of Central Asian Islam has ended due to greater contact between this region and foreign countries, particularly the Muslim ones. With this globalization, Central Asian Islam has fused into worldwide Islam and the extremist element has gone along for the ride.

As you can see, the rise of Islam (and along with it the rise of extremism) is complex and quite regional in the Central Asian arena, just as it is in the Middle East. Chechnya is a particularly important example of this, as it is a crystal-clear picture of a former superpower struggling to contain an Islamic crisis within its borders.

RUSSIA (VIS A VIS CHECHNYA)

Recognized as a distinct people since the 17th century, Chechens were active opponents to the Russian conquest of the Caucasus during the period 1818–1917. Chechens are predominantly Sunni Muslim. They possess different cultural and religious beliefs than their non-Muslim neighbors. Chechens have historically been subdued by external rule or empires, first by the brutal Russian Czarist Empire and thereafter by the Soviets. It is easy to understand why they resent Russia as they did the Soviet Empire. During World War II, Chechens collaborated with the invading German Nazis. As a result, in 1944, Stalin deported many Chechens to Central Asia and Siberia. The circumstance of the deportation and hostility toward the Chechens has ramifications into the present. The mass deportation of Chechen people, among others, is estimated in the range of 400,000 to 800,000 with perhaps 100,000 or more of these people dying due to the extreme conditions. This legacy helps explain why

Chechen nationalism has been more radical and anti-Russian than that of Russia's other Muslim ethnic minorities.[169]

With the Soviet Union's collapse in 1991, a number of regions (including Eastern European countries and the "stan" countries discussed earlier) managed to break away and gain independence. Chechnya was most probably not granted independence for geopolitical and economic reasons. Oil is a significant factor in this region. A major oil pipeline carries oil from the fields in Baku on the Caspian Sea and Chechnya toward the Ukraine.[170] Grozny's major oil refinery along this pipeline (and consequently, Russia's necessity to secure their own source of oil from it) led them to be more concerned that pipeline discussions by major western oil companies have not involved them. As long as Chechnya is a part of Russia, Moscow has a say in the oil that flows through it.[171] Tensions between the Russian government and that of then Chechen President Dzhokhar Dudayev escalated into warfare in late 1994. When Russia invaded Chechnya, a bloody war ensued. Intending to crush separatist forces, this was President Yeltsin's first major confrontation. However, the supposed awesome Russian military strength inherited from the Soviet Union turned into a humiliating disaster. Grozny was devastated. Some 70,000 to 80,000 people died, mostly Chechen civilians. In 1996, Russia withdrew in defeat. Russia tried to succeed in Chechnya as America had in Iraq in its 1991 war to free Kuwait. It failed miserably, revealing how poor Russian military capabilities were in certain, non-nationstate situations. Chechnya provided Islamic radicals another example of how guerilla and terror warfare can overcome the great military machines of the superpowers.

Following the 1994-1996 war, the Chechen government's control over the militias was further weakened while local warlords gained strength. The devastated Chechen economy created record unemployment numbers. Brutalized by war and the atrocities committed by Russian troops, Chechens were easily radicalized.

While it is easy to comprehend why Chechnya desires independence from Russia, the issue of separatism versus terrorism is complex. Russia, for obvious reasons, wishes to label the
Chechens as "extremists" or "terrorists," reasoning that they'll
gain more world support in a heavy-handed approach to sup-
pressing this threat. However, Russia has come under great international criticism due to what many consider to be oppressive military actions in Chechnya. On the other hand, there is
a great deal of evidence that there really is an Islamic extremist
component and presence in Chechnya, evidenced by the per-
petration of terror against civilians, as well as the conspiring of
Chechen radicals with known terrorists groups, including al-
Qaeda. Consider the next two lists: the first a summary of terror
attacks; the second a summary of links to al-Qaeda.

Civilian attacks widely believed to be perpetrated by Chechens: [172]

- In October 2005, at least 85 people were killed in
street fighting in the southern Russian city of Nalchik
after Chechen rebels assaulted government buildings,
telecommunications facilities, and the airport.

- A three-day attack on Ingushetia in June 2004, which
killed almost 100 people and injured another 120.

- A December 2002 dual suicide bombing attack on
the headquarters of Chechnya's Russian-backed government in the Chechen capital, Grozny. Russian officials
claim that international terrorists helped local Chechens mount the assault, which killed 83 people.

- Two Chechen men armed with grenades and other
explosives were arrested in a Grozny market in December 2002.

• The October 2002 seizure of a Moscow theater where some 700 people were attending a performance. Russian Special Forces launched a commando raid, and the opium-derived gas they used to disable the hostage-takers killed more than 120 hostages, as well as many of the terrorists. Shamil Basayev, one of the most radical Chechen commanders, took responsibility for organizing the Moscow theater raid.

• A bomb blast that killed at least 41 people, including 17 children, during a military parade in the southwestern town of Kaspiisk in May 2002; Russia blamed the attack on Chechen terrorists.

• In Moscow, an August 1999 bombing of a shopping arcade, a September 1999 bombing of an apartment building that killed 64 people, and two more terrorist bombings in September 1999 in the neighboring Russian republic of Dagestan and the southern Russian city of Volgodonsk. Controversy still exists in determining whether these attacks were conclusively linked to Chechens.

Experts cite several ties between known Islamic terrorists and Chechnya: [173]

• The connection between the late Chechen warlord Khattab, a Jordanian-born fighter who was killed in Chechnya in April 2002 and Osama bin Laden. Khattab apparently first met bin Laden while both men were fighting the 1979–89 Soviet occupation of Afghanistan. The U.S. ambassador to Russia, Alexander Vershbow, said shortly after September 11, 2001, "We have long recognized that Osama bin Laden and other international networks have been fueling the flames in Chechnya, including the involvement of foreign commanders like Khattab."

• Zacarias Moussaoui, whom U.S. authorities have charged with being the "20th hijacker" in the 9/11 attacks, was reported by *The Wall Street Journal* to be formerly "a recruiter for al-Qaeda-backed rebels in Chechnya."

• Chechen militants reportedly fought alongside al-Qaeda and Taliban forces against the U.S.-backed Northern Alliance in late 2001. The Taliban regime in Afghanistan was one of the only governments to recognize Chechen independence.

• In 1999, the Russian government of Vladimir Putin accused the Chechen leadership of supporting extremist Islamic militants in Dagestan. While denied by the government, local warlords (generally but not completely independent of the central government) did support militant Islamic groups there.

• Following the Chechen defeat in Dagestan, Moscow and other Russian cities suffered bomb blasts that killed more than 300 people. Chechens were blamed for the attacks, though it was never proven.[174] This has also led to a rise in racism directed toward people from the Caucasus regions. The response by Russian President Vladimir Putin was brutal.[175]

• Russia's full-scale war with Chechnya included many bombing raids by Russian forces. Some one-third to one-half of the 1.3 million Chechen people are said to have fled from Chechnya. Civilian casualties were high and there was an international outcry toward the brutal Russian crackdown, of which indiscriminate bombing and targeting of civilians were used as tactics.[176] In conclusion, Russia has its own sordid and complex problems with Islam and Islamic extremism that bleeds into the global conflict.

COMMON SENSE MESSAGE

Asia has not been spared the ravages of Islamic extremism. Radical Islam shares certain common or core beliefs, techniques, and philosophies regardless of where in the world they operate. The triggers and goals of these groups, however, vary greatly on a regional basis. In some regions Islamic extremism and/or terrorism is engaged for ideological reasons, in others economic ones. The important point is that for these fundamentalist Islamists, the death of themselves, their children, and their enemies is a far less abhorrent prospect than it is for Westerners. Yes, this sounds rather harsh, but consider all that we have covered. Radical Islam is a culture that celebrates death; martyrdom is taught to hundreds of thousands of young children, photos of suicide bombers hang in markets and shops all over the Islamic world, thousands of such suicide bombers have been taught their trade throughout the Middle East, hijackers crash planes into buildings believing that 72 virgins await them in paradise, and so on. This is not the exception but rather the rule for Islamic terrorists. Is it uncomfortable for us to think in these terms? Yes, but let us see it for what it is—only in this way can we defeat it.

CHINA

Ever since China took control of the Xinjiang province (home to a substantial portion of China's Muslims) in 1949, Muslim separatist movements have threatened the area. For more than 50 years, there has been an ongoing Muslim rebellion led by the indigenous Uighurs.[177] Xinjiang is surely not China's most important national concern when compared to the Taiwan matter; however, the province is a microcosm of the largest challenge facing Beijing: maintaining internal cohesion. To hold onto power, Beijing feels that it must prevent any tolerance of dissent within its boundaries. Capitulating to Muslim separatist demands would further empower Taiwan, Tibet, and other areas demanding more independence. Beijing has decisively shown its readiness to use force and repression to control this area. The question, and the security challenge, revolves around how long China can repress its Muslim communities and keep them separated from the global Muslim movements in Central Asia and the rest of the world. China's attempts to control dissident elements in Xinjiang have provoked the largest uprisings since the Tiananmen incident of 1989. In 1993, protests over a Chinese book that defamed Islam incited several months of riots, well-engineered protests, and the forcible occupations of mosques. Finally, when the People's Liberation Army (PLA) stepped in "demonstrators were arrested, beaten, and restrained from going to Beijing to take their protest to the halls of the central government."[178]

In 1996, Chinese public security officials said, "Separatism in Xinjiang and other areas is the number one threat to China."[179] This fear was realized in 1997, when the city of Yining burst into riots as the Muslim majority clashed with the Han Chinese militia members. State reports suggest that about 10 people died. However, Amnesty International estimated that the number was closer to 200 as the local police officials arrested approximately 500 people whom they, in Amnesty International's report, "tried to freeze."[180] From then until 1999, 190 people were executed, many of them for convictions of terrorism. It should come as no surprise that Amnesty International identified Xinjiang as one of the "five global trouble spots where violence is escalating."[181] Since early July 2009, there has been serious rioting in Xinjiang, where at least 156 people have been killed. While segregation-related separatist desires on the part of the Uighurs play some role, it seems that the Chinese Hans are also partly responsible for a heavy-handed response to Uighur protestations, which profess that the Hans are marginalizing them and through intentional relocation of non-Muslims, diluting their presence in their own home land.

Similar to Chechnya's economic importance to Russia, Xinjiang has similar importance to China; Xinjiang is estimated to be the second largest domestic source of energy in China. Over the next five years, the region is expected to verify oil reserves of 3.3 billion tons and gas reserves of 1.16 trillion cubic meters. It plans to increase its annual crude oil production to 24 million tons and annual gas production to 18 billion cubic meters. These quantities have earned the region the title of "the Sea of Hope, as it is the second largest oil production centre."[182] Additionally, Beijing has begun construction of a major pipeline that will run from Xinjiang to Shanghai and carry an estimated 25 billion tons of oil and 25 million cubic tons of natural gas each year. In its quest to increase its indigenous supply of energy, this pipeline is an obvious priority for Beijing. China's interests in the oil-rich areas of Central Asia are not supported by the local populations. In Central Asia, there is a considerable demographic that identifies much more closely with Muslim society than with Chinese culture.

Beijing has expressly stated that it will not allow Islamic extremism to threaten Chinese natural resources. Interestingly, China has found a novel way to reduce Muslim influence in this area. The Muslim Uighurs, once 93 percent of Xinjiang's population, now total only 40 percent of the estimated 17 million people in Xinjiang.[183] This percentage drop is a result of Beijing's relocation of many Han (non-Muslim) people to the area. China's security is further threatened by the networks of Muslims separatists located outside China. Many of the Uighurs have received some form of military training from the states surrounding China, including training from the Taliban and al-Qaeda in Afghanistan and Pakistan. Both Russia and China are plagued with their own brand of Islamic extremism to vex them; however, in their cases the differentiation between Islamic extremism versus Muslim separatism is more ambiguous.

COMMON SENSE MESSAGE

In China, there is a very strict society with an authoritarian government that has little interest in political correctness. Islamist activities in China are mostly of an economic nature. Due to the Chinese propensity to be very heavy-handed and unapologetic in their use of military force, their Islamic extremist "problem" is not as threatening as in the West, although it is growing as radical Islam is globally growing.

Russia and China have both exploited the label of "Islamic terrorism" to categorize their Islamic problem as strictly one of extremism, although in reality there is a separatist quality to both of them. In any event, it can be said that Islamic terror against innocent citizens has become global, and the practice of using terrorism to address even legitimate concerns that Muslims may have with America, Russia, or China must not be allowed to further cultivate. It is also clear that both Russia and China deal with Islamic extremism much more aggressively than America does, and this may help to explain why the West appears more plagued than Asia by radicalized Islam.

Now let's answer our question: Why is it worse now? Islamic extremists and Islamic separatists (in Chechnya, China, and elsewhere) have discovered the violent efficiency of terrorism: a small number of people, if brutal enough, can wield great power. This coupled with the apparent lenience by the West, particularly in Europe (and increasingly in America), has resulted in a perception on the part of Islamic extremism that the West is too frightened, too weak, and too fragmented to fight back.[184] This has fueled Islamic extremism, which is in turn fomented by thousands of imams and hundreds of madrassas espousing extremism. They teach a fundamentalist and violent form of

Islam where hatred and intolerance of Christians, Jews, and all infidels is indoctrinated from the youngest ages; vicious hostility against these infidels is encouraged. In 2004, Secretary of State Colin Powell demanded that Islamic governments stop this practice, as it is "indoctrinating children in the worst aspects of religion... teaching hatred will not help bring peace to societies."[185]

Islamic extremists perceive the "relative tolerance" of the West to the barbaric acts of violence perpetrated by Muslims against innocent civilians as weakness. Osama bin Laden boasts that the 1992 bombing of a hotel that Americans had occupied in Aden, Yemen, by Jihadists, the Beirut, Lebanon bombing of the Marine barracks in 1984, and the Somalian "Black Hawk Down" debacle in 1999 all resulted in prompt U.S. retreats. These retreats underscore the Jihadists' belief that America is "exquisitely sensitive to casualties," and that such a strongly ingrained weakness will prove to be their demise.[186]

Unfortunately, weakness invites aggression. This is true in the jungle, the corporate boardroom, the classroom, and even in the home. Just ask any CEO, teacher, or parent. If we know this to be a universal trait, then why it is so widely misunderstood with respect to the radicalization of Islam in recent decades? In other words, why is it not apparent that the West's timid response and forbearance of violence against civilians has greatly augmented this horrific behavior? Why is it that Israel, a small country that has had few if any options but to become militarily superior and forceful in response to terror, still pines for peace? Can it be that due to Israel's consistently strong response to terror attacks that it still exists at all? Consider this oft-forgotten history of the modern Middle East: Jordan, a country consisting of 80 percent of Palestinians, was forced to make a monumental decision in September of 1971. The Palestinian Liberation Organization, headed by Yassir Arafat, invaded and developed a stronghold in the militarily weak country of Jordan.

From there, it launched attacks into Israel, much like what is occurring with the Hezbollah in Southern Lebanon today. King Hussein, feeling his kingdom threatened by these Palestinians and despite his own country being largely Palestinian, viciously attacked the invading PLO with great force. This intense, 10-day battle resulted in thousands of casualties, including huge civilian losses in the adjacent Palestinian refugee camps where many PLO fighters resided.[187] The memory of this violent resistance has prevented further attempts to annex part of Jordan, despite the fact that many in the Arab West Bank believe they have every right to immigrate to Jordan.

COMMON SENSE MESSAGE

The lesson here is an ancient one. Once burned by a match the first time, most people avoid it the next. Pain and adverse consequences are great behavior modifiers. King Hussein made it quite clear that the Palestinians had no claim to Jordan, after which the refugees turned their attention turned squarely to Israel afterwards. I am not condoning the appropriateness of Jordan's brutal attack on the Palestinians, or lack thereof, I am only commenting on the consequences of it. If the world were to rise up in unity and unequivocal intolerance of terrorism, Islamic terrorism would no longer be a growth industry.

ARE THERE MUSLIMS WHO REJECT EXTREMISM AND TERROR?

Most certainly, there are Muslims who reject terrorism. Most people, including Muslims, are decent, well-intentioned, and simply wish to live in peace and prosperity for themselves and their loved ones. If this is so, how is it that Islamic extremists have sowed so much death and destruction and yet continue to grow? The last century provides us some good explanations.

The German peoples, like all peoples, are presumed to be fundamentally decent and yet the Nazis were principally responsible for more than 42 million deaths in World War II, according to the Hitler Historical Museum and the *Twentieth Century Atlas'* WWII statistics.[188] How is this possible? History is replete with examples of a "decent majority" relegated to spectator status while a "violent, hateful, and weaponized minority" wreaks havoc upon the world. Nazism, Bolshevism, the Khmer Rouge in Cambodia, the conflicts of the Hutu and Tutsi tribes in Africa, and the current Sudanese Muslims in their ethnic cleansing of non-Muslim Sudanese are but a few examples.[189] Life, however, isn't a spectator sport, and the "silent, decent majority" must never allow themselves to be consigned to the sidelines while a minority of evildoers spin their webs of hate. The "silent majority" issue is very important and there is a section devoted to this in the "Solutions" chapter. As Irish statesman and philosopher Edmund Burke stated more than two centuries ago, "All that is necessary for the triumph of evil is that good men do nothing." Ironically, the author of this incisive statement was a longstanding and patriotic British House of Commons member and yet he supported the American Revolution in the name of liberty and defiance of tyranny—even if that tyranny was perpetrated by his own beloved government.

In this spirit, there are a number of organizations that exemplify a growing group of Muslims who reject terrorism. The Free Muslims Coalition and the American Islamic Forum for Democracy, each of which are a group of American Muslims who "feel that religious violence and terrorism have not been fully rejected by the Muslim community," and they seek to educate the evils that radical Islam portend to the world and to Islam itself. The Free Muslims Coalition can be found at www.freemuslims.org. Their mission statement claims that "nearly all Islamic leaders and Intellectuals advocate violence, terrorism, and repress anyone who casts doubt upon this." This organization, headed by

Kamal Nawash, is a source of great hope to those who believe that to defeat Islamic terrorism we must convince Islam itself to forsake violence upon innocents for the peaceful and political dialog upon which most of the world depends to address grievances. The other Islamic organization espousing the virtues of Islam as a non-political and peaceful religion, the American Islamic Forum for Democracy (AIFD), is chaired by the aforementioned Dr. Zuhdi Jasser, an internist practicing in Phoenix, Arizona. The AIFD can be found at www.aifdemocracy.org. This organization is committed to promoting the ideology that American Muslims can and should embrace democracy, the U.S. Constitution, and assimilate into the fabric of America while practicing Islam peacefully. Dr. Jasser is also a retired United States Navy Lieutenant Commander.

There are, of course, other so-called moderates, including some less moderate but still espousing at least some moderate positions that can be found in the Islamic world—particularly online. One example is Muqtedar Khan, Ph.D., from Adrian, Michigan, who writes that "Muslim militants are sowing seeds of poison and hatred between Muslims and the rest of humanity by committing egregious acts of violence in the name of Islam."[190] Although he speaks out against terrorism, he is less clear in condemning the peaceful (nonviolent) conversion of Western societies to Islam through "Ijtihad" as he describes in his article, "Who are the Moderate Muslims?" for the website Islamfortoday.com.[191] In the current somewhat confusing Muslim environment we find in 2009, it is important that we in the West find and nurture the so-called moderate voices of Islam as enthusiastically as possible. It is of paramount importance that we in America and the West seek out and support the millions of moderates in the Islamic world who reject terror, violence, and nonviolent Jihad. Ultimately, it is they, not we, who will expunge this evil aberration of Islam that we refer to as Islamic extremism.

COMMON SENSE MESSAGE

There are many rays of hope and much of it emanates from the Muslim community. As stated above, Edmund Burke said it best, "All that is necessary for the triumph of evil is that good men do nothing." There are a number of individuals and groups within Islam, particularly in America, no surprise, that understand (better than me) all that I have covered in this book and also have the courage to promulgate their message. We must, as a nation and a global community, join hands with these folks—they will have greater sway with the "silent majority" than us infidels.

CHAPTER FIVE

The Costs: Economic & Social

THE ECONOMIC COSTS OF THE GLOBAL WAR ON TERROR (VIOLENT JIHAD)

The cost of the Global War on Terror (GWOT) can be measured in human loss (casualties) and in financial loss. There is no question that every single death and injury, on all sides, is tragic and devastating. This chapter, however, addresses the financial ramifications of terrorism to America, and our approach to eradicating it. While the direct and indirect military expenses account for the majority of these costs, the non-military expenses are also very significant. Let's address those first.

NON-MILITARY COSTS:

One of the "hidden" expenses the American public funds are the losses incurred by insurance companies due to acts of terrorism. Robert P. Hartwig, Ph.D. & C.P.C.U., senior vice president and chief economist for the Insurance Information Institute in Washington, D.C., recently presented a lecture to the insurance industry. He described the Terrorism Risk Insurance Act (TRIA). Basically, TRIA is a system where the federal government pays 90 percent and private insurers pay 10 percent of insurance losses from acts of terror. The government caps its losses at $100 billion. After the 9/11 attack on the World Trade Center, insurers paid out $52 billion more in loss and associated expenses than they earned in premiums. This loss, with premium attached, is passed along to the average American in the form of insurance premium increases.

Tom Ramstack wrote an article for *The Washington Times* describing other indirect costs that Americans sustain as a result of terrorism. He explained, "No industry felt the financial pinch of security as quickly and severely as the airlines." Almost immediately following the 9/11 attacks, the Federal Aviation Administration required carriers to spend more money on security, even as their businesses teetered on the edge of bankruptcy. Recent additions to security requirements have included reinforced cockpit doors, transponders, and cabin videos that allow air-traffic controllers to track airplanes with greater precision. Congress has spent more than $100 million to help airlines pay the bill, but analysts warn that the aid won't cover the price tag. "There's no question that our immediate costs will easily surpass this $100 million; probably [by] several hundred million," said John Heimlich, research director for the Air Transport Association, which represents major airlines. Other costs result from the $2.50 security tax on domestic and international airplane tickets, free airline seats for federal sky marshals, and slower flight schedules that allow time for delays caused by enhanced luggage screening and other security procedures.

Another area of great concern is the nuclear industry. The Nuclear Regulatory Commission (NRC) is trying to respond to reported threats that terrorists might crash airplanes into American nuclear power plants or attack them in other ways, such as by car and truck bombs. The enhanced security costs are partially paid by the government (ultimately the taxpayer, of course) and also add to the cost of electrical power in the U.S to the tune of $2 billion annually; this may significantly increase if enhanced barriers are deemed necessary in the future.

Other industries are also beginning to feel the effects of higher security costs. "Everyone anticipates that the additional security measures to make our chemical facilities more secure are going to increase our costs," said Chris Van den Heuvel, spokesman for the American Chemistry Council. Similarly, the railroad industry is asking the federal government for legislative assistance to drive down its ever-increasing insurance that is passed along to Americans in the form of increased train ticket prices. The Transportation Department requires the railroad industry to carry insurance against terrorist acts. Since the attacks, anti-terrorism insurance has become prohibitively expensive. A Federal Communications Commission (FCC) task force has been commissioned to assess security risks to the nation's telecommunications network. One priority is securing wireless communications systems for emergency personnel. The FCC is also involved in Internet security, which has attracted the interest of Congress. At a 2004 hearing before the Senate Judiciary subcommittee on Administrative Oversight and the Courts, Richard Clarke, chief of the White House's Office of Cyberdefenses, warned that a terrorist attack over the Internet was likely. "Terrorists could gain access to the digital controls for the nation's utilities, power grids, air traffic control systems, and nuclear power plants," said the subcommittee chairman, Charles E. Schumer (D-NY). President George W. Bush's proposed fiscal 2003 budget allocated about $38 billion for new terrorism-related domestic security expenses. The 2007 budget for these expenses is addressed in the Department of Defense (DOD) data presented below. "September 11th dealt a very serious blow to the economy, demonstrating the cost of inaction," said White House spokeswoman Claire Buchan two years after 9/11. New security measures are needed "for the sake of the economy and the safety of the American people." While price tags for these disparate security enhancements are still wanting, it is fair to say that they total in the scores of billions of dollars, all of which are eventually shouldered by all Americans.

MILITARY COSTS

The military costs of the Global War on Terrorism (GWOT) are staggering. Much of the data in this section is from the Library of Congress Congressional Research Service (CRS) document, dated March 14, 2007. The U.S. Government breaks down the Global War on Terror into three categories. They are:

1. Operation Enduring Freedom (OEF), covering Afghanistan and other Global War on Terror (GWOT) operations ranging from the Philippines to the little-known northeastern African nation of Djibouti that began immediately after the 9/11 attacks.

2. Operation Noble Eagle (ONE), providing enhanced security for U.S. military bases and other homeland security that was commenced in response to the attacks.

3. Operation Iraqi Freedom (OIF), which began in the fall of 2002 with the build up of troops for the March 2003 invasion of Iraq and continues with counter-insurgency and stability operations.

Including Fiscal Year 2007 (FY2007) appropriations, Congress has approved a total of about $510 billion for military operations, base security, reconstruction, foreign aid, embassy costs, and veterans' health care for the three categories defined above that were initiated since the 9/11 attacks. The $510 billion total includes the $70 billion in DOD's regular FY2007 bill, intended to bridge the gap between the first part of the fiscal year and passage of both supplemental and war-related appropriations for other agencies, which were included in the FY2007 Continuing Resolution (H.J. Res 20/P.L.110-5). Of the $510 billion appropriated thus far, CRS estimates that Iraq will receive about $378 billion (74 percent), the OEF about $99 billion (19 percent), enhanced base security about $28 billion (5 percent), and about $5 billion that CRS cannot allocate (1 percent). Generally, about 90 percent of these funds are for DOD, about 7 percent for foreign aid programs and embassy operations, less than 1 percent for medical care for veterans, and 1 percent unallocated.[192]

Although these figures include DOD's contractual obligations for pay, goods, and services, they do not capture all appropriated funds or all funds obligated. For example, DOD acknowledges that these figures do not capture about $27 billion in classified activities. Other funds—such as those to create more modular fighting units—may also not be represented in Defense Finance Accounting Service (DFAS) reports because these are treated as part of DOD's regular programs. DOD also estimates that there are about $56 billion in funds still to be obligated as of this writing. Obligations figures also do not reflect outlays or payments made when goods and services are delivered (shipping and handling, if you will), and these costs are in the billions also.

Supplemental requests are very common, as one might imagine. A good example is the February 5, 2007 request by the Defense Department that submitted for a $94.4 billion FY2007 supplemental request. As of FY2008 war requests, total funding for Iraq and the Global War on Terror equaled about $752 billion, counting about $564 billion for Iraq, $155 billion for Afghanistan, $28 billion for enhanced security, and $5 billion unallocated.[193]

As it is plain to see, the economic costs (however insignificant when compared to the human costs) of the ongoing war on terror are an enormous drain on our economy. When one considers the ever-increasing global business competition that America faces, and that we carry the world's burden of fighting a Global War on Terror, we as a nation are paying a high pecuniary price.

COMMON SENSE MESSAGE

In this age of financial and industry bailouts and economic stimulus packages, $1 trillion may not seem like much—but it is. Private sector and government expenses directly linked to Islamic extremism actually exceed this number. Clearly, compared to the human cost this is insignificant, but it all adds up and these costs are doing nothing to advance our economic recovery. Of interest, there has never been a nation that lost its economic standing and maintained its military strength. Like it or not, our economic and military strength are forever linked, rendering this topic quite salient.

THE *REAL* COST IF WE DON'T FIX THIS? WHAT WILL AMERICA BE LIKE?

THE AMERICA MOST OF US DO NOT WISH TO SEE

If the present Islamization of Europe and America is not stopped, the world as we know it will undergo an irreversible change. The goal of Jihadists is absolutely clear and they state it in no uncertain terms. They wish to bring about a world where Islam is universal as a religion, a culture, and as a comprehensive way of life. They aspire to a world where the Western infidel's culture is abolished as it "submits" to the ways of Islam. What are those ways? As a summary of what you have read, consider the Europe and America that radical Islam is striving hard to achieve. As radical and brutal as these examples seem to be, they actually exist in Muslim majority countries all over the world today.

Women have few if any civil and legal rights. To varying degrees, they:

- Do not attend school other than Islamic education.

- Do not work outside of the home.

- Do not have access to professional training and practice.

- Do not leave home without being attended by a man.

- Do not have the right to marry whom they wish or divorce their spouse—they do so at the peril of their very life.

- May not expose body parts in public beyond parts of their face and hands, depending upon how strictly the Islamic code is enforced.

- Do not own businesses or work in the corporate environment except as subservient laborers.

- Do perform sexual duties at the demand of their spouse.

- Are subject to corporal punishment, stoning, and death if they are deemed by religious councils as having committed adultery.

Non-Muslims do not enjoy the same privileges and rights as Muslims. In terms of property ownership, religious worship, and political power, infidels are unempowered and at the mercy of Islamic religious leaders. Such as:

- Non-Muslims' immigration and emigration rights are curtailed and subject to the control of Muslim religious councils.

- Shari'a rules the business world and Sheikhs and other Muslim leaders control business and personal loans and the banking industry.

• Pigs are considered unclean and all forms of porcine meats (bacon, pork, etc.) are outlawed or severely restricted.

• Pornography (all forms) is outlawed.

• Music, television, movies, books, internet, and all other forms of media is subject to the approval of Islamic religious councils. If content is not consistent with the promotion of traditional Islamic culture it is challenged if not outlawed.

• Government and more importantly the military is used as a tool to promote the world's submission to Islam—consider the long and violent history of Islam revisited in this book.

• America's long-standing support of allies including India and Israel will give way to their Muslim majority nemeses.

Admittedly, this alternative reality seems an unlikely version of one possible future for America. Make no mistake that this scenario, however severe we think it to be, is *Islam Lite* in the eyes of the Islamists. It is the future that millions of radical Muslims hope for, work toward, and pray will one day materialize. Fortunately, there are a number of devout American Muslims vigorously oppose this future for our nation and they are in the forefront of the fight against it. These Muslims desire an America where all religions, faiths, and cultures "live and let live" in harmony and celebration of our diversity.

COMMON SENSE MESSAGE

The message here is simple. If this isn't the future for America that you aspire to see, work with me and the thousands of others who are combating the Islamization of America. The next and last section of this book is aptly labeled "Solutions." In it you will find simple, even intuitive suggestions on how you can play a role in reuniting our nation and making a difference in this present-day fight to preserve the America that so many have sacrificed so much to create.

III

SOLUTIONS

CHAPTER SIX

The Way Out

UNDERSTANDING THE PERIL

Of particular importance is to understand that the modern Western world, including America, is at much greater risk from the Islamic extremist threat than most realize. Our society's technological complexity and economic inter-dependence is frighteningly vulnerable to terrorist attacks. If a single American city falls victim to a serious biological or nuclear attack, even just a single dirty bomb, the consequences would be devastating. Our stock market would likely crash, investment in America would cease, and our Armed Forces and National Guard would be overwhelmed for years to come. The effect on our insurance industry would be ruinous and the relocation of hundreds of thousands of people would be immeasurably costly in terms of both economics and human suffering. Now imagine the consequence of the typical al-Qaeda tactic of simultaneous attacks.

All it would take is one of these weapons in the backpack of some misguided and brainwashed young Islamic extremist who believes that he will be rewarded by Allah and delivered to paradise. This is no exaggeration. Hundreds of thousands of young Muslims, if not millions, actually believe this.[194] Unlike in past centuries, America is no longer protected by the insulation provided by vast oceans. The average time span between major al-Qaeda attacks is more than five years, so we should not misinterpret our relative success in averting recurrent attacks here in the U.S. as evidence that the danger is diminishing. We are at immeasurable risk, despite our vastly superior military and our incalculably greater wealth, as compared to our Islamic extremist enemy. The 2006 radical Islamic plot in Great Britain to explode 10 aircraft that was fortunately uncovered, to the great credit of the British security services, should be enough to send shivers down all of our spines, and particularly those of us who travel by air. We have extensively discussed the issue of nonviolent or stealth Jihad and what it means to America. The very freedoms that define us and our way of life are at stake and as pointed out repeatedly, this may represent an even greater threat to America's "survival" than violent terrorism.

HISTORY REPEATS ITSELF

We have all heard that adage time and time again. Like so many proverbs, this one is often true. It is so very important that we as individuals, as nations, and as a world learn from yesterday's mistakes. Those who forget the lessons of the past are destined to repeat them. Another old adage is, "Fool me once, shame on you; fool me twice, shame on me." In that spirit, consider these many examples of the similarities between Islamic extremism and fascist Nazi Germany:

- Nazi Germany was fascist and intolerant of all but the pure Aryan race. Islamic extremists are intolerant of all but Muslims.

- The Nazis justified horrific violence and murder against non-Aryans because they were viewed as sub-human. Extremists kill as many innocent infidels as they can without remorse since in their twisted interpretation of Islam, Allah does not recognize infidels as "human."[195]

• Both the Nazis and the Islamists were/are pathologically anti-Semitic.[196]

• This item is included for its intriguing value only, and not necessarily as a valid example of the resemblance of Nazi Germany and Islamic extremism. Though strange (and few are aware of this fact), Hitler's military designed a "Wunderwaffen," or "miracle weapon," called the Amerikabomber in 1944. This large, bomb-filled plane, described in *Die Deutschen Flugzeuge* (magazine) in the 1940s, had no landing gear, as its purpose was to suicide-attack civilian targets on the eastern coast of the United States. Dieter Wulf tells its story in *The Atlantic Monthly*, May 2004.[197]

• Great Britain and the world had an opportunity to stop Hitler in 1938, prior to it becoming a global threat and a worldwide nightmare. Neville Chamberlain, Britain's Prime Minister, essentially abandoned Czechoslovakia to Hitler and also relinquished control of key naval ports to Germany, which facilitated the threat of Nazi submarines. He did this hoping that the aggression and disregard for the sovereignty of other nations would stop with those events, sparing England from going to war because, after all, who wants to go to war? This was a classic "path of least resistance" choice that resulted in a terrible missed opportunity to prevent the horror of World War II. Although many saw the danger that the megalomaniacal and hate-mongering Hitler posed, the world largely looked the other way because it was easier to ignore evil and hope for the best. It is my opinion that this is even more apparent today than it was in 1938.

Only when the world and the U.S. united did the Allies finally begin to win the war against the fascists in both Germany and Japan. Hopefully, this historical victory will be repeated yet again and in time to prevent another worldwide maelstrom.

In the end, radical Islam must be made to understand that their entry ticket to have influence and relevance in the modern world will not be attained by repeating the fascism of yesteryear, or by any number of market and mall suicide bombings. Nor will it be by a Sarin gas attack on European subways, or by blowing up passenger airplanes over the Atlantic, or by detonating a nuclear "dirty bomb" in an American city. They simply need to join the rest of us in seeking education, competing in business, tolerating (if not celebrating) the various ethnicities and religions of the world, and seamlessly integrating into this modern and exciting global New World. Conquering and converting the infidels is an antiquated dream that must be abandoned. It is not really necessary, although it would be desirable, that Islam "modernizes," adopts capitalism, or embraces some form of democracy. It is only necessary that Islamic extremists within Islam abandon their ancient yearning to dominate and "Islamicize" the world. Finally, let us consider solutions.

A PRESCRIPTION FOR AMERICA

Now we know how we got here. How do we get back?

Common sense dictates finding the *common ground* that unites Americans. Most people desire peace, tolerance for ethnic, religious, and racial differences as well as believe in the sanctity of life. They also deplore the injustice of terror and indiscriminate murder of innocents for political purposes. These virtues are a common thread connecting most Americans (and indeed most people). In 1995, a terrorism expert by the name of Professor Paul Wilkinson wrote for the Canadian Security Intelligence Service a set of general principles for defeating terrorism. These very reasonable but basic principles are often praised by many experts on terrorism. They are as follows:

a. No surrender to terrorists and an absolute determination to defeat them within the framework of the rule of law and democracy.

b. No deals and no concessions, even in the face of the most severe intimidation and blackmail.

c. An intensified worldwide effort to bring the terrorists to justice.

d. Tough measures to penalize state sponsors who give terrorists safe haven, weapons, money, and diplomatic support.

e. A determination never to allow terrorist intimidation to block or derail international diplomatic efforts...the suppression of terrorism is in the common interests of international society.[198]

12 x 12 Step Rehab Plan

This section's 12 x 12 step plan is a roadmap for national rehabilitation or "rehab" that goes beyond Professor Wilkinson's basic doctrine. The first dozen are national goals; the latter are personal goals that Americans can make a reality if they so choose. It is in this fashion, where the actions of the individual affect the many, that a nation is transformed over time.

NATIONAL GOALS (THINK GLOBALLY, ACT NATIONALLY)

Nations, like people, are imperfect and as such are subject to bad habits. We have covered the division of both America and Americans in prior chapters. The intransigent nature of people who steadfastly support one political side or another is, essentially, a habit. I would argue it is a bad habit, since it usually closes the individual's mind to honest deliberation of what the other side has to say. This obstinacy requires behavior modification, as individuals and as a nation, if we are to break the current stalemate and move forward. Although overcoming our egos will require some national soul-searching, the result will be an indefatigable America that will finally rise to the threat we have lived under for too long. Once again, the world will benefit from American strength ethically, economically, and, if necessary, militarily. The following list of suggested solutions is offered as national "talking points," or a starting place from which average Americans can reform our dialogue into productive, and eventually successful, discourse.

As stated in the Introduction, these talking points are offered as fresh, logical, and achievable next steps that will move the American people toward each other as we heal the national breach. If *we the people* can improve the dialogue as we come together, this will bleed into the psyche of our nation and our leaders will be obligated to do similarly. The end result will validate the premise that ordinary Americans can and will extraordinarily impact our nation and the world.

NATIONAL REHAB 12 STEP

Step 1. Politics (America)
Behavior: Increasing political divisiveness.
Therapeutic goal: Recognize the trend and then combat it.

A third of this book addresses the deterioration of both the decorum and the function of our elected leaders and our mainstream media, due in large part to ever-increasing partisan politics. The media plays a role in advancing this dysfunction by deceptively inflating the divisions between conservatives and liberals. Many believe it is no accident that by encouraging

Americans to choose sides, both the media and the politicians have benefited by "fueling the substitution of national rhetoric for national debate," which enhances their relevancy by increasing exposure for the politicians and increasing audience for the media.

While few activities are more American than national debate, intentional incitement by demonizing our differences in opinion results in a further polarization of Americans, which prevents our ability to take productive steps forward. Americans are beginning to separate into well-differentiated camps of like-minded folks by following the example they read in the newspaper, hear on talk radio, and see on their television screens. At the same time, the pundits and the politicians are preoccupied with supporting their parochial positions and denigrating their opposition. Somehow Americans have come to condone or at least accept the reality that the political party in power is primarily interested in retaining it, and the party out of power is primarily interested in gaining it. This perpetual tug-of-war between our leaders and the media is diverting our attention from many issues, including the very real dangers that Islamic extremists pose.

All Americans must come to realize that beating our collective chests, trying to convince each other that our position is the right one is counterproductive. Rather, it is in our common interest to find and nurture the harmony in our positions and seek ways to narrow the divide. In this way, America will regain its former stature and benefit the world as it has so many times in the past. Americans must embark on a road of reconciliation, founded upon a mutual respect of each other's positions, as we move toward, rather than away, from each other and the ultimate goals we seek. *We the people* must demand this sea change from our leaders and the media as we stake claim to the common ground that unites us.

Step 2. Politics (World)

Behavior: International preoccupation with short-term national self-interests. This results in global disunity with respect to radical Islam.

Therapeutic goal: Individual nations must cease to appease and enable Islamic extremism to achieve short-term national interests.

It is not only the West that is at risk from Islamism. Both China and Russia are plagued by Islamic extremism, although the root cause of each may be somewhat different. The security and safety of the people of all of our nations are threatened, and the quality of our lives is diminished as Islamic extremism continues to thrive. America is heavily burdened in Iraq and Afghanistan where we are fighting Islamic extremism at a high cost in terms of our blood and treasure. This expenditure of our national resources is to our economic disadvantage relative to other countries. The U.S. exceeds our fair portion in combating Islamic extremism, while many of our allies can preserve their national coffers. Still, it should be more important to these nations that our shared interests be served by globally uniting in the battle against Islamic extremism.

Iran uses its proxies, Hezbollah and Hamas, to perpetrate terrorism on its behalf. Yet, because Iran provides sweetheart oil deals with France, Russia, and China in an attempt to buy their goodwill, these nations appear to look the other way when the U.S. tries to hold Iran accountable.

It is in the interest of the entire world to suspend petty politics and wholeheartedly declare a unified front against Islamic extremism and terror. This danger is potentially too great to the world and it would behoove us to join our considerable powers in order to end this threat definitively. The people of all of our nations must pressure our governments to recognize that the greater good will be served by international cooperation in a worldwide effort to overcome this threat. In America and the West, we can and should vote for leaders who articulate this viewpoint. We also vote with our readership and viewership, and by supporting the pundits and media outlets that broadcast a message of constructive dialogue, they will flourish and the ideologues will weaken. When America, in a united fashion, promulgates the importance of rejecting Islamism even to the detriment of some short-term national interest, the world will listen; such is still the power of the U.S.

Step 3. Complacency
Behavior: Appeasement and pandering.
Therapeutic goal: Develop an uncompromising stand against Islamism.

Much of the modern age of terrorism began in Israel. For decades, the world's response to the murdering of Israeli civilians has been largely silent. The reason for this silence has a lot to do with anti-Semitism, but that is a complex topic and not our focus here. Needless to say, the lack of world outrage to this terrorism has only encouraged radicalized Palestinians and other Islamic extremists to grow increasingly bold and violent. The world, in "allowing" anti-Jewish terrorism to grow with modest objection, has encouraged a widening of this behavior beyond Israel. As declared earlier, weakness invites aggression. Appeasement only encourages continued and even more contemptible behavior. Unity amongst all civilized nations to condemn the murdering of innocents from any quarter, be it Arab, Muslim, Jew, or Christian, is absolutely necessary. Continued worldwide complacency in response to horrific terrorist acts by Islamic extremists against innocents only emboldens these killers. Terrorism must be answered with painful penalties imposed upon the perpetrators and those countries, leaders, financial backers, and any others who support them, without exception. If not, consequences will not be feared and behavior will not change.

A good example of what should be done occurred in July 2008 when the American people rose up and persuaded the U.S. Government to change course and send a powerful message to Islamic extremists. This story involves the immigration to America of students from a Hamas school (Gaza University) on a Fulbright scholarship to America.

In June 2008, the United States State Department granted visas for three students from Gaza University, a known hotbed of Hamas/Islamic extremism.[199] Visas for the three Fulbright students along with a fourth Gazan student coming to the U.S. under a different program were approved for entry and until the State of Israel, Brigitte Gabriel (ActForAmerica.org), and others began a campaign to prevent the entry of these students to our shores.

Surprisingly (and to her eventual chagrin), Secretary of State Condoleezza Rice personally lobbied for these visas despite a number of anti-Islamic terrorism organizations crying foul. Due to mounting pressure, eventually all four of their visas were rescinded.[200] As the previous provost of Stanford University, the educational nature of this story probably struck a chord within her. I have absolutely no doubt that Secretary Rice acted upon only good, if misguided, intentions.

Particularly disturbing is that one reason the State Department decided to offer visas to these students was that they believed them to be "victimized" by the high-tech fingerprinting equipment employed at Israeli checkpoints as a security measure. This equipment facilitates visa interviews for Gaza residents in Israel much like the ones certain Americans in business and government use at select American security installations to facilitate their travel.[201] In other words, the proven security measures used by Israel to prevent terror attacks upon its citizens were viewed by certain people within the U.S. State Department as a form of victimization.

In the end and only due to public pressure, the U.S. did the right thing by revoking these visas. "There were four Palestinians who were issued visas about whom we then received additional information," State Department spokesman Gonzalo Gallegos said. "We decided that we needed to take a closer and harder look at them in light of the additional information we received," said Gallegos.[202] He also stated that their visas were withdrawn under a "prudential revocation clause" in U.S. immigration rules that allows them to be canceled based on information garnered about the holders after they were granted.

When an organization, in this case Hamas, has killed hundreds of people (including Americans) and unabashedly promotes terrorism and the premeditated murder of non-combatant civilians, should America reward them by welcoming their leaders, supporters, financiers, or students? I hope we can all agree that the answer is a resounding no.

This event serves as a paradigm of how grassroots efforts by the American public can make a difference. It also illustrates that by combating political correctness and appeasement, America can deliver a message to the Muslim world that extremism will increasingly create a barrier for Muslims to the rest of the world and that these doors will open when the greater Muslim community endorses the eradication of extremism within their ranks.

The real lesson is that average Americans like you and I really can make a difference by expecting, and at times like this demanding, that our leaders consistently and fairly wield the political power we have entrusted to them by protecting us from Islamic extremism—in all its forms.

Step 4. Isolationism and Segregation

Behavior: Isolation can splinter a nation into incompatible subpopulations—in this case the Muslim population. Non-

Muslim immigrant populations embrace the "American first" concept but at least 25–50 percent of Muslim immigrants consider themselves Muslims first and do not accept America as it is but rather for what it will be as Islam grows.

Therapeutic goal: Segregation encourages radicalism and fractures societies—the goal is to discourage and, if necessary, disallow it.

The West must find ways to discourage Islamic isolation within Western nations. Ending Islamic segregation within Western societies while simultaneously respecting and preserving the multicultural (including Muslim, of course) integrity of America and Europe must be achieved. Our nations must achieve Muslim integration by not tolerating its segregation. The isolation of Muslims in Western nations, as exemplified in France and England, only increases the divisions between Islam and its host society by facilitating and incubating radical and seditious Islamic elements within them.[203] Virtually all other religions and ethnicities immigrate to the West with the intention of assimilating. This is not to say that each group's unique cultural attributes are not preserved and celebrated in the host country, but the goal is to become part of the fabric of their adopted society. Islamic extremism is not interested in "integration," but rather in planting Islamic seeds that will grow within the host society until it can convert that society to Islam.[204] In many instances, this "seeding" is part of a grand plan of a loosely organized mandate by the Islamic extremists to spread Islam to the four corners of the world. This "dominate by population growth and immigration" policy is clearly articulated in the Muslim Brotherhood Manifesto, uncovered by the FBI and also documented in live videos from all over the world by imams (religious priests) and other Islamist leaders. In other situations it is more hapless or random but dangerous nonetheless as a segregated and radical subpopulation grows in host nations. Either way, no nation is obliged to allow so traitorous and/or perilous an element to exist unchallenged within its borders.

Two recent examples of Europe pushing back against the Islamic fracture in their societies are noteworthy and encouraging. The first is in Denmark. After the murder of Theo Van Gogh, Vincent Van Gogh's great nephew, who wrote an article critical of Danish Muslims, Denmark expelled radical imams and demanded an end to Muslim isolationism and radical teaching within its borders. This is particularly remarkable because Denmark is widely viewed as the most liberal nation on the generally liberal continent of Europe. The second example is in France. Consistent with recent actions on the part of the French government to limit Islamic segregation, a French court rejected the citizenship application of a 32-year-old Moroccan woman on July 26, 2008.[205] Faizi Silmi's petition for citizenship was irrevocably denied in a far-reaching and encouraging decision by the French government. Ms. Silmi, who reveals only her eyes in public, observes a severe brand of Islam. The nation's supreme appellate body, the Council of State, ruled that Ms. Silmi's "radical" practice of Islam conflicts with equality of the sexes and other French values. The ruling upheld a 2005 decision that the woman exhibits "insufficient assimilation." A legal expert who advised the Council of State said the woman's interviews with social services revealed, "She lives almost as a recluse, isolated from French society." The report further said: "She has no idea about the secular state or the right to vote. She lives in total submission to her male relatives. She seems to find this normal and the idea of challenging it has never crossed her mind."[206] French Urban Affairs minister Fadela Amara firmly supports the decision against Silmi, who is married to a French national with whom she has three children. They had resided in France for eight years when this final decision was rendered. "The burqa is a prison; it's a straightjacket," said Amara, a practicing Muslim. "It is not a religious insignia, but the insignia of a totalitarian political project that advocates inequality between the sexes and which is totally devoid of democracy."[207]

This is not the first time that France has denied citizenship due to Islamic extremism. However, it is the first time that the French courts have denied citizenship based upon someone's incapacity to be assimilated into France and private religious practice.

These both serve as very encouraging examples that non-violent Jihad can be rejected by the West. It also speaks toward the recognition, at least by some, that allowing a segregated sub-population of radicalized Muslims within any nation is danger-ous and counterproductive to a cohesive and integrated society. Welcoming Muslims into host nations must be encouraged and applauded, but subversive isolationism must not be tolerated. It is by definition divisive. President Theodore Roosevelt had this to say regarding immigration to America: "In the first place, we should insist that if the immigrant who comes here in good faith becomes an American and assimilates himself to us, he shall be treated on an exact equality with everyone else, for it is an outrage to discriminate against any such person because of creed, or birthplace, or origin. But this is predicated upon the person's becoming in every facet an American and nothing but an American... There can be no divided allegiance here. Any man who says he is an American, but something else also, isn't an American at all. We have room for but one flag: the Ameri-can flag."[208]

In that spirit, consider this story. Prompted by a rather shocking development in the United Kingdom, U.S. congress-man Tom Tancredo (R-Co) introduced the Jihad Prevention Act, the first legislation of its kind in the U.S.[209] The U.K., in a 2008 legislative decision, allowed Shari'a courts to adjudicate a wide variety of legal cases in a half-dozen of its cities. In other words, England (in limited areas) has submitted to pressure from British Muslims advocating separatism to allow Shari'a law, not

English law—the very foundation of American and Western freedoms—to rule. Congressman Tancredo's bill would prevent the U.S. from falling victim to this type of "nonviolent" Jihad— the insidious infusion of fundamentalist Islamic tenets into the American justice system and society. The bill would bar entry of foreign nationals who advocate Shari'a law and also render the advocacy of Shari'a law by Islamic extremists already in the U.S. a deportable offense.[210]

Shari'a law, advocated by Islamic extremists, frequently imposes brutal and misogynistic policies and punishments—from the stoning of women who are found guilty of adultery to the amputation of the hands of thieves. Shari'a heavily favors men, well exemplified by requiring women to provide numerous witnesses—a very difficult thing to do—to prove rape allegations against an accused rapist.[211] One must assume that these extreme penalties will not be sanctioned in the U.K., nonetheless, this totally misguided form of Western "broad-mindedness" in legitimizing Islamic religious justice is divisive, dangerous, and obsequious.

"This is a case where truth is truly stranger than fiction... today the British people are learning a hard lesson about the consequences of massive, unrestricted immigration," said Tancredo.[212] Considering the Centre for Social Cohesion poll mentioned earlier where 40 percent of Muslim students in the U.K. support Shari'a law and 33 percent support imposition of Islamic Shari'a law worldwide, it not so surprising although very disturbing that the U.K. capitulated to this pressure.[213] "We need to send a clear message that the only law we recognize here in America is the U.S. Constitution and the laws passed by our democratically elected representatives," said Tancredo. "If you aren't comfortable with that concept, you aren't welcome in the United States." Congressman Tancredo is most widely known for his tough, and some say extreme, positions regarding immigration to the U.S. So far, this bill has garnered neither wide support nor wide condemnation.[214] Political correctness is staying the tongues of our leaders in Washington. We must overcome this type of weak-mindedness cloaked as "tolerance" if we are to succeed in thwarting Jihadism in America and the West.[215]

These Islamist tactics of "lawfare," or aggressive legal maneuvers, intended to carve out a Muslim sub-society within America (and other non-Muslim nations) is a growing and insidious threat. We must unequivocally rise up and firmly denounce these tactics and demand that Muslims integrate into the fabric of America. Once again, *we the people* must shed our complacency and insist that our representatives protect the true interests of America by preventing the type of dangerous legislative nonsense that the U.K. has enacted.

Two stories out of Israel nicely portray the importance of combating Muslim segregation within non-Muslim societies. Each of them demonstrates how economic (and social, when possible) inter-dependence and interactions promote peaceful coexistence.

In the fall of 2008, I was traveling in the northern Israeli city of Akko, whose rich history dates back to the days of Alexander the Great. I was told a story that exemplifies the need for multicultural integration and the dangers of segregation in societies. In 332 B.C. when Alexander the Great resided in Akko, there was a small community of Jews that lived there alongside various other peoples. In Akko, Muslims and Jews have coexisted for centuries, but more so since November 1947 when Israel was granted a separate Jewish safe haven by the U.N. The war that immediately ensued resulted in Israel declaring its sovereign-state status a few months later. While the Jews accepted this U.N. resolution gleefully, the Arabs did not. For the Jews, this was their first homeland in 2,000 years and in light of the Nazi Holocaust just a few years earlier where 11 million people, including six million Jews, were murdered—the U.N. resolution was a long-awaited blessing. The Arabs on the other hand refused to accept this partition as they felt that their autonomy was threatened. In 1948 when Israel won its war of independence, the Arabs in Akko lost their battles with the new Jewish state. This was soon followed by Jews moving back into this ancient city—the oldest continually inhabited city on Earth.

The intensity of the Arabs' fight in Akko was rather anemic compared to most of Israel, where the Arabs fought hard to expel or destroy the Jews in the civil war that began the night the U.N. ruled to divide Palestine into a Jewish and Arab sector. Because the Arab threat was minimal in Akko, so was the Jewish response to their resistance. The result is that most of the Arabs in this ancient city did not flee as they did in Jerusalem, Jaffa, Tiberia, Ramle, Lad, Haifa, and so much of the new State of Israel. As a result, the Arabs and Jews have lived in relative peace in Akko ever since.

Although it would be inaccurate to describe the Jewish and Muslim communities as integrated in Akko, it would be fair to describe them as inter-dependent—integration that is more economic than social. In any event, this city depends upon tourism for its survival and the two communities understand this. As a result, this is generally a peaceful area where these two populations go about their business with little, if any, overt animosity. It is still Israel, however, and Akko does not exist in a vacuum where it is unaffected by the world around it.

While my wife and I were traveling with a professional guide in Akko who knows the locals well, a Muslim shopkeeper joined into a conversation that we had over a cup of incredibly strong Arab (Turkish) coffee. The story goes like this: In September 2008 on the holiday of Yom Kippur, a frightening event took place that seriously threatened the peace of this place. Yom Kippur is the holiest Jewish holiday, where Jews around the world fast for 24 hours and consider their actions of the past year as they ask for repentance from God and strive to become better people. Even non-religious Jews who rarely practice other Jewish rituals respect Yom Kippur. The religious Jews take this holy day very seriously. On Yom Kippur this year a militant young Muslim man stole a car and drove it recklessly into the Jewish section of Akko, honking its horn and screaming profanities at the Jews who were praying. A group of Jewish men eventually removed the Arab from the car and began to beat him—apparently severely. Others called the police and in the end, the man sustained moderate albeit temporary injuries. While this was happening, the religious Muslim broadcaster, who in Akko broadcasts over a loudspeaker the "call to prayer" five times a day, learned of the beating of this Arab while it was occurring. He immediately, over the loudspeaker, encouraged other Arabs to attack the "Jews" in retaliation. Hundreds of Arab men and women did exactly that—they went to the Jewish section and began beating any Jews they could find. Eventually Israeli security forces gained control over the situation and luckily no one was killed in the fiasco. Clearly, there is plenty of culpability on everyone's part here, the Arab man who started this riot, the Jews for vigilantism, and the Muslim leader who accelerated this into a riot by his call for violence. Here is the interesting part. Tourism dropped sharply after this incident when word of this spread throughout Israel and the world. The Arab leaders of Akko, fully aware of the economic impact of this, decided to quietly resolve this situation so they could put it behind them and once again regain the confidence in the safety of their city. Despite the fact that the Muslim leader and his family have been residents of Akko for generations, the Muslim city leaders decided to banish him from the city permanently—there simply is no place for Islamic extremism in Akko and they want all to know this. Just as this story ended, the call to prayer began to boom over the city, fairly packed with tourists and the shopkeeper looked at me with a prideful satisfaction that was well justified. This is a great example of how inter-dependence, if not actual integration, encourages peaceful coexistence.

In a similar story I was told during this same trip to the Middle East, when Islamic extremists make their way to Jerusalem, it seems, they are rapidly forced out of town in recent years. This is not because Jerusalem is so peaceful and happily integrated by its Christian, Jewish, and Muslim inhabitants. It is due to the simple fact that all of these peoples are inter-dependent on each other and on their primary source of income: tourism. The Arabs of Jerusalem depend heavily on tourism for their economic success. Although there is no shortage of young Islamic extremists who, often at the direction of elder radical Muslim leaders (or handlers) are prepared to self-detonate for a "cause greater then themselves," the city elders will have none of this. Simply put, economic prosperity trumps extremist ideology. Once again, while this is certainly not integration it is at least an economic inter-dependence and this seems to be enough to reduce extremist violence. The lesson learned is that common ground ideologically, economically, politically, and socially should be encouraged if not demanded of Muslims by their host nations. Segregation must be discouraged.

On balance, America has been far more successful than most of Europe in avoiding the extreme segregation of Islam from the rest of society. There are a few large Muslim quarters in the U.S., particularly in Detroit and its suburbs, where little English is spoken or written and a large segment of the Muslim population is unusually segregated for an American city. The largest Muslim population in America resides in metropolitan Detroit, which is home to 350,000 Muslims, about 78,000 Jews, and also 60,000 Chaldeans (Iraqi Catholics) against a backdrop that is predominantly Christian. Importantly and ironically, in Detroit one may also find inspiring examples of a very integrated Muslim and Arabic population into the fabric of American society. Although this social fusion of cultures is a work in progress and buoyed by the great promise of the "American Dream," with rare exceptions, they get along quite well. My own experience exemplifies this type of peaceful coexistence seen throughout America. In my private medical practice, I have numerous Chaldean and Muslim patients, a Lebanese physician assistant, and my hospital staff includes scores of Arab and Muslim colleagues. This successful and inclusive social diversity serves as a testament to the brilliance of the American Founding Fathers who designed the Constitution and Bill of Rights. These documents and the spirit behind them are the glue that binds our society together through the reverence of each individual's liberty and freedom. Even the Thousand Year War is no match for the eternal hope that Americans enjoy by virtue of the tolerance, opportunity, and prosperity afforded to all of us who honestly seek it.

Step 5. Political Correctness and National Security
Behavior: Jeopardizing American security due to an obsessive preoccupation with appearing fair-minded and moderate.

Therapeutic goal: Wake up, America, and smell the Turkish coffee.

It cannot be denied that there have been many attempts by Islamic extremists to infiltrate U.S. security, both civilian and military. Some of these penetrations were intended for the purpose of spying and others to facilitate terror attacks. Despite this trend, there have been many dangerous breaches in American security by Islamic extremists gaining high-level or otherwise dangerous posts in America. Many experts place the blame for this squarely on political correctness—our national obsession to appear tolerant. Let's look at six examples of both successful and unsuccessful infiltrations, all of which have occurred post-9/11. All are a consequence of overzealous politically correct behavior that prevented proper background checks.[216]

Aafia Siddiqui, Ph.D, a 30-year-old Pakistani mother of three and alumna of MIT, was charged for working for al-Qaeda and attempting to kill American soldiers in New York in 2008. Well-placed infiltrators can wreak great damage according to a former CIA chief of Counterintelligence, Michael Sulick: "In the war on terrorism, intelligence has replaced the Cold War's tanks and fighter planes as the primary weapon against an unseen enemy." Islamist moles, he explains, "could inflict far more damage to national security than Soviet spies." He goes on to point out that the U.S. and Soviet Union never actually fought each other, whereas now "our nation is at war."[217]

The U.S. Air Force discharged Sadeq Naji Ahmed, a Yemeni immigrant, when his superiors learned of his pro-al-Qaeda statements. Ahmed *subsequently* became a baggage screener at Detroit Metro Airport, which terminated him for hiding his earlier discharge from the Air Force. He went on to be charged and convicted of making false statements and sentenced to 18 months in jail.

Mohammad Alavi, an engineer at the Palo Verde nuclear power plant in Arizona, was accused of taking computer access codes and software to Iran that provide details on the plant's control rooms and plant layout. He subsequently pleaded guilty to transporting stolen property.

Nada Nadim Prouty, a Lebanese immigrant living in Detroit who worked for both the CIA and FBI, was actually a mole for Hezbollah. She pleaded guilty to charges of fraudulently obtaining U.S. citizenship and accessing a federal computer system to unlawfully transmit information about her relatives and Islamic terrorist organizations to Hezbollah as she engaged in a conspiracy to defraud the United States.

Waheeda Tehseen, a Pakistani immigrant who was an expert in parasitology as it relates to public water systems, worked as a toxicologist for the Environmental Protection Agency when she was arrested. Another red flag missed was that her husband worked for Pakistani intelligence—an organization with a long history of supporting al-Qaeda. She pleaded guilty to fraud and was deported.[218]

Weiss Rasool, aged 31, was an Afghan immigrant who worked as a police sergeant for Fairfax County, Virginia. He pleaded guilty for checking police databases without authorization, thereby jeopardizing at least one federal terrorism investigation.

All of the above individuals have actually been charged and pleaded guilty. They represent just a few of the scores of Islamists already convicted of a host of conspiracy crimes against America. According to U.S. intelligence there have been between 40 and 200 such cases, with many investigations ongoing. While it is reassuring that U.S. intelligence appears to be picking up the pace on finding these moles, it is disturbing that so many people of, at the very least, questionable intent gain access to our companies and security grid. Elsewhere in this book we have covered many examples of political correctness. The common thread here is that radical Islam has successfully thwarted nearly all criticism of Islamic extremism except, perhaps, actual acts of terrorism and even that reporting is "filtered" to avoid the appearance of "insensitivity" or "stereotyping" of Muslims. The solutions to this are going to be complex. It is not the American way to indict all people based solely upon their nationality or faith. It is equally un-American, however, to be negligent with the keys to our kingdom, as we fear the label of Islamophobia more than we fear actual terrorism within our shores. These people should never have gained the access they did, but due to a fear of appearing to "target" Muslims they were not properly vetted. America must stop pretending that there is no war with Islamic extremists as we capitulate to the idealists who cling to the fiction that it is only a very few in the Muslim community that represent a threat to the West. One of the first steps in our national rehabilitation must be to jettison the burden of unreasonable political correctness and idealistic appeasement.

Step 6. Education

Behavior: Hateful propaganda bombarding much of the Islamic and Arab world. Even America and the West are not spared.

Therapeutic goal: Adopt a zero-tolerance policy of this abomination, at home and abroad.

This may well be the decisive key to the long-term, successful eradication of Islamic extremism and I will devote considerable time on this solution. Most cultures hold education sacred. In the West, we strive to find the most educated teachers and sages to educate our young. It would be outrageous for a priest, rabbi, or grade school teacher to promote the hatred and killing of anyone based upon their ethnicity, religion, or creed. In the Islamic world this is, sadly, an everyday occurrence. In the schools, in the media, and in the mosques an endless barrage of hateful propaganda exists. Tragically, millions of Arab and Muslim children worldwide are fed a steady diet of hateful diatribes and xenophobia. This is difficult for Americans to believe, but burying our heads in the proverbial sand (whether that sand is Middle Eastern or domestic) is only adding to our complacency. As stated in the Introduction, Islamic fundamentalists celebrate the antiquated thinking of ancient Islamic customs and rulers. They are greatly threatened by democratic thinking and particularly the separation of *politics* from *religion* that defines most modern-day non-Muslim nations. To succeed, they must persuade young and vulnerable Muslims into hating all things non-Muslim. Indoctrination under the guise of education is their most potent tool, and we simply must find ways to combat this.

In an article by social psychologist Brad Bushman, a faculty member at the Institute for Social Research at the

University of Michigan, he concludes that reading violent religious texts increases aggressive behavior.[219] "To justify their actions, violent people often claim that God has sanctioned their behavior," says Bushman. Later, the author says, "Christian extremists, Jewish reactionaries, and Islamic fundamentalists all can cite scriptures that seem to encourage or at least support aggression against unbelievers."[220] As discussed previously, in the modern world, the religious-based promotion of intolerance and violence against non-adherents is almost exclusive to the Islamic faith. Bushman concludes, "Our results further confirm previous research showing that exposure to violent [scriptures] causes people to behave more aggressively if they identify with the violent characters than if they do not." This is not to say that both the New and Old Testament aren't also replete with violent and "dark" passages; indeed, many scholars point out that there is more violence cited in the Bible than the Qur'an. The difference is that Christian and Jewish leaders and the Western world, in general, simply do not dwell upon, promote, or even tolerate actions based upon the literal interpretation of these words. The West certainly does not teach these violent messages to our young in the hope that they will perpetrate violence against Muslims.

Examples of violent intolerance within the Bible include:
Deuteronomy 7:1-2:"... the seven nations greater and mightier than thou; And when the LORD thy God shall deliver them before thee; thou shalt smite them, and utterly destroy them; thou shalt make no covenant with them, nor show mercy unto them." Also, in Exodus 35:2: "Six days may work be done; but in the seventh is the Sabbath of rest, holy to the LORD: whosoever doeth any work in the Sabbath day, he shall surely be put to death."

Examples of similar passages in the Qur'an include:

"A disgraceful chastisement" (4.102) and "the fire of hell"(9.6) for "unbelievers," it urges Muslims not to "take the unbelievers for friends" (3.28). Worse, it commands Muslims to "fight those of the unbelievers who are near to you and let them find in you hardness" (9.123). Elsewhere it says to "kill them wherever you find them, and drive them out from whence they drove you out... Such is the recompense of the unbelievers" (2.191).[221]

The Muslim scholar Fareed Zakaria puts it this way: "The Qur'an is a vast, vague book, filled with poetry and contradictions (much like the Bible). You can find in it condemnations of war and incitements to struggle, beautiful expressions of tolerance and stern pictures against unbelievers."[222] Others, including Dr. Samuele Bacchiocchi, note that tolerance on the part of Muhammad in his earlier life was replaced by increasingly violent teachings. Consistent with Muhammad's initial mindset are passages such as these in the earliest days of Islam: The Qur'an says, "Invite [all] to the way of thy Lord with wisdom and beautiful preaching; and argue with them in ways that are best and most gracious: for thy Lord knoweth best, who have strayed from His path, and who receive guidance" (16:125). "Nor can goodness and evil be equal. Repel (evil) with what is better" (41:34).[223] Once Muhammad secured his power, however, he explicitly ordered offensive warfare against unbelievers, often referred to as "Sword Verse": "But when the forbidden months are past, then fight and slay the pagans wherever ye find them, and seize them, beleaguer them, and lie in wait for them in every stratagem [of war]; but if they repent, and establish regular prayers and practice regular charity, then open the way for them: for God is Oft-forgiving, Most Merciful" (9:5).[224] It is unfortunate that Muhammad's later years were marked by an increasingly violent tone toward infidels, because these late-period texts are used by extremists in the form of educational indoctrination as justification for much of today's Islamic terror.

EIGHT EXAMPLES OF HATRED IN EDUCATION:

a. Excerpts from a *Washington Post* article summarizing a Fox News Live report from Ken Adelman in Islamic teaching of hatred in U.S. schools.

- First grade textbook in U.S. Muslim schools (Saudi Arabian authors): "Every religion other than Islam is false."[225]

- Fourth grade textbook: "True belief means that you hate the polytheists and infidels."[226]

- Sixth grade textbook: "It is forbidden to be a loyal friend to someone who does not believe in the Prophet."[227]

- Eighth grade textbook: "The apes are Jews and the swine are Christians."[228]

- Eleventh grade textbook: "Do not yield to Christians and Jews on a narrow road."[229]

- Twelfth grade textbook: "Jihad in the path of God consists of battling against unbelief... [and] is the summit of Islam."[230]

b. Kenneth Adelman reported this story in an earlier report: Near Washington, D.C. at an Islamic Center, 11th grade textbooks state that "the day of judgment can't come until Jesus Christ returns to Earth, breaks the cross and converts everyone to Islam, and until Muslims start attacking Jews."[231]

c. **There exists an endless stream of hateful anti-American, anti-West, anti-Semitic TV, video, and articles throughout the Islamic world.** The depiction of Jews, Christians, and Americans doing and saying horrific things are commonplace in Arabic and Muslim societies the world over. Examples include the persistent depiction of the West as plotting the murder of Muslim children for sport amongst other heinous crimes against humanity. A common cartoon that appears in Middle Eastern newspapers is one of former President Bush and the Israeli prime minister drinking Arab blood in a toast to success. Another image is former Secretary of State Rice's hands dripping with the blood of Arabs as she smiles. It is notable that the source for many of these examples is an Arabic woman who is bravely speaking out against Islamic extremism to increasing numbers of Muslim and non-Muslim audiences. Her name is Nonie Darwish, and she has authored books on this subject (*Now They Call Me Infidel* and *Cruel and Unusual Punishment*) and also appears frequently on American television telling her story.[232] In recent months I have discussed these issues with Ms. Darwish. It is heroic people like her who represent our greatest hope for global tolerance and the peace that it will one day foster.

d. **Nonie Darwish, an Arab and Middle East expert, describes in her book, *Now They Call Me Infidel*:** "I was brought up to hate Christians and Jews... Martyrdom is dying for the cause of Jihad against the infidels...terrorists and Suicide Bombers are the heroes of Islamic society."[233]

e. **Walid Shoebat, former Arab terrorist, discusses the state-sponsored songs he learned in school:** "I was six years old. In school we were taught the song that Arabs are Beloved, Jews are Dogs... By High School the songs taught us that all Jews are killers. I had never even met a Jew."[234]

f. Similarly, the current president of Iran freely spews his hatred for infidels and endless threats against America and Israel. These are quotes between 2005 and the time of this writing in 2007 from various interviews on television and in print that are ascribed to President Ahmadinejad:

> *"The United States thinks they are the absolute rulers of the world... Soon there will be a world without America."*[235]

> *"Israel must be wiped off the map; it will be annihilated in a single storm."*[236]

> *"The wave of Islamic Revolution will soon reach the entire world."*[237]

> *"Iran is ready to transfer nuclear know-how to the Islamic countries due to their need."*[238]

g. On Iranian TV, as secretly captured on tape by Glenn Beck, an American journalist when the Iranian president did not realize the camera was recording.

President Ahmadinejad: "America should acknowledge the right and might of the Iranian people...we will force you to bow and surrender...as the crowd of hundreds of thousands screams "Death to America, Death to Israel." Interestingly, the death chant was conveniently left out of most of the world's reporting of that speech.[239] This serves as a good example of a significant omission of fact due to the "politically correct" reporting standards much of our mainstream media adhere to, according to Bernard Goldberg, Liz Trotta, and Glenn Beck—all well-known watchdogs of American media.[240]

The comments that President Ahmadinejad makes on and off camera are remarkably different. "He is very clever in appearing 'loving,' 'caring,' and 'reasonable' for Western media while fomenting great hatred for America, Jews, and the West off-camera," according to Beck.[241]

h. The same is true in many Palestinian schools. Consider these textbook phrases from books in current circulation in the Palestinian territories:

"All Jews are treacherous and disloyal..."[242]

"Christians and Jews are enemies of the Prophets and Believers..."[243]

"The Jews are usurpers of Allah's people, they must be and will be exterminated, Allah has declared they will be exterminated."[244]

"Children should aspire to be martyrs; any child who commits a suicide bombing is Allah's dearest and brings honour to their family. No child can aspire to anything better than to be a suicide bomber or, join a terrorist unit to wage war against Jew and Westerner."[245]

i. Brigitte Gabriel, Arab author of the book *Because They Hate*, puts it this way: "In Arabia and America, Muslim school books teaching hatred are popular." Consider this example: an eighth grade textbook (2001) for Saudi Arabian and American Islamic schools on page 43 states, "Jews and Christians are cursed by Allah and will be turned into Apes and Pigs for not adhering to Islamic Law." Gabriel says that the stated goal, as iterated by al-Qaeda, countless imams, and many others is that Islamic radicalism will result in the caliphate (Islamic world ruler) establishing Islamic rule throughout the world. Gabriel concludes, "They intend to establish this by spreading fear and hatred of infidels."[246]

I have also had the opportunity to discuss some of these issues with Ms. Gabriel, who is another courageous and successful advocate against Islamic extremism. No one that I have encountered is more passionate, dedicated, or successful in focusing attention on the issues presented in this book.

We cannot—we must not—allow the Islamic extremist agenda, including so-called "religious education," to be sheltered under the protection of Constitutionally guaranteed religious freedom. Radicals have successfully merged *political* Islam with the legitimately sacrosanct *religious* Islam resulting in their insulation from scrutiny in America and much of the world. In other words, Islamic radicals craftily use our revered Constitution (freedom of religion) against us to deflect any criticism of the Islamist political agenda. Many Muslim organizations in the U.S. use this tactic, according to Dr. Zuhdi Jasser, himself a devout American Muslim. Their hate-filled schoolbooks and vitriolic anti-Western Friday night sermons promoting the soft Jihad (Islamization of the West) and sometimes the hard Jihad (violence) shouldn't be tolerated, let alone insulated from legitimate censure. We as a nation working with the world at large must begin to differentiate *political* from *religious* Islam thereby empowering us to challenge, combat, and eventually defeat Islamic extremism at its core by ending this odious programming of the children of Islam. It is difficult to overestimate the virulence of inculcating hatred into the malleable minds of successive generations of Muslims. Unless and until America and the wider world adopts the position that we must not allow the Islamists to continue poisoning the minds of our children, Western life as we know it will end. If they succeed in continuing to promote intolerance, hatred for infidels, and the creation of endless future generations of warriors whose mission in life is to spread a virulent brand of Islam to the four corners of the Earth, then we lose—it is that simple.

It isn't surprising that from Saudi Arabia to Egypt and from the West Bank to Pakistan, civic leaders, educators, and imams (religious leaders) teach this appalling kind of xenophobic propaganda intended to instill hatred in their children. Millions of Arab and Muslim children are taught that the only *guaranteed* way to be admitted to the kingdom of heaven is to kill infidels. In the Qur'an (3:169), it states that, "If anyone fights Allah's path... Paradise will be assured him."[247] Obviously, most Muslims do not interpret these lines as the Jihadists do, but the extremists use this to recruit an endless stream of radical haters to kill for them.[248] Devoutly following the edicts of Islam is another way to heaven, but it is not as assured a path as Jihad. [249]

It is even more disturbing that within America this type of perverse teaching is widespread. A recent study suggests that in the U.S., as many as three out of every four Saudi-funded Islamic centers were found to teach widespread radicalism. This is according to a February 23, 2008 undercover survey by the World Net Daily that examined more than 100 mosques and Islamic schools in America. There are more than 2,000 mosques in the U.S. The article went on to note that the Mapping Shari'a in America Project (MSAP), which is sponsored by the Center for Security Policy in Washington, D.C., relies upon trained former counterintelligence and counterterrorism agents from the U.S. military, CIA, and FBI.[250]

"So far of 102 mapped, 75 should be on a watch list," said an official with the project. Frank Gaffney, a well-known former Pentagon staffer who now heads the Center for Security Policy, notes that the results of the survey have not yet been published. He did confirm, however, that "the vast majority" are inciting insurrection and Jihad by Saudi-trained imams and anti-Western literature, videos, and textbooks.[251] The MSAP director is David Yerushalmi, an expert on Shari'a law. Yerushalmi, also an attorney, claims that almost 80 percent of the group exhibits a high level of Jihadist threat. Examples include:

- Sermons that preach that women are inferior to men and can be beaten for disobedience.

- Non-Muslims, particularly Jews, are infidels and inferior to Muslims.

- Jihad, or support of Jihad, is not only a Muslim's duty, but the noblest and most direct way to secure an eternity in heaven. Suicide bombers and other so-called "martyrs" are worthy of the highest praise and that the Islamic caliphate should one day encompass the U.S.

- Solicitation of financial support for Jihad.

- Bookstores that sell books, CDs, and DVDs that promote Jihad and martyrdom.[252] A few of the 9/11 hijackers are confirmed to have received aid and counsel from one of the largest mosques in the Washington, D.C. area.

Despite this data, the U.S. government has not undertaken its own structured investigation of U.S. mosques, although the European Union has begun to examine the issue.[253] Even if one assumes this study to be biased and/or greatly exaggerated, it is still cause for concern and perhaps further scrutiny and consideration.

Is it surprising that so many of these children grow up despising us? This simply must stop. Why we in America and the West tolerate this so willingly is beyond reasonable understanding. If a Muslim country allows this preposterous fomenting of hatred to occur, they should be considered an enemy of the global community and treated as such, whatever the consequence. We will not win this conflict if each new generation of Muslims is taught that Americans, Christians, Jews, and all infidels are agents of the devil who must be annihilated, and that killing us is more important to Allah than for they themselves to live.

We can better understand this issue by confronting a simple fact: responsible leadership and world citizenship demands that

religious and academic leaders of all faiths and cultures impart
the virtues of peaceful tolerance of others to their children.
Imams and other Muslim leaders must be stopped from planting the seeds of hatred based upon the literal interpretation
of antiquated verses from the Qur'an, which sanction violence
based solely upon non-Muslim status. Until this ceases, both
here and abroad, can we really expect that this or any future generation similarly barraged with antipathy toward non-Muslims
will champion the virtues of respecting others and working towards global peace? As the wise Ben Franklin said, "An ounce
of prevention is worth a pound of cure." The West must act
with purpose to end this sinister violation of the tacit code of
civilized humanity, even if we must suspend trade and travel,
impose other penalties, or take any number of other actions
against these countries and their leaders. Until they conform
to the basic rules that humanity and modern civilization has
carved out of our violent history over thousands of years, we
owe it to future generations to remain vigilant until this conflict
is finally extinguished for all time.

Step 7. Freedom of Religion and Speech

Behavior: Providing protection for speech that includes
the promotion of sedition and encourages violence against
innocents.

Therapeutic goal: Reasoned compromise on the limits of
"free speech" where advocating hate and treason are not afforded the same level of protection as other speech—while still
respecting the First Amendment.

The issue of protected hate speech is another important one
that America and the West must grapple with if we are to prevail
in the war that is being waged upon us from Islamic extremism.
We must separate the true religious portion of Islam (which is
to be considered sacred and protected) from the political arm

of Islamic extremism (which must be unconditionally defeated). On its face, this appears to tread close to violating America's sacred Constitution, as some might argue it opposes the freedoms of speech and religion. In reality, opposing Islamists' political attacks pose no threat to the Constitution—the Constitution does not allow for sedition, treason, and overthrow of our government. After WWII, General MacArthur recognized the need to respect legitimate Japanese religions, but refused to tolerate the teachings of the Shinto creed that advocated continued war with the West. This serves as an example of what is necessary for us today. We must avoid being so politically correct in interpreting and upholding an unreasonably broad interpretation of the Constitution such that we cannot protect ourselves against the heinous and dangerous teachings of Islamic extremism within our own borders. Surely, the Founding Fathers did not intend to handicap future generations of Americans in this manner. Tolerating intolerant, hate-inspired sedition under the cloak of "religious freedom" may well prove catastrophic for America in this age of WMDs. We would do well to realize that if these extremists were to succeed, there would be no freedom of religion, no tolerance of varied cultures and ethnicities, and few (if any) rights for females in the society they would impose upon us.

We are obligated to come to terms with the idea that it isn't a violation of our values to redefine political correctness and religious tolerance to *exclude* the toxic hatred that inspires violence. At what point does the constitutional protection of free speech cease to apply to those who encourage others to perpetrate violent Jihad? What about nonviolent Jihad? Brigitte Gabriel, in addressing this issue puts it this way: "Lawyers who we have talked to say the question comes down to an assessment of whether or not the call to Jihad is incitement to violence that amounts to an 'imminent threat.' Yelling 'fire' in a crowded theater is an example of speech that creates an imminent threat of injury to the moviegoers, and is thus not protected speech.

At what point does calling for Jihad become the equivalent of yelling 'fire' in a crowded theater?"

Americans attach great importance to our right to free speech. How are we to reconcile that benchmark of our Constitution with the risk that we are facilitating our own destruction by extending these protections to those who would use them to destroy us? In America this debate is currently raging on in the media, on talk radio, and television talk shows throughout the nation. Defining what is, and what should never be, protected speech under the umbrella of "religion" in America is critical to our success in overcoming this evil. Other nations must also address this issue, as we are not fighting Islamic fundamentalism alone.

At a conference in 1775 Benjamin Franklin stated, "They who give up essential liberty to obtain temporary safety deserve neither liberty not safety." Many use this quote out of context to justify their position that the American government must not suspend ANY freedoms at all, whatever the consequence. Yet, we acquiesce to being searched and half-stripped before boarding aircraft, disarmed of personal firearms at public events, forced to prove our identity when withdrawing funds from a bank account, and many other compromises in our privacy. Although some Americans object to these intrusions and inconveniences, exploding in an aircraft somewhere over the Atlantic would be even more objectionable—so we endure it. Clearly, in order to augment safekeeping, certain liberties sacrificed have become reluctantly accepted, thereby proving that forgoing certain freedoms for security is a relative concept.

No doubt this issue will require thoughtful deliberation by our people, legislation by our Congress, and (eventually) interpretation by our courts. Such is the greatness of America. Our government is designed with the tools to adapt to future circumstances beyond even the Founding Fathers' grand vision. This is one such circumstance that will require careful interpretation and perhaps new amendments to preserve the sanctity of legitimate religion and our right to free speech, but not at the expense of our right to live in a secure and free society, or for that matter, to live at all. We, and our government, must never forget that the first duty of every government is the security of its people.

Step 8. The Silent Majority

Behavior: Recognize our failure to engage the "silent majority" of Muslims.

Therapeutic goal: Reaching out to the world's moderate Muslims to reject the intolerant and expansionist goals of Islamic extremists and finally join the global community in peace.

We have established that there exists both violent and nonviolent Islamic extremism. A critical component to America and the West's victory of tolerance over hatred will be predicated by our ability to persuade the "silent majority" of Muslims to recognize and reject the radicalized element within their societies. They must come to realize that by their tacit acceptance of Islamic fundamentalism, both violent and nonviolent, they are not only failing to be part of the solution, they are part of the problem. Their enemy within doesn't allow them the luxury to be "innocent bystanders"—they must choose sides in this epic battle of our times.

NONVIOLENT ISLAMIC EXTREMISM

A significant segment of Muslims living in Western nations oppose Islamic terrorism but support nonviolent aspects of Islamic fundamentalism. In other words, although they do not wholly embrace the murdering of innocents for political gain, they welcome efforts to nonviolently Islamicize Western societies. Therefore, the ambivalence toward their host nations manifests as a type of dual allegiance, one to the host nation for providing an opportunity for a better life than most Muslim nations, another supporting the conversion of that nation to Islamic law and culture.

In America, the overwhelming majority of Christian, Jewish, Hindu, atheist, and agnostic Americans regard themselves as Americans who "happen to be" Christian, Jewish, etc. As such, they bring with them their religious, ethnic, and/or cultural characteristics, creating the mosaic that is America. Too many Muslim Americans are mixed in their loyalty—they are Muslims living in America but wish to pattern America into a progressively more and more Islamic nation. The root of the problem is that Muslims the world over are subjected to a lifetime of indoctrination due to the toxic invective from radical Islamists. Well-known patriotic American Muslims authorities in recent months have confessed a frustration with their own Muslim community with respect to this issue. Many American Muslims, they say, are torn between the opportunities these host nations provide and their desire to move these societies toward Shari'a law. Examples of this duality include political lobbying to achieve the broadcasting of the Muslim call to prayer five times daily throughout the major cities of America (already occurring in Hamtramck, Michigan since May 2004), hijabs to be worn in public schools, foot baths in universities, female-only gymnasium days at universities and public parks, prohibiting television shows and movies depicting Muslims as terrorists, demanding that Islam never be blasphemed by congressmen and congresswomen, demanding and forcing online video games that do not flatter Islam to be recalled, and so on.[254]

I suggest that America and the West need to send a very clear message to the silent majority of Muslims, as Denmark and Australia have in recent years. In February 2006, Australian Prime Minister John Howard addressed this issue in a refreshing, unequivocal, and non-politically correct fashion. He said, "...radical elements within the country's Islamic community need to be confronted. It is not a problem we have ever faced with other immigrant communities, who become easily absorbed into the mainstream. We want people, when they come to Australia, to adopt Australian ways, [but] sections of Australia's Muslim population are antagonistic to Australian culture. We don't ask them to forget the countries of their birth, we respect all religious points of views and people are entitled to practice them, but there are certainly things that are not part of the Australian mainstream."[255] He added, "There is within some sections of the Islamic community an attitude towards women which is out of line with mainstream Australian society [and] there is really not much point in pretending it doesn't exist."[256]

The solution to nonviolent Islamism is actually rather simple. America and the West must shed its obsessive fear of appearing intolerant and demand that Muslims, like all other peoples, respect and adopt the culture and laws of nations they reside in or choose to migrate to. The West must acknowledge this unapologetically. We should stipulate without equivocation that Muslims reject their Islamist leaders' commands to "Islamicize" or subvert our nations toward Islamic law and traditions.[257]

A good example for America to follow is developing in England. Finally, in Great Britain there appears to be a growing awareness that nonviolent Jihad is real and dangerous. In the past, it was considered too intolerant for the government to be critical of nonviolent Jihadists and they were just given a pass. The British felt that they had their hands full just dealing with terrorists so why upset a whole other group of Muslims? Up until now, the British government was actually hopeful that if they supported the Islamic extremists that wished to *peacefully* convert England into a Muslim state, these so-called moderates with their "street cred" (social credibility in Muslim circles) would marginalize the violent terrorists. Over time, the terrorist's power over the Muslim population would wane. As it is said, make a deal with the devil and eventually you will pay the price. Britain is now recognizing the price they paid. Their efforts to contain violent Jihad by supporting the nonviolent Islamic extremists have failed miserably.[258] The government has been "underwriting the very Islamist ideology which spawns an illiberal, intolerant, and anti-Western worldview" according to a March 2009 report by the Great Britain Policy Exchange. This report stated, "Not only is it failing to achieve its stated objectives; in many places it is actually making the situation worse." They further noted, "A new generation is being radicalized, sometimes with the very funds that are supposed to be countering radicalization."[259] It appears that Britain has finally accepted the reality that nonviolent Jihad is as serious a threat to them as is terrorism. Their updated criteria for the definition of Islamic extremism includes these criteria: advocating a caliphate or one rule of a pan-Islamic state in Europe, the promotion of Shari'a law, and the support of armed resistance or violent Jihad anywhere in the world. Another promising sign is the government's recent suspension of ties with the Muslim Council of Britain—an organization very much like CAIR in America.[260] Hopefully Americans will learn from our allies across the pond, who are further along the curve of radical Islam and will adopt a stronger stand against nonviolent Islamic extremism. Global harmony on this subject must begin somewhere, let it be here, let it be now, and let it be America that leads the way.

VIOLENT ISLAMIC EXTREMISM AND TERROR

Most people believe that humanity is fundamentally decent. Is it possible that after more than 1,000 years of relative failure and stagnation in a progressive world, the Muslim "silent majority" actually prefers infamy (via terror) to anonymity? This is very important and worthy of deeper discussion. Obviously, this doesn't suggest that all Muslims are guilty of this, but enough seem to be, as there is apparently no worldwide Muslim outrage against terrorism. Recall the Pew Research Center poll percentages of Muslims who justify suicide bombings and other acts of terror to avenge the name of Islam. According to that poll, when extrapolated to the entire Islamic faith, at least 200 million Muslims support suicide bombings and other acts of terror against civilians for simply committing the offense of not "respecting" Islam. How many others, without actually supporting this aberrant behavior, are guilty of tolerating it? Consider this excerpt from a *Washington Post* article on July 20, 2007 (which quotes a poll in *The London Times*): 37 percent of Britain's two million Muslims agreed that all 268,000 members of the London Jewish community were legitimate targets for physical attack because of Israel's policies.

Basically, the fundamentalist and maybe not-so-fundamentalist Islamic mindset seems to be this: "After a 1,000 years of being marginalized (although it may be regrettable that innocent Americans, Christians, and Jews are being killed by terrorism), at least the world is finally listening to Muslims."[261] Isn't it strange and telling that a Danish cartoon causes millions of Muslims to rise up in anger, demonstrating their disdain around the world, yet these same Muslims fall silent when Islamic extremists kill civilians by detonating explosives in planes, trains, and automobiles?

When in December 2006 the pope quoted a 14th-century pundit who was criticizing that period's Islam for spreading religion by the sword and not positively contributing to society, millions of Muslims demonstrated in scores of cities while others threatened his life and Christianity in general. More recently, Muslims in Sudan arrested, convicted, and threatened with death and bodily harm a 54-year-old British schoolteacher for "blasphemy and insulting the Prophet Muhammad."[262] Ms. Gillian Gibbons' young class was due to study the behavior of bears, so she instructed that pupils bring in a teddy bear to provide the class a case study. One girl brought in her cuddly toy and the class proceeded to name him. After considering several names, including Abdullah and Hassan, they decided upon the name Muhammad. This obviously innocent event, once again, outraged Muslims to the point of arresting and convicting Ms. Gibbons of blasphemy. Sentencing options included 40 public lashes and six months in prison, but due to international outrage she was ultimately sentenced to fifteen days in prison and deportation. Sudan's influential Council of Muslim Scholars had urged the government not to pardon Gibbons, saying it would injure Khartoum's reputation among Muslims around the world. The event inflamed passions among thousands of Sudanese, some of whom publically called for her execution.[263] Ultimately, capitulating to global indignation, which included some Muslim countries, the president of Sudan pardoned Ms. Gibbons and she was returned to Great Britain.

On 9/11, when Islamofascists killed 3,000 Americans in New York, hundreds of thousands of Muslims celebrated the attacks and no notable Islamic demonstrations of condemnation occurred despite this culture's predilection to demonstrating with very little provocation. Why? It would appear that the silent (Islamic) majority either secretly supports these actions or lacks the courage to denounce it. Either way, this is unacceptable; the Muslim majority, in their relative silence, is part of the problem rather than the solution.

The greatest hope of engaging this silent majority is to assist organizations including the American Islamic Forum for Democracy (aifdemocracy.org), Muslims Against Shari'a (reformislam.org), and the Free Muslim Coalition (freemuslims.org) mentioned earlier. These Muslim activists have the courage and conviction to speak out against the ignorance of intolerance and the madness of terrorism. An added benefit is that Islamic extremists are probably more apt to follow their pleas than those of non-Muslims. In whatever ways are necessary, the silent majority must either adopt a position in opposition to terrorism or be made to pay a steep price for tacitly tolerating, if not quietly promoting, the murderous and barbaric behavior being perpetrated by a segment of their society. The world must rise up and demand that they root out their own cancer within or move aside so that America, the West, and others may do it for them. Many believe this is exactly what is happening in Afghanistan, the Philippines, Northern Africa, and Iraq today. As stated previously, when the West is prompted or otherwise cajoled to act militarily against Islamic extremism, it often contributes to the problem due to the extremists' ability to spin these actions as a war against Islam and not one against terrorism or the states that support it. This allows the extremists to convince young Muslims that they must join them in Jihad, further swelling their ranks, resulting in escalating acts of terror that we are then obligated to avenge in a cycle of violence. One way or another, we must find a way to convince Muslims to rise up against the extremists in their midst, thereby taking us out of the equation.

Currently, dozens of Islamic and Arab nations offer extremists safe harbor. They are provided secure anonymity, welcomed into their mosques, venerated by political leaders, imams, and teachers, and thereby given safe quarter and high social status. It stands to reason that as the tide turns against them in their own nations and communities, fewer young and impressionable Muslims will aspire to a vocation that is abhorred by their community at large. It is also reasonable to expect that without the support of these communities, it will be much harder for them to hide from the many nations searching for them. Then and finally, the terrorists will receive little comfort from the religious and secular leaders of Islam; they will be shunned from within.

It is necessary to encourage, nourish, and support the so-called "moderate Muslims" who are, no doubt, melded into the silent majority but have the capacity to refute and resist the extremist's messages. Through financial, militarily, and other means, we and our allies must shore up this segment of Islam. It is the old reward-versus-punishment philosophy. We evaluate our needs and decide whether incentive or punishment will best fit the situation. The U.S. has been fair (though some say aggressive) in its wielding of the punishment via military interventions, but less than stellar in its use of the reward system in encouraging Muslims to oppose the extremists within their midst. According to psychologists, more people respond favorably to positive reinforcement than negative. If this is so, it is even more critical to buoy this aspect of our foreign policy. Many would argue that this is the greatest missed opportunity of the last (George W. Bush) administration. Being that as it may, we must focus on looking forward while also learning from the past; if we have ignored the Islamic moderates to our disadvantage, we must recognize and correct this oversight.

If, despite all of these efforts, worldwide Islam cannot be persuaded to cooperate with the global non-Muslim community in its efforts to end Islamic extremism, penalties must be exacted by an indignant and united world. It is necessary to convince the silent majority to assume their duty and responsibility to work with the world in ending this Islamic reign of terror. Justice served in this regard will go a long way toward bringing a resolution to this madness.

Step 9. War, Borders, and Safe Havens

Behavior: Treating national borders and even mosques as sacrosanct while executing the war on terror and the wider war against Islamic extremism is folly.

Therapeutic goal: Recognize that a nation's borders are relative demarcations that vary between peacetime and wartime. Similarly, places of worship lose their "untouchable" status when they are used as storage depots for weapons and safe havens for Jihadists. Terrorists must not be allowed to simply cross a border or enter a mosque into a safe haven to avoid pursuit from American and coalition forces.

In wars, national boundaries are obscured. The enemy is the enemy, wherever he or she resides. When necessary, borders are crossed to achieve strategic goals. This is a very tricky issue and one that is wrought with controversy. Nonetheless, it is important for the world to decide just how far the defenders (America, NATO, coalition forces, and others) can go geographically in responding to the war declared upon them by those who hide behind host countries, borders, mosque walls, and far too often women and children. Obviously, working with nations is paramount if we are to win this fight, but when a nation is unwilling to stop the instigation, recruiting, indoctrinating, organizing, and harboring of the "Extremist Army" within its borders, the defenders must allow themselves to follow the killers wherever they take refuge. If not, how is the West ever to abolish the insulation the terrorists enjoy by hiding behind the veil of false religious protection (discussed above) and from the protection afforded the terrorists by their host countries' "sovereign nation" statuses? Once again, this will require careful national and international deliberation to ferret out a just and reasonable set of rules to guide these endeavors, but the notion of impenetrable borders for rogue states must be eliminated.

Step 10. The Predicament of "Moderate" Arabs and Muslims

Behavior 1, international moderates: Failing to recognize the danger that moderate Muslims endure if they resist extremism.

Behavior 2, American moderates: Too many Americans wrongly consider all Muslims who do not wear homicidal bomb vests as "moderates." Most Americans fail to appreciate the shades of Islamic extremism which results in non-violent Jihadists not being held accountable. Admittedly, some Americans are distrustful and even hateful of ALL Muslims, which is a bigotry that must also be expunged.

Therapeutic goal 1, international: Aggressively support and protect moderate Muslims abroad.

Therapeutic goal 2, inside America: We must develop the sensitivity to discriminate the good from the bad and the bad (nonviolent extremists) from the really bad (violent extremists). The simple metric of "Do they want to kill me?" isn't enough. We must also ask ourselves, "Do they strive to deprive me of my religious and cultural freedom?"

Let's first look at the international quandary of moderate Muslim leaders. The very definition of a "moderate Arab" is elusive. Does "moderate" define any leader that will make peace with Israel? Or does "moderate" refer to those who do not support terrorism? Or perhaps "moderate" is defined as leaders who accept secular law (for example, in Turkey) rather than Islamic (Shari'a) law? For the sake of argument, let us accept any and all of these definitions as accurate. A common worldwide predicament is that those Arab and Muslim leaders who do not support Islamic fundamentalism and its primary weapon, terror, are threatened with both bodily harm and regime overthrow by brutal extremists. This form of coercion can be quite persuasive and it prevents those moderate Muslims from winning the hearts and minds of their people. We need to look no further than one of the greatest leaders in recent times, Anwar al-Sadat. It was Egyptian President Sadat who forged a peace agreement with Prime Minister Menachem Began of Israel—the first such pact in the Arab world. His reward was to be assassinated by an Egyptian Islamic Jihad. Many experts believe that the current second-in-command of al-Qaeda, Dr. Ayman al-Zawahiri, was involved in this assassination. Al-Zawahiri was arrested for this crime, but released some time later due to a lack of evidence. As exemplified by Sadat's murder, being killed is a potential consequence of boldly defying Islamic extremists. More recently, past Pakistani President Pervez Musharraf, in working with America and NATO against the extremists in his country, was the target of countless assassination attempts. Tragically, former Pakistani Prime Minister Benizar Butto was assassinated on December 12, 2007, and it is widely believed that extremists were responsible.

Her husband, Asif Ali Zardari, is currently the Pakistani president. It is incumbent upon all world leaders to support these moderate Muslim leaders to the best of our ability. What we must not do is support corrupt or oppressive Muslim leaders and their regimes solely because they oppose Islamic extremism and terrorism. It was exactly this folly (America's support of Muhammad Reza Pahlavi, former Shah of Iran) that brought us the 1979 Iranian Revolution, which provided the spark for much of today's Islamic extremism. Again, it is difficult to over-emphasize the importance of remembering yesterday's mistakes so that we don't repeat them. Muslim leadership in the current Islamic world is complex, and it is not always easy to differentiate the good guys from the bad. This notwithstanding, the global community that rejects terrorism must search out ways to encourage Muslim leaders to follow President Sadat's example of heroic leadership as we help protect these moderates from the retribution of the extremists so they don't share his fate.

Inside America, the moderate Muslim is a different issue altogether. The adage that "one man's freedom fighter is another man's terrorist" may sometimes be true for terrorism occurring outside of America but for terror acts within our borders, Americans of all political, cultural, and religious persuasions condemn it. Muslims that wish to enjoy the American dream by enjoying their culture and practicing their faith while respecting others to do the same are indistinguishable from the rest of us. Those that practice nonviolent extremism that I have devoted so much of this book is devoted to, however, are quite another

story. We need to much more aggressively support the courageous Muslims who resist the fundamentalists and speak out
against extremism and for America as a free, democratic, tolerant nation. It is my fervent hope that this book will add to the
small but courageous group of these individuals, a few of whose
websites are listed here:

AIFDemocracy.org
ArabsForIsrael.com
ReformIslam.com
FreeMuslims.org

Step 11. Public Relations: America in the Arab and Muslim World

Behavior: Failure by America and the West to promote
the good qualities of our nations and societies to the Muslim
world.

Therapeutic goal: Break the habit of self-centeredness and
consider how we are actually viewed by others and use this perspective to promote ourselves to the Muslim world.

The West has largely failed to make inroads into the endless rhetoric against all things American and Western in the
Islamic world. Much of the Muslim world is bombarded with
anti-American rhetoric on a daily basis. In newspapers (both
state-sponsored and private), television, and perhaps most sadly,
mosques, the diatribe is unyielding.[264] For millions of Muslims,
their main information data stream regarding the West is an
endless tirade that decries the evil, warmongering Americans,
Christians, and Jews. Many Muslims are never exposed to a
counterpoint for the relentless denunciation of infidels, with
Americans being chief among infidels. America and the West
must improve our presence in the Muslim world so that our
viewpoint can also be heard and considered by the millions of

non-radicalized Muslims who have essentially been brainwashed by the extremist element in Islam.

Radio Free Europe was the broadcasting division of the New York-based National Committee for a Free Europe in the late 1940s. In 1950, the U.S. Congress first funded this, and it still broadcasts in Europe and the Middle East today. Although this is a step in the right direction, it is obviously not adequate in today's global multimedia culture to depend entirely on this medium, despite its use of 28 languages in more than 1,000 broadcast hours per week. America needs to increase its presence in the Arab and Muslim world. It is incumbent upon us to offer our perspective to their media including television, radio and print news. I am not suggesting that we propagandize but much of the Muslim worlds young people enjoy American and western music so perhaps entertainment is a gateway to the hearts and minds of Islam? This will be an uphill battle but one very much worth undertaking.

Step 12. Public Relations: America in the <u>Global</u> World

Behavior: Complacency by America and the West in promoting the good qualities of our nations and societies to the non-Muslim world.

Therapeutic goal: Improving our promotion of America to the world at large. This will require breaking the American media and American left's habit of national self-deprecation to the point of a self-destruction. We must learn to better consider how we are actually viewed by others thereby promoting ourselves to the non-Muslim world.

Simply put, America's unprecedented supremacy frightens the world. Never before in modern times has a single nation commanded so great a power and influence over the rest of Earth, notwithstanding the challenges we face while applying military power in asymmetrical anti-terrorism warfare. America's challenge isn't a lack of power but rather how to apply it against an enemy that uses innocents, national borders, and mosques to expertly exploit our desire to minimize collateral damage and respect the sovereignty of nations. America's absolute military spending greatly exceeds that of all other nations on a per capita basis. America's dominance, however, goes well beyond our military preeminence.[265] The U.S. economy exceeds that of Germany, Japan, and Great Britain. We are under 5 percent of the world's population but, as stated above, the U.S. accounts for 50 percent of all research and development, 45 percent of all high technology invention and production, and the majority of Nobel laureates since the inception of the Nobel Prize. As stated previously, America is the birthplace of the telephone, the light bulb, the automobile, the airplane, and electricity as well as most of the world's space exploration, Internet start-up companies, and so on. This dominance alarms much of the world, even our closest allies. Interestingly, in a global survey conducted in 2004, large majorities in nearly every nation believe that if America had a rival superpower, the world would be a more dangerous place.[266] In other words, the world is better off with America as the preeminent power on Earth, however, since "absolute power corrupts absolutely" there also exists considerable fear of and ambivalence toward America in the world today.

Having said all of this, U.S. supremacy is hardly a new phenomenon. America has been the leading world power for nearly a century. So, why all the anti-Americanism now? According to Fareed Zakaria, journalist, pundit, and *Newsweek* contributor, the answer goes back to 1945, when America was beloved after the conclusion of WWII. Franklin Delano Roosevelt and Harry Truman chose not to create an American empire, but to build a world of alliances and multilateral institutions. They formed the United Nations, the Bretton Woods system of economic cooperation, and dozens of other international organizations in an effort to buoy the rest of the world. America helped get the rest of the world back on its feet by pumping out vast amounts of aid and private investment. The nucleus of this effort, the Marshall Plan, provided $120 billion in today's dollars to redevelop Europe.[267] Secretary of State George Marshall demanded that America should not dictate how that money be spent. Rather, Europeans should control these funds as they see fit. Since that time, the United States has provided money, technical expertise, and other assistance across the world to build dams, educate a countless number of people, and stabilize economies throughout the world.[268] These efforts paved the way for a booming global economy in which America also thrives. If all of this is so, what have we done to either instill fear or otherwise cause so many throughout the world to lessen their support of America in recent years?

It is widely believed that the George W. Bush administration has alienated our allies by seemingly flying solo and failing to exert the diplomacy necessary to build coalitions. To some degree this is true, but I believe that the American media so detested George Bush that it unfairly castigated him and his administration so unremittingly that eventually the criticisms and characterization of him as an idiot-president stuck. Examples of diplomatic failures include America's refusal to support international treaties including Kyoto Global Warming Treaty and the 1998 Rome Statute to establish an International Criminal Court (ICC), as well as our handling of the entire Iraq War. In all fairness, the United States' objection to each of these international treaties does have merit (America may have been disproportionately adversely affected by them) as did the invasion of Iraq, depending upon one's perspective. According to many people in this country and too many of our allies abroad, it was the arrogant manner in which the Bush administration behaved in these and other matters that has impugned our reputation and caused our popularity to plummet. Perhaps this is partially true, so is it true that the collapse of the Soviet Union generated concerns of America's unchecked power. In any event, this trend of suspicion and fear of America must be reversed, for many reasons not the least of which is that fighting terror requires international cooperation. Hopefully, the new Obama administration will take great care to nurture the goodwill that America deserves and requires. We must find ways to return to a world where being pro-America is an asset rather than a liability.

There are many ways for the United States to rebuild its relations with the world. It can start, as Fareed Zakaria suggests in his 2004 *Newsweek* article, "The Arrogant Empire," by matching its military buildup with diplomatic efforts that demonstrate its interest and engagement in the world's problems. The ironic part of this is that America truly is a nonexpansionist and egalitarian nation that is a force for good in a tough world. Did we occupy Germany, Japan, Korea, Kuwait or any other nation that we engaged in the last century's wars—none of which were wars that we started? The answer is a resounding no, despite the endless rhetoric from too many far left and foreign zealots. We must "market" this reality to the world in order to recapture our global favor; the same global favor that we acquired at the expense of our blood and treasure over the last century. America can also reevaluate what our critics consider to be protectionist practices in our steel and farming industries, and to further open our borders to goods from poorer countries.[269] Most importantly, we must evoke international faith in the legitimacy and benevolence of America—not only based upon our rich history as a great protector of freedom, fairness, and free trade, but also from our enduring history of being a good neighbor to the world. America truly is the premier protector of freedom in this global war on terror, and it must succeed in rekindling the world's respect and appreciation.

NATIONAL REHAB 12 STEP

PERSONAL GOALS (THINK GLOBALLY, ACT LOCALLY)

The behavior that these personal solutions are intended to correct is the "prisoner of self" that psychologists often talk about. Most people, being creatures of habits both good and bad, are very consistent in their way of approaching most of the activities in their lives. We tend to establish personal behaviors or patterns in the way we eat the same foods, travel the same routes, use the same phrases and mannerisms, etc. One of these habits includes the way we perceive and judge people, situations, and events often in a rote memory sort of way, without even the benefit of thoughtful consideration. Automatic or "knee-jerk" thinking, if you will. For example, if we have previously formed an opinion on, say, a baseball team, a restaurant, a political candidate, or even a political party—for no logical reason we often tend to defend that position to the end, even if the facts surrounding these opinions have entirely changed. Imagine a restaurant changing ownership or a baseball team making major player trades. In these instances, it only stands to reason that an initial opinion may no longer be valid—if only we are open-minded enough to see it again from a new perspective. Each of these goals is intended to encourage you to see things from that new perspective and by doing so, open your mind to what was right there in front of you, although hidden from your view. The threat of Islamization and particularly the nonviolent Jihad described in these pages is one of those subjects that people "own" in a way that renders them inflexible. The political right sees it as a serious threat; the political left doesn't see it at all. The liberal playbook simply doesn't allow this politically incorrect subject to be considered let alone legitimately debated. If *Re-United States* and other books, blogs, websites, and lectures covering this subject can find their way into the American lexicon, real change can occur. In this way, as individuals, we can reshape our viewpoints, open our hearts and minds to each other and eventually heal the divide that threatens to cripple America.

Step 1. Recognition
The first step to any successful rehabilitation is to acknowledge that one has a problem. In this case, of course, we aren't dealing with personal vices. Rather, the problem is often the relative ignorance of the issues facing our nation, a total adherence to one ideology or another, or both. Either way, take a deep breath, close your mouth, open your mind, and allow yourself a fresh look at this issue.

Step 2. Role Reversal
Moving forward, think~really think~from another perspective. Put yourself in the shoes of whomever you may consider an opponent of your beliefs, and don't stop until you understand their point of view. You need not agree with it, but understand what it is they feel and why.

Step 3. Fresh Look: Print
Read newspaper articles (or if you are highly motivated, books) on the subject from the point of view you consider to be the opposite of your own.

Step 4. Fresh Look: View
At least occasionally, watch CNN or MSNBC if you are a FOX News adherent, or vice versa if you identify with a more liberal position.

Step 5. Blogosphere
If you are an Internet user, find a few blogs expressing a variety of viewpoints and visit them regularly, even if for just a few minutes a week. This will help you identify with the "average"

Americans, irrespective of their primary political allegiance. There are literally hundreds of blogs to choose from, here are a few to consider:

   a. **Conservative blogs:**
   i.   http://www.steynonline.com
   ii. http://fallbackbelmont.blogspot.com
   iii. http://hotair.com
   iv. http://www.redstate.com
   v.   http://americanthinker.com

   b. **Liberal blogs:**
   i.   http://www.politico.com
   ii. http://leftyblogs.com
   iii. http://www.ringsurf.com
   iv. http://glenngreenwald.blogspot.com
   v.   http://talkingpointsmemo.com

Step 6. Attendance

If time permits, attend local lectures on topics that we have discussed in this book. If you look for them, you will find them at nearby schools, universities, libraries, or bookstores.

Step 7. Work and Friends

Now that you have begun to expand your knowledge on this subject matter, engage your friends and coworkers in constructive and positive discourse. Start off slow and safe. In time, you just might find that you have a knack for this. You will feel more engaged and more knowledgeable on subjects that we are barraged with but you previously avoided due to relative unawareness. Remember, knowledge breeds awareness and awareness breeds expectations. Eventually, like a pyramid scheme, people are drawn in and in this way our improved national dialogue on this subject can help to rescue our nation and the world from a terrible threat—one person at a time.

Step 8. Family

The same is true with your family except it is often easier and "safer" to speak with family about politics and issues such as these. Speak with both your immediate and extended family on these matters. People you interact with will continue the discussion with others, and so on. Your conversations will, in a grassroots fashion, help to advance the national discourse.

Step 9. The Mighty Pen

Eventually, you will hone your opinions and better understand these subjects through your conversations. At that point you may wish to consider writing editorials in local or national newspapers and magazines when you have an opinion regarding an article you have read, or a program you have watched. Perhaps you can contribute your thoughts or comments to blogs?

Step 10. The Mightier Pen

Write your representatives and share with them your thoughts and expectations.

Step 11. Vote

Always vote, and always vote your conscience.

Step 12. Lighten up

Really. It's not that this subject isn't terribly important, but replacing some of the intensity with levity will lessen your need to be defensive about your political beliefs and enhance productive dialogue. Now that you've got the necessary tools, let's bridge the cracks, and reunite these United States by building a more secure nation and world—together.

CONCLUSION

In this book, I have discussed the background and nature of the fundamentalist Islamic movement and the history of the major religions. I have illustrated the root causes of Islamic extremism and the grave threat that it poses to American and Western civilization. I have addressed the complex divisions and perceived divisions in America and the way that both American and European appeasement of terrorism has exacerbated worldwide radical Islamic activity.

Finally, I articulated two dozen talking-point solutions (national and personal rehabilitation, if you will) to this growing danger. Regardless of whether you consider yourself a(n) liberal, conservative, Democrat, Independent, Libertarian, Republican, all or none of the above, I beseech you to take an active role by expressing your views. Perhaps you are inclined to do so with friends or coworkers? Maybe you prefer to share your points of view in a political environment, or simply in an email or letter to your congressional representative? Become engaged in some fashion and by all means do so in the spirit of collaboration. After all, "this is your land *and* this is my land," and if you have taken the time to read this book you share a love of America, its rich history, and a sense of its place in the world. Above all, *Re-United States* is written to encourage Americans to re-examine our positions, embrace our similarities, and finally, to focus squarely on the challenge of Islamic extremism and the danger it represents to America and the World. Exercise your right and, I dare say, your responsibility to participate in this far-reaching conflict of our time. If we, "average Americans," can do this, our leaders will follow; such is the genius of our great democracy. In this fashion, every American can play a role in supporting our nation as we guide ourselves and the world once again toward peace.

GLOSSARIES

This glossary is alphabetical except for the first six terms. These six will greatly facilitate your reading of the book. Feel free to look up any others along the way or you may wish to just read through the list now—there aren't very many. Note also that you will frequently see these three words and, for the purposes of this book, they have the same meaning: Islamic extremist, Islamic fundamentalist, and Islam<u>ist</u> are essentially the same.

SPECIAL GLOSSARY

Muslim: A person who follows the faith of Islam.

Islam: The religion founded by Muhammad in the 7th century and has 1.2 billion adherents throughout the world today.

Islamic extremist: Any Muslim who holds radical and extreme views against non-Muslims (infidels). Some advocate the murder of all infidels, others prefer a slow Islamization of the planet but all wish for (and work toward) the entire world being converted to a harsh, fundamentalist, and primitive brand of the Islamic faith.

Islamic fundamentalist: Essentially the same as Islamic extremist.

Islamist: (Note this is not the word *Islamic*, which just refers to Islam.) Islamist is essentially the same as Islamic extremist.

Islamism: Essentially the same as Islamic extremism.

Jihad: As referred to in this book this terms means is the struggle against infidels (non-Muslims) which may be violent (terror and war) and nonviolent (known as "lawfare").

GLOSSARY

Ahl al-Dimmah (or Dhimmis): The non-Muslim subjects of an Islamic state who have been guaranteed protection of their rights: life, property, and practice of their religion, etc. Non-Muslims have fewer legal and social rights in most if not all Muslim lands.

Allah: The greatest and most inclusive of the names of God. It is an Arabic word of rich and varied meaning, denoting the one who is adored in worship, who creates all that exists, who has priority over all creation, who is lofty and hidden, who confounds all human understanding. It is exactly the same word as, in Hebrew, the Jews use for God (Eloh), the word which Jesus Christ used in Aramaic when he prayed to God. God has an identical name in Judaism, Christianity, and Islam; Allah is the same God worshipped by Muslims, Christians, and Jews.

Caliph: Successor (literal translation). Refers to the successor of the Prophet Muhammad, the ruler of an Islamic theocratic monarchy.

Dar al-Harb (Domain of War): Refers to the territory under the hegemony of unbelievers, which is on terms of active or potential belligerency with the Domain of Islam, and presumably hostile to the Muslims living in its domain. Literally means, and this is very important, "House of War" because it will take war to bring it to a "House of Submission" or Dar al-Islam.

Dar al-Islam (House of Submission): The abode, or land, of Islam, in submission to Islamic rule and culture.

Dhimmi: Jews and Christians under Islam. These infidels have fewer legal and social rights than Muslims.

Fatwa: Legal opinion of an (alim) binding on him and on those who follow his taqlid.

Hadith: Speech (literal translation). Recorded saying or tradition of the Prophet Muhammad. These are validated by isnad; with sira these comprise the Sunna and reveal Shari'a.

Hajj: Pilgrimage to Mecca. Sunnis regard this as the fifth pillar of Islam Hajj (Major Pilgrimage). Hajj is one of the five pillars of Islam, a duty one must perform during one's lifetime if one has the financial resources for it.

Imam: 1. Imam signifies the leader, and in its highest form, refers to the head of the Islamic state. 2. It is also used with reference to the founders of the different systems of theology and law in Islam. 3. A person who leads the prayer.

Islam: Submission to God. The Arabic root word for Islam means submission, obedience, peace, and pure. Also, the religion founded by Mohammad in the 7th century and has 1.2 billion adherents throughout the world today.

Itjtihad: Nonviolent Islamic extremism intended to convert non-Islamic lands into Islamic ones (typically through takyya and lawfare).

Jihad: Struggle. Any earnest striving in the way of God, involving personal, physical, for righteousness and against wrong-doing. The Jihad referred to in this book is the struggle against infidels (non-Muslims) which may be violent (terror and war) and nonviolent (known as "lawfare").

Lesser Jihad: 1. In defense, fighting to protect Islam from attack or oppression. In such fighting, so it is said, no woman, child, or innocent civilian is to be harmed, and no tree is to be cut down. Clearly, this is somehow ignored in the practice of Islamic terrorism. 2. The struggle against infidels (non-Muslims).

Greater Jihad: Internal struggle for the soul against evil, e.g. Lust, Greed, Envy, etc. Also to thrive to do actions that have great value in Islam, and that one has to overcome one's self. For example, overcoming the temptation to sleep when it is time to pray the morning prayer is a greater Jihad.

Madrassa(h): A school, university. Many madrassas teach a radical version of Islam, but the term is more generic than that.

Mecca: The holiest city in Islam, located in Saudi Arabia.

Medina: City. Medinat-un-Nabi means "the City of the Prophet."

Muhammad: The last Messenger of God. The Prophet.

Muslim: A person who follows the faith of Islam. One who submits their will to Allah (God).

Prophet: A person who has had messages from Allah. "The Prophet" refers to Muhammad.

Qu'ran (Koran): The book of divine guidance and direction for mankind, the revelation of God to Muhammad.

Ummah: The global community of all Muslim believers.

Salafism: The radical version if the ideology of Osama bin La-din's al-Qaeda organization. It is a complex ideology that promotes only pure Islam; a fundamental version that is intolerant to all other interpretations. Literal interpretations of the Qu'ran and the Sunna are mandatory.

Shari'a: The body of Islamic religious law. The term means "way" or "path to the water source"; it is the legal framework within which the public and private aspects of life are regulated for those living in a legal system based on Islamic principles of jurisprudence and for Muslims living outside the domain. Shari'a deals with many aspects of day-to-day life, including politics, economics, banking, business, contracts, family, sexuality, hygiene, and social issues.

Shari'ah: Signifies the entire Islamic way of life, especially the Law of Islam.

Sunna: Trodden path (literal translation). The way and the manners of the Prophet. The Sunna and the Qu'ran are, together, the holy scriptures of Islam.

Takiyya: Within the Muslim moral universe, the concept of "takiyya" is religiously sanctioned deception to protect or promote Islam. Although dishonest, it is not only moral but admirable because it comes from the Qu'ran and experiences of Muhammad himself. This is the justification for Muslims living in non-Muslim lands to deceive the "infidel" people and security personnel as they work to Islamicize the host nation.

ENDNOTES

1. Kay, Barbara. "Paving the Way For Soft Jihad." Islamist-Watch.org, July 22, 2008. http://network.nationalpost.com/np/blogs/fullcomment/archive/2008/07/22/barbara-kay-paving-the-way-for-soft-jihad.aspx

2. Langguth, A.J. *Patriots: The Men Who Started the American Revolution.* New York: Simon & Schuster, 1988.

3. Ibid.

4. Ali, S Ahmed. "Mumbai Locals Helped Us Terrorist Tells Cops." *The Times of India.* November 30, 2008. http://timesofindia.indiatimes.com/india/Mumbai-locals-helped-us-terrorist-tells-cops/articleshow/3774106.cms

5. Faraj, Carolyn. "Tape justifies killing." CNN Live, May 18, 2005. Audiophile www.cnn.com/2005/WORLD/meast/05/18/iraq.main/index.html

6. Solomon, S. and E. Alamaqdsis. *The Mosque Exposed.* ANM Press, 2007.

7. Lewin, Tamar. "Universities Install Footbaths to Benefit Muslims and Not Everyone is Pleased." *The New York Times,* August 7, 2007.

7. Schlussel, Debbie. "So Long Church/State Separation: University of Michigan to fund Muslim Footbaths." DebbieSchlussel.com, June 5, 2007. http://www.debbieschlussel.com/1373/exclusive-so-long-churchstate-separation-university-of-michigan-to-fund-muslim-footbaths-2/

8. "Harvard Tries Women-Only Muslim Gym Times." Drudge Report, March 10, 2008. http://www.drudge.com/news/105220/harvard-tries-women-only-muslim-gym-times

Ruzicka, Abbie. "To Accommodate Muslim Students, Harvard Tries Women-only Gym Hours," *The Daily Free Press,* February 5, 2008, http://www.dailyfreepress.com/news/to-accommodate-muslim-students-harvard-tries-women-only-gym-hours-1.582273

9. Henry, Julie and Laura Donnelly. "Female Muslim Medics Disobey Hygiene Rules." Telegraph.co.uk. February 4, 2008. http://www.telegraph.co.uk/news/main.jhtml?xml=/news/2008/02/03/nislam403.xml

10. Panjwani, Radhika. "City Wraps Up Muslim Lifeguard Program," *The Mississauga News.* February 14, 2008, http://www.islamist-watch.org/274/city-wraps-up-muslim-lifeguard-program

11. Bawer, Bruce. "An Anatomy of Surrender." *City Journal.* vol. 18, no. 2, Spring 2008. http://www.city-journal.org/2008/18_2_cultural_jihadists.html

12. Salam, Reihan. "The Sum of All PC." Slate. May 28, 2002. http://slate.com/ID/2066272

13. Steyn, Mark. "Jews Get Killed, but Muslims Feel Vulnerable." *Jewish World Review,* December 8, 2008. http://www.jewishworldreview.com/1208/steyn120808.php3

14. Meryhew, Richard, et al. "The Making of a Suicide Bomber." *The Star Tribune.* May 3, 2009. http://www.startribune.com/local/44231707.html?elr=KArksUUUU

15. Winter, Jana. "Book Based on Prophet Muhammad's Child Bride Yanked At 11th Hour." FOXNews.com, August 19, 2008. http://www.foxnews.com/printer_friendly_story/0,3566,406483,00.html

16. Ibid.

17. Ibid.

18. Beckerman, Gal. "The Sun's Wafer-thin Attack on Elliott's Pulitzer Piece." *Columbia Journal Review.* April 20, 2007. http://www.cjr.org/politics/the_suns_wa-ferthin_attack_on_e.php

19. Steyn, Mark. "Jews Get Killed, but Muslims Feel Vulnerable." *Jewish World Review.* December 8, 2008. http://www.jewishworldreview.com/1208/steyn120808.php3

20. Ibid.

21. Ibid.

22. Ibid.

23. Kay, Barbara. "Paving the Way For Soft Jihad." Islamist-Watch.org. July 22, 2008. http://network.nationalpost.com/np/blogs/fullcomment/ar-chive/2008/07/22/barbara-kay-paving-the-way-for-soft-jihad.aspx

23. Stillwell, Cinnamon. "The Mumbai Atrocities: Where is the Outrage?" SFGate.com, December 17, 2008. The Middle East Memo Forum. http://www.meforum.org/article/2038

24. Imm, Jeffry. "Islamism and Free Press." Counterterrorismblog.org, March 10, 2008. http://counterterrorismblog.org/2008/03/islamism_and_free_press.php

25. Gioia, Vincent. "The Time for Appeasement of Islam is Over." *Right Side News.* July 12, 2008. http://www.rightsidenews.com/200807121407/culture-wars/the-time-for-appeasement-of-islam-is-over.html

Imm, Jeffry. "Islamism and Free Press." Counterterrorismblog.org, March 10, 2008. http://counterterrorismblog.org/2008/03/islamism_and_free_press.php

26. Stillwell, Cinnamon. "The Mumbai Atrocities: Where is the Outrage?" SFGate.com, December 17, 2008. The Middle East Memo Forum. http://www.meforum.org/article/2038

27. Hitchens, Christopher. "Jefferson Versus the Muslim Pirates." *City Magazine.* Spring 2007. http://www.city-journal.org/html/17_2_urbanities-thomas_jefferson.html

28. Gioia, Vincent. "The Time for Appeasement of Islam is Over." *Right Side News.* July 12, 2008. http://www.rightsidenews.com/200807121407/culture-wars/the-time-for-appeasement-of-islam-is-over.html

29. Ibid.

30. Hitchens, Christopher. "Jefferson Versus the Muslim Pirates." *City Magazine.* Spring 2007. http://www.city-journal.org/html/17_2_urbanities-thomas_jefferson. html

31. Trifkovic, Serge. "Islam: The Folly of Appeasement." *FrontPage Magazine.* December 10, 2002. http://97.74.65.51/readArticle.aspx?ARTID=20757

32. Ibid.

33. Ibid.

34. Pipes, Daniel. "The Voice of America, Silenced on Radical Islam." DanielPipes. org. March 6, 2009. http://www.danielpipes.org/6215/the-voice-of-america-silenced-on-radical-islam

35. Ibid.

36. Glaberson, William. "U.S. Won't Label Terror Suspects as 'Combatants'." *The New York Times,* March 14, 2009. http://www.nytimes.com/2009/03/14/us/politics/14gitmo.html

37. Douglas, William and Carol Rosenberg. "Obama Administration Dropping 'Enemy Combatant' Term." *The Miami Herald.* March 14, 2009. http://www.miamiherald.com/news/politics/story/949260.html

38. Pipes, Daniel. "Islam and Islamism-Faith and Ideology." *The National Interest.* Spring 2000. http://www.danielpipes.org/article/366

39. Editors. "Combat Street and Fort Hood Gunman." *The New York Times,* November 6, 2009. http://roomfordebate.blo-gs.nytimes.com/2009/11/06/combat-stress-and-the-fort-hood-gunman/?em

40. Ibid.

41. "Obama: Don't Jump to Conclusions." CBS News, November 6, 2009. http://www.cbsnews.com/stories/2009/11/06/national/main5551286.shtml

Feller, Ben. "Obama says don't jump to conclusions on shooting." Associated Press (replicated on Yahoo! News). November 6, 2009. http://news.yahoo.com/s/ap/20091106/ap_on_go_pr_wh/us_obama_fort_hood

42. Bowen, Catherine Drinker. *Miracle at Philadelphia: The Story of the Constitutional Convention May-September 1787.* Boston: Back Bay Books. 1966.

43. Ibid.

44. Ibid.

45. Solomon, S. and E. Alamaqdsis. *The Mosque Exposed.* ANM Press, 2007.

46. Lewis, Bernard. *What Went Wrong: The Clash Between Islam and Modernity in the Middle East.* Oxford University Press, 2002.

47. Solomon, S. and E. Alamaqdsis. *The Mosque Exposed.* ANM Press, 2007.

48. Lewis, Bernard. *What Went Wrong: The Clash Between Islam and Modernity in the Middle East.* Oxford University Press, 2002.

Black, Antony. *The History of Islamic Political Thought: From the Prophet to the Present.* Routledge: Edinburgh University Press, 2001.

49. Lewis, Bernard. *The Crisis of Islam, Holy War Unholy Terror.* The Modern Library, 2003.

Gourley, Bruce. "Introduction to Fundamentalism." *Islamist Ideology.* 2005. http://www.brucegourley.com/fundamentalism/islamicfundamentalismintro2.htm

50. Pipes, Daniel. "Islam and Islamism-Faith and Ideology." *The National Interest* (Spring 2000). http://www.danielpipes.org/article/366

51. Ibid.

52. Hoffman, Bruce. *Inside Terrorism.* Columbia University Press, 1998.

53. Jenkins, Brian Michael. "Does Terrorism Work?" *The Mercury News.* The Rand Corporation. 2004. http://www.rand.org/commentary/032104MN.html

54. "Beyond Red Versus Blue." Pew Research Center Poll. May 2005. http://people-press.org/reports/display.php3?ReportID=242

55. Ibid.

56. Page, Susan. "The Great Divide: How Westerners and Muslims View Each Other." *USA Today,* June 2006. http://pewglobal.org/reports/display.php?ReportID=253

57. Ibid.

58. Solomon, S. and E. Alamaqdsis. *The Mosque Exposed.* ANM Press, 2007.

59. Pipes, Daniel. "Moderate Muslims Slam CAIR, Congratulate the FBI." DanielPipes.org, April 4, 2009. http://www.danielpipes.org/blog/2009/03/moderate-muslims-slam-cair-congratulate-the-fbi.html

60. Solomon, S. and E. Alamaqdsis. *The Mosque Exposed.* ANM Press, 2007.

61. Ibid.

62. Ibid.

63. Solomon, S. and E. Alamaqdsis. *The Mosque Exposed.* ANM Press, 2007.

Hudson, Daniel. "Taqiyya and Kitman: The Role of Deception in Islamic Terrorism." DanielPipes.org. September 1, 2005. http://www.danielpipes.org/comments/25320

64. Zeidan, David. "The Fundamentalist View of Life as a Perennial Battle." *Middle East Review of International Affairs*. Vol. 5, no. 4, December 2001. http://meria.idc. ac.il/journal/2001/issue4/jv5n4a2.htm

65. Solomon, S. and E. Alamaqdsis. *The Mosque Exposed*. ANM Press, 2007.

66. IPT News. "Hizb Ut-Tahrir: Shariah Takes Precedence over U.S. Constitution." The Investigative Project on Terrorism. July 20, 2009. http://www.investigativeproj-ect.org/1100/hizb-ut-tahrir-shariah-takes-precedence-over-us

67. Ibid.

68. Ibid.

69. Ibid.

70. Solomon, S. and E. Alamaqdsis. *The Mosque Exposed*. ANM Press, 2007.

Fitzgerald, Hugh et al. "The Myth of the 'Moderate' Muslim." JihadWatch.org. July 26, 2005. http://jihadwatch.org/archives/007376.php

71. Solomon, S. and E. Alamaqdsis. *The Mosque Exposed*. ANM Press, 2007.

72. Fitzgerald, Hugh et al. "The Myth of the 'Moderate' Muslim." JihadWatch.org. July 26, 2005. http://jihadwatch.org/archives/007376.php

73. Cengiz, Orhan Kemal. "The Real Danger Awaiting Turkey is Not Takiyya." *Turkish Daily News*. September 1, 2007. http://www.hurriyetdailynews.com/h. php?news=the-real-danger-awaiting-turkey-is-not-takiyya-2007-09-01

74. Ibid.

75. Ibid.

76. Beshear, Robin. "Karachi Kids." Accuracy in Media. July 23, 2008. http://www. aim.org/briefing/karachi-kids

77. "Keeping An Eye on the Karachi Kids: Documentary Follows the Experiences of Pakistani-American Brothers at Religious School." CBSnews.com, July 11, 2008. http://www.cbsnews.com/stories/2008/07/11/earlyshow/leisure/boxoffice/ main4253344.shtml

78. Beshear, Robin. "Karachi Kids." Accuracy in Media. July 23, 2008. http://www. aim.org/briefing/karachi-kids

79. "Keeping An Eye on the Karachi Kids: Documentary Follows the Experiences of Pakistani-American Brothers at Religious School." CBSnews.com, July 11, 2008. http://www.cbsnews.com/stories/2008/07/11/earlyshow/leisure/boxoffice/ main4253344.shtml

80. Ibid.

81. Beshear, Robin. "Karachi Kids." Accuracy in Media. July 23, 2008. http://www. aim.org/briefing/karachi-kids

82. "Keeping An Eye on the Karachi Kids: Documentary Follows the Experiences of Pakistani-American Brothers at Religious School." CBSnews.com, July 11, 2008.

http://www.cbsnews.com/stories/2008/07/11/earlyshow/leisure/boxoffice/main4253344.shtml

83. Beshear, Robin. "Karachi Kids." Accuracy in Media. July 23, 2008. http://www.aim.org/briefing/karachi-kids

84. Ibid.

85. Sayeh, Reza, et al. "Terror School Turns Out to Be Moderate Madrassa." CNN. July 30, 2008. http://www.cnn.com/2008/WORLD/asiapcf/07/30/karachi.boys/index.html

86. Ibid.

87. Ibid.

88. Alexiev, Alex. "Karachi Kids in CNN's 'Crooked Mirror.'" *FrontPage Magazine.* August 19, 2008. http://97.74.65.51/readArticle.aspx?ARTID=32057

89. Ibid.

90. Ibid.

91. Ibid.

92. Lewis, Bernard. *What Went Wrong: The Clash Between Islam and Modernity in the Middle East.* Oxford University Press, 2002.

Stock, Barbara. "The Long, Bloody History of Islamic Terrorism." July 2005. Chronwatch.com. http://www.chronwatch-america.com

93. Bawer, Bruce. "An Anatomy of Surrender." *City Journal* vol. 18, no. 2 (Spring 2008). http://www.city-journal.org/2008/18_2_cultural_jihadists.html

Beck, Glenn. "Exposed: The Extremist Agenda." CNN. December 2006.

94. PewResearchCenter. "America's Image Slips, but Allies Share U.S. Concerns of Iran, Hamas: No Global Warming Alarm in U.S., China." Pew Global Attitudes Project. June 2006. http://pewglobal.org/reports/display.php?ReportID=252

95. Goldberg, Bernard. *Crazies to the Left of Me, Wimps to the Right: How One Side Lost Its Mind and the Other Lost Its Nerve.* New York: HarperCollins, 2007.

96. Noonan, Peggy. "A Separate Peace: America is in Trouble—and Our Elites Are Merely Resigned." *The Wall Street Journal*, October 2005.

97. "Beyond Red Versus Blue." Pew Research Center Poll. May 2005. http://people-press.org/reports/display.php3?ReportID=242

98. Ibid.

99. Ibid.

100. Ibid.

101. Freedom House. "Saudi Hate Ideology." The Center for Religious Freedom. 2005. http://www.freedomhouse.org/uploads/special_report/45.pdf

102. Schmidt, Susan. "Spreading Saudi Fundamentalism in the United States." *The Washington Post*, October 2, 2003. http://www.washingtonpost.com/ac2/wp-dyn/A31402-2003Oct1?language=printer

103. Gienger, Viola. "Saudi Academy's Books Promote Violence, Intolerance, Panel Says." Bloomberg.com. June 11, 2008. http://www.bloomberg.com/apps/news?pid=20601116&sid=aBqRU9kr7vc4&refer=africa#

104. Ibid.

105. Ibid.

106. Kanes, Tim and James Carafano. "Debunking The Myth of the Underprivileged Soldier." *USA Today*, November 27, 2005. http://www.usatoday.com/news/opinion/editorials/2005-11-27-soldier-edit_x.htm

107. Goldberg, Bernard. *Crazies to the Left of Me, Wimps to the Right: How One Side Lost Its Mind and the Other Lost Its Nerve.* New York: HarperCollins, 2007.

Noonan, Peggy. "A Separate Peace: America is in Trouble—and Our Elites Are Merely Resigned." *The Wall Street Journal*, October 2005.

108. Nye, Joseph. "America Represents Global Capitalism." *The Boston Globe*, September 16, 2001.

109. Zakaria, Fareed. "The Arrogant Empire." *Newsweek*, June 2004.

110. Bennett, William J. *Why We Fight: Moral Clarity and the War On Terrorism.* Regenery Publishing Co., 2002.

111. Harper, Jennifer. "Fifty percent of U.S. says Iraq had W.M.D.'s." *The Washington Times*, July 25, 2006.

112. Taft, William H. IV. "9/11 Attack on America: U.S. Military Commissions: Fair Trials and Justice." The Avalon Project at Yale University. March 2002. http://www.yale.edu/lawweb/avalon/sept_11/taft_001.htm

113. Ibid.

114. Ibid.

115. U.S. Congress. Military Commissions Act of 2006. S.3930. Cong., 2nd session. http://dpc.senate.gov/dpc-new.cfm?doc_name=lb-109-2-145

116. Ibid.

117. "Bush Signs Law for Tough Interrogation of Terror Suspects." FOX News, October 17, 2006. http://www.foxnews.com/printer_friendly_story/0,3566,221480,00.html

118. Office of the Presidential Press Secretary. "President Discusses Creation of Military Commissions to Try Suspected Terrorists." September 2006, http://www.whitehouse.gov/news/releases/2006/09/print/20060906-3.html

119. Zengerle, Patricia. "Bin Laden's Driver is not POW, U.S. Judge Says." Reuters, December 20, 2007. http://www.reuters.com/article/topNews/idUSNCK5075812

0071221?pageNumber=2&virtualBrandChannel=0

120. Ibid.

121. Burton, John. "U.S. Supreme Court Upholds Habeas Corpus for Guantanamo Bay Prisoners." *World Socialist*, June 13, 2008. http://www.wsws.org/articles/2008/jun2008/cour-j13.shtml

122. Ibid.

123. Ibid.

124. Ibid.

125. Markon, Jerry. "Military Tribunal Splits First Guantanamo Bay Verdict." *The Washington Post*, August 6, 2008. http://www.startribune.com/world/26361894.html?elr=KArksD:aDyaEP:kD:aUnOiP3UiD3aPc:_Yyc:aUU

126. "Hamdan gets 5 ½ years on terror charge," Associated Press and MSNBC. August 7, 2008, http://volokh.com/posts/1218142290.shtml

127. Markon, Jerry. "Military Tribunal Splits First Guantanamo Bay Verdict." *The Washington Post*, August 6, 2008. http://www.startribune.com/world/26361894.html?elr=KArksD:aDyaEP:kD:aUnOiP3UiD3aPc:_Yyc:aUU

Williams, Carol J. "Verdict is Mixed in First Guantanamo Trial." *The Los Angeles Times*, August 7, 2008. http://articles.latimes.com/2008/aug/07/nation/na-hamdan7

128. Williams, Carol J. "Verdict is Mixed in First Guantanamo Trial." *The Los Angeles Times*, August 7, 2008. http://articles.latimes.com/2008/aug/07/nation/na-hamdan7

129. Hayes, Stephen F. "Not Right: The Obama Administration Grants Miranda Rights to Detainees in Afghanistan." *The Weekly Standard*, June 10, 2009. http://www.weeklystandard.com/Content/Public/Articles/000/000/016/605iidws.asp

130. Ibid.

131. Ibid.

132. Ackerman, Spencer. "Petreas Speaks to CNAS." washingtonindependent.com, June 11, 2009. http://washingtonindependent.com/46472/petraeus-speaks-to-cnas

133. Star, Penny. "Obama's Assistant Attorney General Tells Senate: Terrorists Captured on Battlefield Have Constitutional Rights." CNSNEWS.com. July 8, 2009.

134. Ibid.

135. Feyerk, Deb and Terry Frieden. "Ex-Gitmo Detainee Pleads Not Guilty in Embassy Bombings." CNN politics.com. June 9, 2009. http://edition.cnn.com/2009/POLITICS/06/09/guantanamo.detainee/index.html?iref=topnews

136. Goodwin, Doris Kearns. *Team of Rivals: the Political Genius of Abraham Lincoln.* New York: Simon & Schuster, 2005.

137. Lewis, Bernard. *What Went Wrong: The Clash Between Islam and Modernity in the Middle East.* Oxford University Press, 2002.

138. Ibid.

139. Hamzway, Amr. "The Real 'Arab Street'." *The Washington Post.* February 4, 2005. http://www.washingtonpost.com/wp-dyn/articles/A6a4963-2005Feb4.html

140. Ibid.

141. Ibid.

142. Ibid.

143. Qaddafi, Muammar. "The One-State Solution." *The New York Times.* Op-Ed. January 22, 2009. http://www.nytimes.com/2009/01/22/opinion/22qaddafi.html

144. "Nobel Laureates." *The Jewish Magazine.* February 2006. http://www.jewishmag.com/99mag/nobel/nobel.htm

145. Noll, Mark. *A History of Christianity in the United States and Canada.* 2nd ed. William. B. Eerdman's Publishing, 1993.

Warren, Tony. "What is Reformed Christianity?" The Mountain Retreat. June 1999. http://www.mountainretreatorg.net/articles/what_is_reformed_theology.shtml

146. Ojeda, Auriana. "Introduction." *At Issue: Islamic Fundamentalism.* San Diego: Greenhaven Press, 2004. http:/www.enotes.com/Islamic-fundamentalism-article/38718

147. Lewis, Bernard. *What Went Wrong: The Clash Between Islam and Modernity in the Middle East.* Oxford University Press, 2002.

148. Ojeda, Auriana. "Introduction." *At Issue: Islamic Fundamentalism.* San Diego: Greenhaven Press, 2004. http:/www.enotes.com/Islamic-fundamentalism-article/38718

149. Center for Muslim-Jewish Engagement. "A Brief Chronology of Muslim History." University of California. http://www.usc.edu/dept/MSA/history/chronology

150. Ibid.

151. Ibid.

152. Ibid.

153. Ibid.

154. Hahn, Gordon M. "Introduction." *Russia's Islamic Threat.* Yale University Press, 2007.

Myers, Steven Lee. "Russia's Struggle Over Islam's Place." *International Herald Tribune.* November 8, 2005. http://www.iht.com/articles/2005/11/07/news/islam3.php

"Muslim Birthrate Worries Russia." *The Washington Times.* November 20, 2006. http://www.washingtontimes.com/news/2006/nov/20/20061120-115904-9135r/

155. Myers, Steven Lee. "Russia's Struggle Over Islam's Place." *International Herald Tribune*, November 8, 2005. http://www.iht.com/articles/2005/11/07/news/islam3.php

156. Myers, Steven Lee. "Russia's Struggle Over Islam's Place." *International Herald Tribune*, November 8, 2005. http://www.iht.com/articles/2005/11/07/news/islam3.php

"Introduction China Country Study." *Central Intelligence Agency World Fact Book*. Washington, D.C., 2008. https://www.cia.gov/library/publications/the-world-factbook/geos/ch.html#People

157. "Demographics of Islam." Wikipedia. 2005. http://en.wikipedia.org/wiki/Demographics_of_Islam

158. Lewis, Bernard. *What Went Wrong: The Clash Between Islam and Modernity in the Middle East*. Oxford University Press, 2002.

159. Lewis, Bernard. *What Went Wrong: The Clash Between Islam and Modernity in the Middle East*. Oxford University Press, 2002.

Atkine, Norville de. "Why Arabs Lose Wars." *Middle East Review of International Affairs*. Vol.4, no.1, 2000. http://meria.idc.ac.il/journal/2000/issue1/de-atkin.pdf

Dunnigan, James. "Why Arabs Lose Wars." Strategypage.com, September 2002. http://www.strategypage.com/dls/articles2002/20020909.asp

160. Lewis, Bernard. *What Went Wrong: The Clash Between Islam and Modernity in the Middle East*. Oxford University Press, 2002.

161. Atkine, Norville de. "Why Arabs Lose Wars." *Middle East Review of International Affairs*. Vol.4, no.1, 2000. http://meria.idc.ac.il/journal/2000/issue1/de-atkin.pdf

"Islamic Radicalism." StrategyPage.com. September 2002. http://www.strategypage.com/qnd/iran/articles/20020902.aspx

162. "1 in 3 Muslim Students Approve Killing for Islam." WorldNetDaily.com. July 26, 2008. http://www.worldnetdaily.com/index.php?fa=PAGE.view&pageId=70673

163. Ibid.

164. Ojeda, Auriana. "Introduction." *At Issue: Islamic Fundamentalism*. San Diego: Greenhaven Press, 2004. http:/www.enotes.com/Islamic-fundamentalism-article/38718

Rusin, David J. "No French Citizenship for Veiled Muslim." IslamistWatch.org. July 26, 2008. http://www.islamist-watch.org/blog/2008/07/no-french-citizenship-for-veiled-muslim

165. "The Rise of Islamic Extremism in Central Asia." UCLA Center for European and Eurasian Studies. April 28, 2005. http://www.international.ucla.edu/euro/article.asp?parentid=23631

166. Ibid.

167. Ibid.

168. "Policy Watch: Russia's Role in the World." TerraDaily. November 28, 2005. http://www.terradaily.com/reports/Policy_Watch_Russias_Role_In_The_World.html

169. "Policy Watch: Russia's Role in the World." TerraDaily. November 28, 2005. http://www.terradaily.com/reports/Policy_Watch_Russias_Role_In_The_World.html

"Russia and its Muslim Population: A Balancing Act, Power and Interest." PINR News Report, September 2004. http://www.pinr.com/report.php?ac=view_report&report_id=222&language_id=1

170. "Russia and its Muslim Population: A Balancing Act, Power and Interest." PINR News Report, September 2004. http://www.pinr.com/report.php?ac=view_report&report_id=222&language_id=1

171. Shah, Anup. "Crisis in Chechnya." GlobalIssues.org, September 4, 2004. http://www.globalissues.org/Geopolitics/Chechnya.asp?p=1

172. Ibid.

173. Ibid.

174. Human Rights News. "No Financing for Russia's War in Chechnya: Rights Group Presses World Bank to Withhold $100 Million." Human Rights Watch, December 14, 1999. http://www.hrw.org/hrw/press/1999/dec/chech1211.htm

175. Human Rights News. "No Financing for Russia's War in Chechnya: Rights Group Presses World Bank to Withhold $100 Million." Human Rights Watch, December 14, 1999. http://www.hrw.org/hrw/press/1999/dec/chech1211.htm

176. Valasek, Tomas. "The Plight of Chechen Civilians Turns From Bad to Worse." Center for Defense Information. Weekly Defense Monitor 4, no. 2, January 2000.

177. Nankivell, Nathan. "China's Muslim Separatists: Terrorist or Terrorized?" 2002. http://cache.zoominfo.com/CachedPage/?archive_id=0&page_id=778149998&page_url=%2f%2fwww.cancaps.ca%2fcbul32.html&page_last_up dated=8%2f6%2f2008+11%3a01%3a21+AM&firstName=Nathan&lastName=Nankivell

178. Ibid.

179. Canadian Security Intelligence Service. "Islamic Unrest in the Xinjiang Uighur Autonomous Region." Ottawa, Ontario: Spring 1998. http://www.oss.net/dynamaster/file_archive/040319/023539ebdbd64ed648eb562d65081223/OSS1999-P2-27.pdf

180. Fincher, Leta Hong. "China-Yining Riots." Voice of America. September 2000. http://www.fas.org/news/china/2000/prc-000915a.htm

181. Lawrence, Susan V. "Where Beijing Fears Kosovo." Far Eastern Economic Review. September 2000. http://www.feer.com/articles/2000/0009_07/p22region.html

182. "Xinjiang to Become China's 2nd Largest Oil Production Center." People'sDaily.com. December 2000. http://english.peopledaily.com.cn/200012/09/eng20001209_57364.html

183. Pomfret, John. "Muslim Chinese Fear for Rights." *Washington Post*, October 2001. http://www.encyclopedia.com/doc/1P2-476393.html

184. Lewis, Bernard. *What Went Wrong: The Clash Between Islam and Modernity in the Middle East.* Oxford University Press, 2002.

185. Beck, Glenn. "Exposed: The Extremist Agenda." CNN. December 2006.

Ojeda, Auriana. 2002. "Introduction." *At Issue: Islamic Fundamentalism.* San Diego: Greenhaven Press. August 2004. http:/www.enotes.com/Islamic-fundamentalism-article/38718

Spencer, Robert. "Powell: Clean up the Madrassas." Jihad Watch. 2004. http://www.jihadwatch.org/archives/000707.php

186. Jenkins, Brian Michael. "Does Terrorism Work?" *The Mercury News.* The Rand Corporation. March 21, 2004. http://www.rand.org/commentary/032104MN.html

187. Gubser, Peter. *Jordan: Crossroads of Middle Eastern Events.* Boulder, CO: Westview Press, 1983.

188. Bawer, Bruce. "An Anatomy of Surrender." *City Journal.* Vol. 18, no. 2 (Spring 2008). http://www.city-journal.org/2008/18_2_cultural_jihadists.html

"Introduction." Hitler Historical Museum. http://www.hitler.org

Keegan, John ed. "National Death Tolls for the Second World War." *HarperCollins Atlas of the Second World War,* 1997.

189. Solomon, S. and E. Alamaqdsis. *The Mosque Exposed.* ANM Press, 2007.

190. Kahn, Muqtedar. "Who are the Moderate Muslims?" IslamForToday.com. http://www.islamfortoday.com/khan08.htm

191. Ibid.

192. Belasco, Amy. "The Cost of Iraq, Afghanistan, and Other Global War on Terror Operations Since 9/11." Library of Congress: CRS Report for Congress, 2007. http://nefafoundation.org/miscellaneous/FeaturedDocs/CRS_GWOTCosts.pdf

193. Ibid.

194. Darwish, Nonie. *Now They Call Me Infidel: Why I Renounced Jihad for America, Israel, and the War on Terror.* Sentinel, 2006.

195. Mudeiris, Sheik Ibrahim. "The Palestinian Authority Friday Sermon." The Middle East Research Institute TV. May 2005. http://switch5.castup.net/frames/20041020_MemriTV_Popup/video_480x360.asp?ClipMediaID=60227&ak=null

196. Kuntzel, Mathias. "Islamic Anti-Semitism and Its Nazi Roots." April 2003. http://www.matthiaskuentzel.de/contents/islamic-antisemitism-and-its-nazi-roots

Lewis, Bernard. *Semites and Anti-Semites: Inquiries into Conflict and Prejudice.* New York: W.W. Norton and Co., 1987.

197. Wolf, Dieter. "Hitler's Amerikabomber." *The Atlantic Monthly,* 2004.

198. Canadian Security Intelligence Services. "Terrorism: Motivations and Causes." Commentary: Professor Paul Wilkinson. January 5, 1995. http://www.csis-scrs. gc.ca/pblctns/cmmntr/cm53-eng.asp

199. "U.S. Revokes Visas for 3 Gaza Fulbright Scholars." MSNBC News, August 5, 2008. http://www.msnbc.msn.com/id/26035526/

200. Ibid.

201. Ibid.

202. Ibid.

203. Bawer, Bruce. "Not all Muslims want to integrate." *The Christian Science Monitor*, November 2005. Quoted by Hugh Fitzgerald. November 2005. http://jihad-watch.org/dhimmiwatch/archives/2005_11.php

204. Adelman, Kenneth. "U.S. Islamic Schools...Teaching Hate." FOX News Live, February 27, 2002.

Bawer, Bruce. "Not all Muslims want to integrate." *The Christian Science Monitor*, November 2005. Quoted by Hugh Fitzgerald, November 2005. http://jihadwatch. org/dhimmiwatch/archives/2005_11.php

Beck, Glenn. "Exposed: The Extremist Agenda." CNN. December 2006.

205. Rusin, David J. "No French Citizenship for Veiled Muslim." Islamist-Watch. org. July 26, 2008. http://www.islamist-watch.org/blog/2008/07/no-french-citizen-ship-for-veiled-muslim.html

206. Ibid.

207. Ibid.

208. Clark, Lillian P. *Federal Textbook on Citizenship Training, Part III: Our Nation. U.S. Department of Labor.* Washington, D.C.: U.S. Government Printing Office, 1931.

209. Shaidle, Kathy. "The Jihad Prevention Act." *FrontPage Magazine.* September 24, 2008. http://97.74.65.51/readArticle.aspx?ARTID=32468

210. Bartholomew, Richard. "Tancredo's 'Jihad Prevention Act.'" September 25, 2008. http://barthsnotes.wordpress.com/2008/09/25/tancredos-jihad-prevention-act/

211. Shaidle, Kathy. "The Jihad Prevention Act." *FrontPage Magazine.* September 24, 2008. http://97.74.65.51/readArticle.aspx?ARTID=32468

212. Ibid.

213. "1 in 3 Muslim Students Approve Killing for Islam." WorldNetDaily.com. July 26, 2008. http://www.worldnetdaily.com/index.php?fa=PAGE.view&pageId=70673

214. Shaidle, Kathy. "The Jihad Prevention Act." *FrontPage Magazine.* September 24, 2008. http://97.74.65.51/readArticle.aspx?ARTID=32468

215. "Tancredo Proposes Anti-Shari'a Measure in Wake of U.K. Certification of Islamic Courts." September 27, 2008. ReformIslam.org. http://www.reformislam.org/

Formerly: http://muslimsagainstShari'a.blogspot.com/2008/09/tancredo-proposes-anti-Shari'a-measure.html\

216. Pipes, Daniel. "The West's Islamist Infiltrators." Jewish World Review. August 12, 2008. http://www.jewishworldreview.com/0808/pipes081208.php3?

217. Ibid.

218. Fitzgerald, Hugh, et al. "Is the U.S. government infested with jihadist moles?" JihadWatch.org, November 21, 2007. http://jihadwatch.org/archives/018878.php

219. Swanbrow, Diane. "When God Sanctions Violence, Believers Act More Aggressively." The University Record Online. The University of Michigan. http://www.ur.umich.edu/0607/Mar12_07/04.shtml

220. Ibid.

221. Bacchiocchi, Samuele. "Violence in the Koran and the Bible." FreeRepublic.com. June 7, 2002. http://www.freerepublic.com/focus/f-religion/696408/posts

222. Ibid.

223. Ibid.

224. Ibid.

225. Adelman, Kenneth. "U.S. Islamic Schools...Teaching Hate." FOX News Live, February 27, 2002.

226. Ibid.

227. Ibid.

228. Ibid.

229. Ibid.

230. Ibid.

231. Spencer, Robert and Hugh Fitzgerald. "Teaching Children to Hate and Kill." Jihad Watch. 2005. http://jihadwatch.org/archives/007662.php

232. Darwish, Nonie. Now They Call Me Infidel: Why I Renounced Jihad for America, Israel, and the War on Terror. Sentinel, 2006.

Darwish, Nonie. Cruel and Usual Punishment: The Terrifying Global Implications of Islamic Law. Thomas Nelson, 2009.

233. Ibid.

234. Shoebat, Walid. "Raised to Hate." CNN Live. October 2006.

235. Beck, Glenn. "Exposed: The Extremist Agenda." CNN. December 2006.

236. Ibid.

237. Beck, Glenn. "Exposed: The Extremist Agenda." CNN. December 2006.

Ojeda, Auriana. "Introduction." *At Issue: Islamic Fundamentalism.* San Diego: Green-haven Press, 2004. http:/www.enotes.com/Islamic-fundamentalism-article/38718

238. Beck, Glenn. "Exposed: The Extremist Agenda." CNN. December 2006.

239. Ojeda, Auriana. *"Introduction."* At Issue: Islamic Fundamentalism. San Diego: Greenhaven Press. 2004. http:/www.enotes.com/Islamic-fundamentalism-article/38718

240. Beck, Glenn. "Exposed: The Extremist Agenda." CNN. December 2006.

241. Ojeda, Auriana. "Introduction." *At Issue: Islamic Fundamentalism.* San Diego: Greenhaven Press, 2004. http:/www.enotes.com/Islamic-fundamentalism-article/38718

242. Ibid.

243. Ibid.

244. BrooksNews Bulletin. "U.N. Funding the Indocrination of Children into Isla-mo-Nazi Terrorism." BrooksNews.com. August 14, 2006. http://www.brookesnews.com/061408unterror.html BrooksNews Bulletin. "U.N. Funding the Indocrination of Children into Islamo-Nazi Terrorism."

245. Ibid.

246. Beck, Glenn. "Exposed: The Extremist Agenda." CNN. December 2006.

247. Ibid.

248. "Study: 3 in 4 U.S. Mosques Preach Anti-West Extremism: Secret Survey Exposes Widespread Radicalism." WorldNetDaily. February 23, 2008. http://www.worldnetdaily.com/index.php?pageId=57141

249. Ibid.

250. Ibid.

251. Kay, Barbara. "Paving the Way For Soft Jihad." Islamist-Watch.org. July 22, 2008. http://network.nationalpost.com/np/blogs/fullcomment/ar-chive/2008/07/22/barbara-kay-paving-the-way-for-soft-jihad.aspx

"Lawfare." Islamist-Watch.org. 2007. http://www.islamist-watch.org/articles/

Lewin, Tamar. "Universities Install Footbaths to Benefit Muslims and Not Every-one is Pleased." *New York Times.* August 7, 2007. http://www.religionnewsblog.com/18965/islamification-4

Schlussel, Debbie. "So Long Church/State Separation: University of Michigan to fund Muslim Footbaths." DebbieSchlussel.com. June 5, 2007. http://www.debbi-eschlussel.com/1373/exclusive-so-long-churchstate-separation-university-of-michigan-to-fund-muslim-footbaths-2/

252. Mercer, Phil. "Australian Prime Minister Worries Over 'Extremist' Muslim Immigrants." VOANews.com. February 20, 2006. http://www.voanews.com/english/archive/2006-02/2006-02-20-voa7.cfm?CFID=218158569&CFTOKEN=71938473

Christiansen, Melanie. "Howard Comments Unhelpful, Say Islamic leaders: Interview with Prime Minister Howard John." PM. February 20, 2006. http://www.abc.net.au/pm/content/2006/s1574311.htm

253. Mercer, Phil. "Australian Prime Minister Worries Over 'Extremist' Muslim Immigrants." VOANews.com. February 20, 2006. http://www.voanews.com/english/archive/2006-02/2006-02-20-voa7.cfm?CFID=218158569&CFTOKEN=71938473

Christiansen, Melanie. "Howard Comments Unhelpful, Say Islamic leaders: Interview with Prime Minister Howard John." PM. February 20, 2006. http://www.abc.net.au/pm/content/2006/s1574311.htm

"PM's Muslim Comments 'Offensive." The Sydney Morning Herald. February 20, 2006. http://www.smh.com.au/news/national/pms-muslim-comments-offensive/2006/02/20/1140283978611.html

254. "Terrorism, What Do We Need to Know?" FamilySecurityMatters.com. http://www.familysecuritymatters.org/terrorism.php?id=1387130

255. Rusin, David J. "Glimmers of Hope in Great Britain." Islamist-watch.org. April 3, 2009. http://www.islamist-watch.org/blog/2009/04/glimmers-of-hope-in-great-britain

256. Ibid.

257. Ibid.

258. Ibid.

259. Ibid.

260. Ibid.

261. Lewis, Bernard. What Went Wrong: The Clash Between Islam and Modernity in the Middle East. Oxford University Press, 2002.

262. Crilly, Rob. "The Blasphemous Teddy Bear." TIME Magazine. November 26, 2007. http://www.time.com/time/world/article/0,8599,1687755,00.html

263. "Thousands in Sudan Call for British Teddy Bear Teacher's Execution." FOX News. November 30, 2007. http://www.foxnews.com/story/0,2933,314111,00.html

264. Ojeda, Auriana. "Introduction." At Issue: Islamic Fundamentalism. San Diego: Greenhaven Press, 2004. http:/www.enotes.com/Islamic-fundamentalism-article/38718

Nawish, Kamal. "Modern Islam, Positions." Free Muslim Coalition. http://www.FreeMuslims.org

265. Zakaria, Fareed. "The Arrogant Empire." Newsweek, June 2004.

266. Ibid.

267. Zakaria, Fareed. "The Arrogant Empire." *Newsweek*, June 2004.

268. Ibid.

269. Ibid.